4 KEYS

to

HEARING

GOD'S VOICE

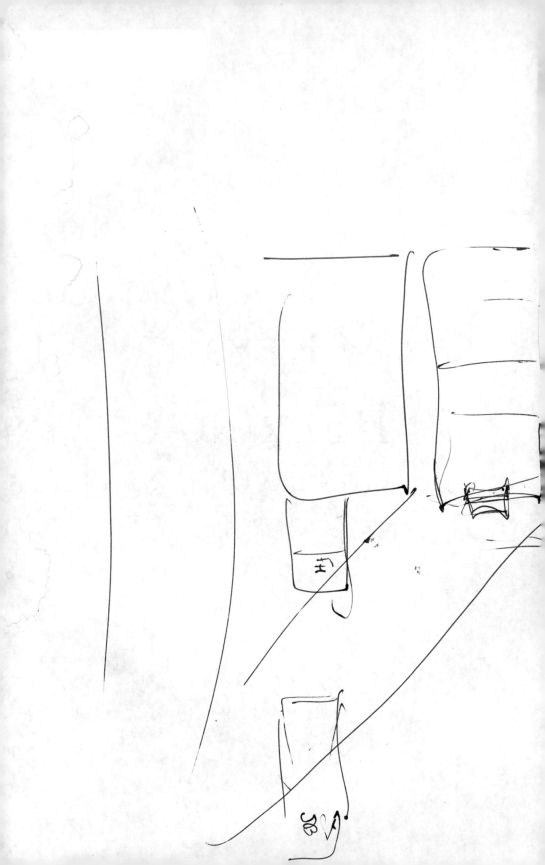

4 KEYS
—to—
HEARING
GOD'S VOICE

MARK AND PATTI VIRKLER

DESTINY IMAGE® PUBLISHERS, INC.

P.O. Box 310, Shippensburg, PA 17257-0310

"Speaking to the Purposes of God for This Generation and for the Generations to Come."

This book and all other Destiny Image, Revival Press, MercyPlace, Fresh Bread, Destiny Image Fiction, and Treasure House books are available at Christian bookstores and distributors worldwide.

For a U.S. bookstore nearest you, call 1-800-722-6774.

For more information on foreign distributors, call 717-532-3040.

Reach us on the Internet: www.destinyimage.com.

Trade Paper ISBN 13: 978-0-7684-3248-0

Hardcover ISBN 978-0-7684-3436-1

Large Print ISBN 978-0-7684-3437-8

Ebook ISBN 978-0-7684-9121-0

For Worldwide Distribution, Printed in the U.S.A.

6 7 8 9 / 17 16 15 14

Endorsements

Oh my, I am speechless...I have completed only the first several lessons in the course on *4 Keys to Hearing God's Voice* and my life has been totally, totally transformed. He is such a wonderful, wonderful God. A few months ago I told Him I was desperate for more of Him...I had no idea His answer to my prayer would be so exceedingly abundantly above anything I could ever have imagined. My days and nights are now filled with His presence. Thank you for your service to Him, Mr. Virkler.

Amy

4 Keys to Hearing God's Voice is very, very rich and wonderful. I am going to study personally with it. I praise God for your ministry and important contribution to the Body of Christ. If you have written other study manuals, would you kindly send a copy of each one of them to me?

Dr. Paul Yonggi Cho
Founder, Yoido Full Gospel Church of Korea

I have been an active Baptist pastor for 37 years. As far as I am personally concerned, seminars like *4 Keys to Hearing God's Voice*, *Counseled by God* and *Naturally Supernatural* are absolutely fundamental to the building up of the inner life. At this present time we have six ongoing classes in *4 Keys to Hearing God's Voice* using Mark's video series and another class on *Counseled by God*.

Rev. Peter Lord
Former pastor, Park Avenue Baptist Church

Next to salvation and the baptism in the Holy Spirit, Mark Virkler's seminar *4 Keys to Hearing God's Voice* has been my most life-changing experience.

Pastor Lyman Rice

Practical yet inspirational, the Virklers have combined the best of the school of the Word and the school of the Spirit to bring us this landmark work about 4 *Keys to Hearing God's Voice*. This book will help guide and ground multitudes in their adventure to discern the voice of God. Great job!

James W. Goll
Co-founder, Encounters Network
Author of *The Seer, The Lost Art of Intercession,* and
Praying for Israel's Destiny

I didn't realize that it was so easy to hear God's voice, or to see visions, or to have dreams, or to walk in the spirit, or to be healed of deep emotional pain. These teachings must be shared. I can't keep these blessings to myself. They belong to the world. They belong to you. Thank you so very much, Mark Virkler. My life has been changed. I thank God for your ministry.

Tarik Carey
Kingston, Jamaica

I was introduced to a course of study called *4 Keys to Hearing God's Voice* containing a real anointed teaching on drawing closer to God. It is the favorite of all our students, and I don't think I will ever have a school without it.

Dr. Harold Reents
Former Academic Dean, Christ for the Nations

4 Keys to Hearing God's Voice by Mark and Patti Virkler has dramatically changed my prayer life. I have found that I can will to dialogue with Christ on a daily basis, and I do. I believe this inspired approach to be absolutely essential to the growth of every serious Christian. I further believe *4 Keys to Hearing God's Voice* is an excellent example of the uniquely powerful way God is reaching out to His people today.

Dr. Richard Watson
Former professor, Oral Roberts University

The guys from the federal prison camp, as well as the mentors, just couldn't say enough about the materials and what they've learned through *4 Keys to Hearing God's Voice.*

Steve Cronk
South Florida Area Director Prison Fellowship

Learning to hear God through journaling has been the most exciting and revolutionizing thing to happen in my life. It has brought extreme change to my life and that of my family. It has caused me to have constant and lasting joy in my life. It has given me wisdom and guidance in every area of my life. As a woman, I journal about everything from what I wear each day to what His will is for my life. Hearing each day what my Father wants me to eat has helped me to lose 60 pounds. My life will never be the same!

Paulette

This Book Is Dedicated
With Gratitude

To our spiritual advisors, Roger Miller, Maurice Fuller, and Gary Greig, who have encouraged us greatly as we have walked this road of spiritual intimacy with Almighty God.

And to all who have proven this message in their own lives and have begun to hear God's voice, see vision, and journal.

Contents

Introduction

We are going to make something that has been very hard, very simple. I could not hear God's voice for the first ten years of my Christian life, and now I have spent 30 years teaching the Body of Christ how to do so. It is as simple as quieting yourself down, fixing your eyes on Jesus, tuning to spontaneity, and writing! And **all** Christians can do it! **You** can do it! Jesus **promised**, *"My sheep hear My voice"* (John 10:27). So you **can** hear His voice. His voice sounds like spontaneous thoughts that light upon your mind, especially as your heart is fixed on Him.

And you can do this **every day** as part of your morning devotions. You can live out of His voice all day, by simply seeing Him alongside you (He is Immanuel, God with you), and staying tuned to spontaneity all day long. The Bible calls this abiding in Christ (see John 15:4) or *"praying without ceasing"* (1 Thess. 5:17).

And if these four keys sound like something counterfeit groups do, then we get excited, because we know that satan only counterfeits things that are real and have value. So finally we are doing something real enough and valuable enough for satan to take interest in it and counterfeit it. Glory be to God!

Come on, let's get started! Jesus is waiting to share His love with you!

As I began to journal and hear God's voice, it was astounding to me how much He loved me. Being more of a "Martha" than a "Mary," I had always focused on serving and obeying the King of Kings. (There is nothing wrong with serving and obeying; they are just not to be the CENTER of the relationship.) In my journaling, God began pouring His love out to me, telling me how special I am and how precious to Him, and how much He enjoys spending time with me. He said, "Mark, this is the reason I have created you – so that we can spend time together and share love together. This is the center of life to Me. It is not the things you do for Me. It is the time we spend together sharing love. Come and do this daily. This is why I died for you on Calvary, to restore times of wonderful intimacy and love. So come and do this often. Come and do it daily. This is My desire...to spend time sharing love together with you. Come, My child, and do this often. Come, My Child."

Wow! Talk about a world-changing reorientation! So the center of life is not workaholism or obedience. The center of life is sharing love together, and experiencing intimacy and romance with the King of Kings!

As you begin to hear God's voice and journal, you too will experience this same amazing realization of God's love. God's passionate desire is to be intimate with you!

So again I say, come on, let's get started. Jesus is waiting to share His love with you (I Jn. 3:1).

Do you want to intensify your results? Find a few friends who want to learn to hear God's voice, too. We highly recommend that you meet together for 10 weeks with a small group. We have 10 one-hour DVDs in which we teach the key principles of the 10 chapters of this book. During the week you can read the corresponding chapter for additional background and to deepen what you learn on the DVD. You may order DVDs, CDs, and Audio/Video Guides at: www.CWGMinistries.org

Each week's video session will lead you into journaling (writing down what God is speaking to you) and encourage you to share your journaling with one another. These journaling questions are also listed throughout this book, and the page numbers where you can find them **are all listed for you in Appendix D**.

You *must* **enter into the journaling times**! We must "practice truth!" We must be doers of the word and not hearers only (see James 1:22). So journal together weekly in your small groups at the close of each DVD session and then share your journaling with one another or a prayer partner, and ask them if they feel in their heart that this came from the Lord. As they affirm your journaling, your faith is strengthened and you leap forward in spiritual intimacy. If you do this, you will clearly, daily hear His voice. He promised, and I have proven Him true to His Word.

Even if you are not able to be part of a group, we encourage you to still get the CDs and Audio/Video Guide, and to share your journaling with a couple of spiritual friends, or a "Personal Spiritual Trainer" available from Communion with God Ministries.

Chapter 1

How I Discovered
the Four Keys

I Hungered for a Personal Encounter
with the Living God

When I accepted Jesus Christ into my heart at age 15, an immediate hunger to know God sprang up within my spirit. I first attempted to satisfy this desire by devouring the Bible. However, within weeks it was obvious to me that the people in the Bible knew God through hearing Him speak to them and seeing visions of Him. God was their Friend. They walked and talked with Him. Every day, Adam and Eve heard God's voice and lived out of it. What an astounding lifestyle! From Genesis to Revelation, people heard God's voice and saw visions. I wanted that, too! What I didn't know at the time was that this hunger to know God had been placed in my heart by the Holy Spirit, and that God fully intended to satisfy this passion.

I Believed that Christianity Is to Be More than a Religion

One basic distinction between Christianity and the many other religions is that Christianity goes beyond a simple code of ethics, a list of rules and laws that one must follow, and offers direct, spiritual experiences with a loving God. We not only know about God, we experience Him. We not only say the sinner's prayer, and accept by faith that we are saved, but we experience His Spirit bearing witness with our spirits that we are the children of God (see Rom. 8:16). We not only seek direction from the laws of the Bible, we also find guidance through the Spirit granting peace in our hearts. We do not simply read the Bible as a lifeless book with black print on white pages, but we experience it as alive (see Heb. 4:12). God "illumines" or quickens it to our hearts as we pray for a spirit of revelation (see Eph. 1:17). We do not just pray according to our own desires; rather, God "burdens" our hearts to pray in harmony with His will. God has sent His Holy Spirit into our hearts, crying "Abba Father" (see Rom. 8:15), so that we can have a direct ongoing love experience with Him. God has come to dwell within the hearts of humankind!

> *And I will ask the Father, and He will give you another Helper, that He may be with you forever; that is the Spirit of truth, whom the world cannot receive, because it does not behold Him or know Him, but you know Him because He abides with you, and will be in you. I will not leave you as orphans; I will come to you* (John 14:16-18).
>
> *Or do you not know that your body is a temple of the Holy Spirit who is in you, whom you have from God, and that you are not your own?* (1 Corinthians 6:19)
>
> *But we have this treasure in earthen vessels, that the surpassing greatness of the power may be of God and not from ourselves* (2 Corinthians 4:7).

I am sure all Christians have experienced the truth of Philippians 4:13, "I can do all things through Him [Christ] who strengthens me [fuses His strength to mine, literal Greek]." Being too weak to handle a problem, we have called upon the indwelling Spirit to help us and have found His strength overcoming our weakness, His joy overcoming our sorrow, or His peace overcoming our anxiety.

Christianity is much more than a code of ethics; it is much more than a religion. It is a love relationship with the King of Kings. It is a direct encounter with Him through the indwelling work of His Holy Spirit, which we freely receive as His gift to us. This, then, causes

Christianity to ascend far beyond rationalism into the world of direct spiritual experiences. First Corinthians 2:9-10 tells us:

> *Things which eye has not seen and ear has not heard, and which have not entered the heart of man, all that God has prepared for those who love Him. For to us God revealed them through the Spirit; for the Spirit searches all things, even the depths of God.*

We Are to Experience Divine Revelation Within Our Spirits

We come to know truth with our hearts or spirits, rather than with our minds. God reveals things that our natural eyes and ears could never sense through His Spirit speaking directly to our spirits. It is not that our natural eyes, ears, and mind have no place in God's glorious revelation, for they are wonders of His creation as much as our hearts and spirits are. However, each part of us (body, soul, and spirit) has a special function in God's plan.

God says that there are some things that He can only "reveal through the Spirit." Through the indwelling Holy Spirit, God has given us direct communion with Himself. We hear His voice within our hearts. We are led by the Spirit (see Rom. 8:14). We have inner subjective experiences. Through insight, we receive revelation from Him, and He illumines Scripture to us (see Luke 24:32). Through intuition, we sense the promptings of the Holy Spirit and the voice of God. So, our life in the Spirit, our relationship with God, is an inner, intuitive, spiritual, heart experience.

So Let's Not Settle for JUST Doctrine!

We must receive the caution Jesus gave in John 5:39-40: "*You search the Scriptures, because you think that in them you have eternal life; and it is these that bear witness to Me; **and you are unwilling to come to Me, that you may have eternal life.**" We may assume that we can acquire correct doctrine and head knowledge from Scripture. We can learn what the Word says about Christ and become satisfied with that information. But such intellectual exercise does not profit **our spirits** at all. We must take a **further step** of loving trust in Jesus as a Person who is alive right now and yearns to be part of our lives. Only through heart faith can we experience the things that the Scriptures testify about Him.

The Bible itself teaches us that in addition to examining Scriptures, we also need a personal relationship with God in which He speaks directly to us. For instance, in Exodus 15:26 the Lord tells the Israelites to listen carefully to His voice and to give heed to His commandments and statutes. Many people think these are all the same thing: we listen to God by paying attention to Scripture. But in the context, there were no commandments to heed. The Hebrews had recently come out of Egypt and had not yet reached Sinai, which is where God gave the Law. *So listening to God's voice came before the Law was given.*

Now that we have readily available printed Bibles, our experience is that we learn through the Bible first and hear God only as an added extra. But this is not the order of Scripture itself. Paul makes it very plain that faith is more important than the Law. Our personal relationship with Jesus through faith, including the ability to hear Him speak to us, is actually more important than following the Law, the Torah, the Scriptures! Not that we abandon one to concentrate exclusively on the other. It is clear that God tells His people to do two related, overlapping, but distinct things—hear His voice and obey the commandments—just as Jesus made a distinction between searching the Scriptures and listening to what He said.

[Handwritten margin note: Romans 10:17 Faith comes by hearing & hearing by the word. Psalm 138:2 I magnified thy word above thy name.]

Charles Finney: Three Classes of Christians

Pastor, writer, and theologian Reverend Charles G. Finney, who was a key evangelist in the Second Great Awakening, wrote this in the late 1800s:

> Many, understanding the "Confession of Faith" as summarizing the doctrines of the Bible, very much neglect the Bible and rest in a belief of the articles of faith. Others, more cautious and more in earnest, search the Scriptures to see what they say about Christ, but stop short and rest in the formation of correct theological opinions; while others, and they are the only

saved class, love the Scriptures intensely because they testify of Jesus. They search and devour the Scriptures because they tell them who Jesus is and what they may trust Him for.

> They do not stop short and rest in this testimony; but by an act of loving trust [they] go directly to Him, to His person, thus joining their souls to Him in a union that receives from Him, by a direct divine communication, the things for which they are led to trust Him. This is certainly Christian experience. This is receiving from Christ the eternal life which God has given us in Him. This is saving faith...The error to which I call attention does not consist in laying too much stress in teaching and believing the facts and doctrines of the Gospel: but consists in stopping short of trusting the personal Christ for what those facts and doctrines teach us to trust Him, and satisfying ourselves with believing the testimony about Him, instead of committing our souls to Him by an act of loving trust.[1]

On the one hand, let's not stop with the doctrine and techniques taught in this book or trust in them. Life and power flow only from Jesus. On the other hand, let's not discard doctrines or techniques. Recognize that they have been given as channels through which the grace of God flows. Let them lead you into a full encounter with your Lord Jesus Christ, allowing you to wholly experience His life.

I Tried Many Approaches that Didn't Work

I read and memorized Scripture. I went to Bible college. I became an ordained pastor. I prayed and fasted. I obeyed the Lord's commands to the best of my ability. And I closely questioned people who professed to hear from God, since I still didn't know what His voice sounded like. Their favorite answer seemed to be, "You know that you know that you know." Well, that didn't help me because I didn't know, and that is why I was asking them! I could not hear Him, see Him, or feel Him, and yet I was taught and believed that I had a relationship with Him. If I were married to someone I could not hear, see, or feel, I would be quite disappointed in my marriage relationship! It appeared to me that my "relationship" with Jesus was rather thin. It sure seemed more like a theology about Jesus than a relationship with Him.

Finally I Focused Intently on Hearing and Seeing for One Year

As I began my 11th year as a Christian, I had a *"thought come to me"* that I should set aside the entire year, and focus intently on learning to hear the voice of God. Well, I was ready to do this, because by this time I had noticed from John 5:19-20,30 that Jesus was anointed because He only did what He heard and saw His Father doing. I wanted desperately to be anointed, and so I was willing to spend an entire year focused on learning to hear and to see. Obviously it was the Lord telling me to set aside this time to learn to hear His voice, but at this point in my life, I had not yet identified God's voice as spontaneous thoughts that light upon my mind as my heart is quiet before the Lord.

Focused effort meant that all my Bible study was on learning to hear and see. All the books I read were on prayer. All the conferences I went to were on prayer, and some were way outside my theological traditions. I was willing to seek out those who were different from me because my theological tradition said God no longer spoke or gave dreams or visions in this dispensation, and my heart had rejected that as being false. All my experimentation was on learning to hear and see. All my preaching was on prayer and hearing and seeing. That year, 1979, I had my breakthrough.

Through a full year of my life devoted to focused prayer and research, the Lord taught me **four simple keys** that unlocked the ability for me to discern the voice of God within me. They would have to be simple, because the Bible says if we want to enter the Kingdom we must become as little children. So hearing God's voice cannot be anything more difficult than an 8-year-old can do! I had made it so much harder. Now I was being stretched because I discovered it was so easy.

Very simply stated, the four keys to hearing God's voice are:

Stillness: Quiet yourself so you can hear God's voice.

Vision: Look for vision as you pray.

Spontaneity: Recognize God's voice as spontaneous thoughts that light upon your mind.

Journaling: Write down that flow of thoughts and pictures.

Now, whenever I need or want to hear from God, I can—as long as I use all four of these keys. I have traveled worldwide teaching what I have learned, and the four keys have worked in every culture and every circumstance and every age group. God's people can recognize His voice, just as He promised, and YOU can hear His voice!

How God Taught Me the 4 Keys

God introduced me to these four keys by awakening me early in the morning with an actual loud voice in my head that said, "Get up, I want to teach you how to hear My voice." When I arrived at my office, the Lord took me to Habakkuk 2:1-3:

> I will **stand on my guard post** and station myself on the rampart; and I will **keep watch to see** what He will speak to me, and how I may reply when I am reproved. Then the LORD answered me and said, "**Record the vision** and inscribe it on tablets, that the one who reads it may run. For the vision is yet for the appointed time; it hastens toward the goal and it will not fail though it tarries, wait for it; for it will certainly come, it will not delay."

As exemplified in Habakkuk 2:1-3, there are four keys to hearing God's voice:

1. I will stand on my guard post (be still).

2. I will keep watch to see (fix your eyes on Jesus).

3. He will speak to me (tune to spontaneity).

4. Then the Lord answered me and said, "Record the vision." (Write the flow of thoughts and pictures that light upon your heart and mind.)

Like me, Habakkuk is seeking a spiritual experience. He wants to hear the voice of God – a *rhema* word – spoken directly into his heart so that he can gain some understanding concerning the calamity he sees around him. So first, Habakkuk goes to a quiet place where he can be alone and become still. He stations himself there, waiting for God to speak.

Second, he quiets himself within by "watching to see" what God will say. Now, watching is something I had never done. I had never used the eyes of my heart as I prayed. I had never looked or watched. The Hebrew words translated, "Keep watch to see" are numbers 6822 and 7200 in *Strong's Exhaustive Concordance*. They carry the following meanings: to look out or about, spy, keep watch, observe, to see, inspect, perceive, consider, have vision, observe, look upon, give attention to, discern, distinguish, gaze at, present oneself.1

I believe Habakkuk had a way of looking specifically toward God. I needed to incorporate this into my prayer time, as I had never done any of this. Habakkuk 1:1 states that this is the "burden which Habakkuk the prophet **saw**." God's spoken word (*rhema*) was couched in vision. As we shall see, focusing the eyes of our hearts upon God (fixing our eyes upon Jesus – see Heb. 12:2 NASB) causes us to become inwardly still, raises our level of faith and expectancy, and makes us fully open to receive from God.

Third, Habakkuk hears God's voice within him. We have defined this as the still small voice of God that is registered within us as spontaneous thoughts that light upon our mind. The Greek term for a spoken word is *rhema*, and we will explore more about its meaning and significance as we go along.

Fourth, when God begins to speak, the first thing He says is, "Record the vision." Habakkuk wrote down the flowing thoughts and flowing pictures that were coming to him from God. This was certainly something new, because I had never written out my prayers up to this point in my life.

These four elements—becoming still, using vision, tuning to spontaneity, and journaling—are the elements used by the prophet Habakkuk to hear the voice of God. I believe this is a divinely ordained pattern that assists us in our approach to God and helps lift us to the level of the Spirit. Until I combined **all four** of these elements in my devotional life, I was not able to discern God's voice and commune with Him. I often had become frustrated and uncertain about what God really wanted. These FOUR elements truly have transformed my devotional life. In my earlier Christian life, I had stopped singing the song "Sweet Hour of Prayer," because I never had sweet hours of prayer. Now I find that I can enjoy dialoguing with God by the hour and leave fully charged with His life and love. I have discovered that almost everyone I teach will hear and recognize God's voice if he or she will use **all four elements at the same time!**

John Used the Same 4 Keys When He Wrote the Book of Revelation

> *I was in the Spirit on the Lord's day, and I heard behind me a loud voice like the sound of a trumpet, saying, "Write in a book what you see..."* (Revelation 1:10-11 NASB).

Being "in the Spirit" suggests that John had quieted himself down. He heard a voice—in this case the voice of an angel—and it is not quite so soft as the "still, small voice" of God! "Writing in a book" is journaling, and "what he sees" indicates the use of vision. So once again we see a prophetic writer in Scripture using all four keys at one time to receive revelation from God—and, in this case, two visions that last 22 chapters!

Now, the four keys are stated in a slightly different order in Revelation than in Habakkuk, and I find it easier for me to teach them in an order different from either prophet. **The order of the keys is not critical. The crucial thing is that you use all four keys at one time!**

Actually These 4 Keys are Found Throughout Scripture

Being still: Elijah stilled himself by going to a cave to listen to God. David commanded his soul to wait in silence for God only. Daniel went alone to his chamber and looked toward Jerusalem three times a day. Jesus regularly took time away from the multitude and even His disciples to be alone to pray. Paul went to the Arabian Desert after his conversion so he could hear from God alone.

Seeing vision: The Bible also shows us repeatedly that before we hear God speak we need to see something of His glory. Seeing God's glory comes before hearing God's voice. Looking precedes listening. From Abraham to whom God 'appeared' before He spoke (we don't know any detail of this appearing), to Jacob seeing the ladder and the angels, to Moses seeing the burning bush, to Elijah seeing the effects of the earthquake, wind, and fire, to Isaiah seeing the seraphim, to Mary, Joseph, and the shepherds seeing the angels, to Peter seeing the animal-filled sheet, to John on Patmos seeing Jesus, the pattern is repeated. These are not 'extraordinary.' In the Bible they are ordinary, as confirmed by Moses in Numbers 12:6 explaining that God's usual way of speaking to prophets is through a vision. In our culture such 'seeing' is deemed extraordinary, but that only shows how much we have to learn.

A voice: Elijah heard God speak in a still small voice, but generally people in the Bible never discuss whether God's voice came as an inner thought or an outer sound. Even though some may believe God's voice came as an audible sound to people in the Scriptures, the Bible does not state that.

Journaling: Many in the Bible wrote down what they were receiving from the Lord. David wrote the Psalms; the prophets wrote their visions and the words the Lord gave them. John wrote the entire book of Revelation as a record of two visions he had. Literally hundreds of chapters of Scripture came from people journaling or writing out their encounters with the living Lord.

After 30 years of teaching this message worldwide to all age groups, I am convinced that anyone who uses all four keys at one time will hear God's voice! *Two or three keys at one time are not enough; all four keys are necessary.* I am so convinced this will work 100 percent of the time that I feel comfortable offering a money-back guarantee whenever we sell our course "Communion with God" from Christian Leadership University. Any student who does not learn to hear God's voice can ask for and receive a refund for the cost of the course. These four keys work! You will hear! Jesus was the One who issued the guarantee. He said, *"My sheep hear My voice"* (John 10:27). A Christian who utilizes the four keys all at the same time will recognize God's voice! Use them and teach them to others:

- Stillness

- Vision

- Spontaneity

- Journaling

Hearing God's voice is as simple as quieting yourself down, fixing your eyes on Jesus, tuning to spontaneity, and writing. Memorize this statement and share it over and over and over with people. Help them break out of a culture of rationalism and discover spiritual intimacy with Almighty God for themselves. I believe it is the greatest gift you can share with people, next to salvation and baptism in the Holy Spirit.

Come On, Let's Stir Up a Passionate Hunger for Spiritual Things!

Creating a desire within for more of what God has to tell you and to give you is the beginning of a new way of thinking, living, and believing. For instance, when Oral Roberts was asked, "How do I go about learning to hear God speak to me?" he replied, "Wanting it badly enough to work on it." You will not learn much about the spiritual world until you take time to be quiet and look within. Relating to the spiritual world is complex and takes as much time and effort as relating to the physical world. Learning to walk in the spiritual world is similar to learning to walk physically. There will be stumbling, falling, and getting back up again. Do you have a passion to live and walk by the Spirit? (See Galatians 5:25.)

Prayer Is a Dialogue, Not a Monologue

Prayer is our link to God. Therefore, prayer is the most important activity in which we can engage. Prayer is supposed to be powerful, effective, and meaningful in our lives. Yet many times it is nothing more than a dutiful recitation of the items on our prayer list. We need to learn how to make prayer what it should be—a dynamic dialogue with the Lover of our souls.

Of paramount importance is learning to break free from the prison of rationalism in which Western culture is locked and relearning how to have spiritual experiences—experiences that come from God's Spirit to our spirit and only secondarily to our brain. We must return to the balance that was so beautifully expressed in Jesus' life who did nothing on His own initiative, but only what He heard and saw the Father doing (see John 5:19-20,30).

I needed to learn some things before prayer became purposeful in my life:

- I can have a relationship with God through spiritual experiences rather than the dry monologue of simple mental prayer.

- The essence of prayer is my love relationship with the King of Kings, not simply going to Him to get things.

- The main purpose for learning to hear God's voice is so that I might really know Him—His heart, His joys, His desires, His hurts, His character, His will.

- The principles from the Bible that relate to prayer and the spiritual realm provide direction and understanding as I travel the road of spiritual experiences.

- The Holy Spirit will mold my prayer life, instead of me taking the principles of prayer God has shown me and reducing them to legalistic bondage.

- Spirit-born specific action and power flow as a natural result of my love relationship, causing the activities of my life to be of the Spirit and not the flesh. This keeps my relationship with the King of Kings from being simply self-indulgent on my part and helps me to realize that many others need to be touched by His love, as well.

Some Reflections on Learning to Hear God's Voice

After many years of successfully teaching these four important keys, I've come to several conclusions:

- Christ often speaks back to us using Scripture. God's voice (*rhema*) is grounded in God's Word (*Logos*).

- Initially, I looked upon my experiences as experiments. I was unsure and only acted on one-half to two-thirds of them. My confidence grew as I saw the positive results.

- I found I could react to God's ideas with my own analytical thoughts and questions, and that Christ would react to my thoughts with His words, which I sensed as spontaneous thoughts. I still recognized a distinction between His spontaneous thoughts and my analytical thoughts.

- When His inner voice lines up with inner thoughts you already have, rejoice. Don't doubt that it is His voice and assume that they are just your own thoughts. You were simply already picking up God's spontaneous thoughts before you began your prayer time. Your journaling has merely confirmed what you already had been sensing from God.

- God does not require more of you than you are ready to give. He will provide an alternate, easier path if you request it. However, He is most pleased when we allow Him to expand our faith and draw us out of our comfort zone.

- When the Lord's words do not come to pass as you expected, go back and ask Him why. He will tell you. If the issue degenerates into a confusing mess that you can't comprehend, that's fine. Just put it on the back burner and maybe someday you will receive understanding about it. If not, you will understand it in eternity.

I have several such issues simmering in my heart. One stayed there for eight years until God finally gave me understanding through another person in the Body of Christ. The Lord had spoken to me through a prophecy that I was going to move to Montana. I have never felt any witness in my heart to go to Montana, so I just let the prophecy sit in the back of my mind. When I was sharing this in a seminar one day, a person explained to me that "going to Montana" was a colloquialism that meant "you are going to a higher plain" (Montana is a high-altitude state). That made sense and bore witness in my heart, as this prophecy was given to me shortly after I learned to journal.

Examples of Two-way Journaling

Key #4 is two-way journaling. You write your thoughts and questions to God, and God responds. The entire conversation is captured on paper. It is two friends, sharing love together. It is not one-way journaling where you share your heart and leave. It is you letting God share His heart back with you. That is why we call it two-way journaling. Throughout the book, we go into great detail about this important key and also provide examples to help you become familiar with this exceptional way to connect more intimately with your heavenly Father. We recommend that you have a journal and a pen nearby as you continue reading. At various junctures within the discussion, writing in your journal will be helpful—and necessary—to keep you moving forward toward hearing God's voice.

All journaling is similar in that you sense the character of Christ permeating it. It is saturated with attitudes of love, joy, peace, faith, gentleness, faithfulness (see Gal. 5:22-23). Your journaling will edify, exhort, and comfort you (see 1 Cor. 14:3). Let the examples throughout this book inspire and encourage you as you note how similar they sound to the journaling you receive from the Lord.

✳✳✳

Della—God Says to Relax

Dear Jesus, what are You telling me today?

Today is a beautiful day and you are in the center of My will. It only feels bad because of what you are holding on to. Breathe deep. Relax. Put your feet up. I am in charge. I still am Head of the universe. And I am the laughing Jesus, or else there would be no laughter on earth. You, My daughter, are very, very serious. It all works out in the end.

Turn your worry into warfare. Turn anxiety into answers. Turn your problems into prayers. Seek Me. I am here waiting. Sit at My feet. I will come. Give up on yourself and your circumstances. I AM is My name. The great I AM.

✳✳✳

God says, "Celebrate the Storms of Life"

Lord, what would You say to me?

You are a beautiful child with innocent eyes. See the clouds forming on the horizon? My arms will keep you safe. Storms are exciting times. Thunder and lightening—not to be feared, for My arms are around you and I'll not let you go.

We can dance to the music of the storms—your feet on Mine; My hands holding yours.

We dance with abandonment. The pounding of your heart is not from fear but pleasure and anticipation. The wind wraps My robes around you. Watch and be amazed at what I do. You will find peace in the midst of chaos.

✳✳✳

Mark—The Process Is Where It Is At!

You feel the immediate victory and slaughter of the evil one is the goal. I feel the process is the goal. You see, I can instantly slaughter the evil one. Yet I have not. I am letting him perform his greatest efforts against My body and then I shall utilize **both his and My efforts together** *to demonstrate My victory. Thus I shall rule over all—both the forces of good and the forces of evil. And My triumph shall be unquestionable.*

Therefore, fear not the process nor the intertwined defeats. I shall in My time thoroughly and totally defeat the enemy and shall be Lord over all.

Has not the process always been integral to My plans? Consider Joseph's many years of slavery before being exalted to Pharaoh's right hand. Consider Moses' 40 years on the backside of a desert before being exalted by My right hand. Is not the process integral to the victory? Consider My Son's death and torment before being exalted to My right hand.

Fear not the process. Fear not for the victory, for it shall surely come SAITH THE LORD.

CELEBRATE the process. CELEBRATE the struggle. CELEBRATE the defeats, for all shall be swallowed up in My victory and I shall be Lord over all. I shall rule over the light as well as the darkness. My glory shall shine forth as never before and all mankind shall see it.

✳ ✳ ✳

Christian Leadership University Student—God Dances Over Us

Lord, I have drifted away and so easily for the last two weeks. You know the whys. I need You. I must have intimacy with You above all else. My life depends on it. Speak to me this morning.

It's hard for you to see Me or to understand when I dance over you with joy. I do not see you as you see yourself. I am not bogged down by the past and the failures. You are My joy. You are a joy to Me.

But what about all my failures, even my most recent ones?

They are gone. Washed away. Forgotten. You have confessed them. I see your heart, My heart in you. There are two choices before you today. To dwell in Me or to dwell in you, on your sins, your failures or your struggles. Choose the better. Sit at My feet and learn of Me. You will find rest for your troubled soul. Come and sit. Dwell. Rest. Relax in My presence.

I know your tendencies toward sin and how easily you stray from Me. I see. I know. As you sit before Me, I cover you with My robe. I place it on you. I lift your head by putting My hand under your chin, and lift your gaze into My eyes. There you see acceptance, and approval.

I know you feel like running, like pulling back. But how long can you go on like this? This is a much better way. Continue in My love. Live in My love and acceptance and in My approval. Nothing, absolutely nothing you can do can win My approval. This is hard for you to grasp. To be free from striving, trying hard to be accepted; to be free is where I am taking you. Total abandonment to Me. To My righteousness, to all that I give you; to receive from My hand. No strings attached.

Remember, I do not see with your eyes, but you can see with Mine. As I touch your eyes, receive sight. This is a new day. Today. Come to Me TODAY. NEW! Fresh. Everyday is a new start. No past. No failure. Covered by My blood. Just as if you have never failed or sinned. That's how I see every morning. My mercies are new every morning! Start this day, every day with that fresh realization. Behold, all things are new. Come away, My beloved. Come.

❊ ❊ ❊

More journaling is available as blogs at www.KoinoniaNetwork.org.

Free Online Resources to Deepen These Truths
Interviews with Mark Virkler

- **100 Huntley Street** www.cwgministries.org/huntley. htm
- **It's Supernatural** www.cwgministries.org/RothTV

Endnotes

1. James Strong, *Strong's Exhaustive Concordance of the Bible* (Peabody, MA: Hendrickson Publishers, first published in 1894), ISBN 0-917006-01-1, 6822 and 7200.

2. Charles G. Finney, "The Psychology of Faith," *The Independent of New York* (April 30, 1874). Taken from protected material, used by permission of the Christian Literature Crusade, Fort Washington, PA 10934. Full text available at http://www.charlesgfinney.com/1868_75Independent/740430_psych_faith.htm.

A Cultural Backdrop for Hearing God's Voice

Very Different From the New Age Movement

Sometimes people ask me what the difference is between what New Age teaches and what I teach. As will be demonstrated, we begin and build from a totally different foundation from that of the New Age movement. Therefore, the differences are immense. I believe it is ludicrous to suggest that people beginning from such totally opposite foundations could end up in the same place. New Agers contact demons, familiar spirits, and evil spirits. Christians who are covered by the blood of Jesus and guided by the Holy Spirit are led into the throne room of God as John was in Revelation. Our goal is to contact Almighty God. Theirs is to encounter **any** spirit out there. We test our revelation **against the Bible**. They don't. **We ask the Holy Spirit to lead and guide us**, since we don't know how to pray as we ought, but He prays through us with groanings too deep for words (see Rom. 8:26). New Agers do not ask for guidance from the Holy Spirit. These are just three foundational differences between what the Church does and what New Agers do. So we have different foundations, different goals, and different processes, and thus we get extremely different results!

Why Is New Age so Attractive?

New Age offers creativity and life to its followers. For example, David Spangler, who has been lecturing and writing about New Age for 25 years, defines New Age as "the condition that emerges when I live life in a creative, empowering, compassionate manner."[1] That's an attractive prospect and goal for both Christians and non-Christians. He goes on to state, "I understand the New Age as a metaphor for being in the world in a manner that opens us to the presence of God—the presence of love and possibility—in the midst of our ordinariness."[2]

The ideals of the New Age mindset are high and lofty and, if they can be achieved in even a small way by the power of humans, they are tremendously enticing to a growing number of people. Therefore, people flock to read and study the literature put out by New Agers.

Why Is New Age so Deceptive?

One reason New Age is so deceptive is that it embraces ideals and values that are very similar to Christianity. This, of course, should be expected, considering the fact that satan is the great counterfeiter. For instance, listen again to David Spangler:

> Inwardly, the New Age continues the historical effort of humanity to delve deeply into the mysteries of the nature of God, of ourselves, and of reality. In the midst of materialism, it is a rebirth of our sense of the sacred.... The New Age is essentially a symbol representing the human heart and intellect in partnership with God building a better world that can celebrate values of community, wholeness and sacredness. It is a symbol for the emergence of social behavior based on a worldview that stimulates creativity, discipline, abundance and wholeness; it is a symbol for a more mature and unobstructed expression of the sacredness and love at the heart of life.[3]

After reading definitions like this, many Christians would respond with a feeling that Christianity itself holds many of these ideals. However, New Agers believe humanity can reach for these goals and achieve them through our own effort, or if we do seek spiritual assistance, it is not restricted to Jesus Christ or God, but to any "good" spiritual energies that are floating around. Remember, the New Age movement is eclectic, and therefore willing to draw from anyone's experiences or insight. They do not have a written standard against which to test all their experiences and teachings, as Christians do.

What Should Be the Church's Response to New Age?

Obviously, we recognize it as a continuation of the deception that began in the Garden of Eden: "Man can become like God" (see Gen. 3:22). It is the age-old lie that we can strive to reach divinity ourselves. Instead, Christians have discovered the freedom simply to rest in the Vine, experiencing the flow of the river of life that wells up within them by the Holy Spirit as they cease from their own labors and simply attune themselves to God.

We respect New Agers' desire to become loving, creative, and fulfilled, and we point them to the only true Source of such a lifestyle, Jesus Christ. New birth is mandatory as they acknowledge Jesus Christ, the Son of God, as their Lord and Savior and receive by faith His atoning work at Calvary.

We recognize that because New Agers are part of the great counterfeit, they may use words, phrases, and techniques that have been borrowed from Christianity or Christian traditions. *Yet, we will not give over either these words or these experiences to the satanic counterfeit, as they are God's forever.*

For example, New Agers have written on "the rainbow," which of course was part of God's covenant with Noah, and on "centering," which is a word and an experience that has been used for decades by the Quaker church. *The New Age Catalogue* even recommends the Christian book *Hinds Feet on High Places* by Hannah Hurnard.

Being eclectic, we should expect them to draw from Christianity as well as everyone else. That does not concern us. We have a standard, the Word of God, and our acceptance of a truth is not based on whether or not a counterfeit group has yet picked it up. We look to see if it is taught in Scripture; and surely such things as centering or quieting our souls before the Lord, as is practiced by the Quaker church, is clearly taught and demonstrated by King David in the Psalms as he states, *"My soul waits in silence for God only"* (Ps. 62:1,5).

Therefore, we will expect New Agers to blur the line between truth and error through their eclectic nature, but we will walk calmly according to the eternal truths and experiences taught in God's Word. We shall not concern ourselves with how many cults are also drawing upon biblical concepts. We shall concern ourselves only with encountering fully and completely the God of the Scriptures.

Rev. Maurice Fuller, one of our long-time friends and spiritual advisors, writes:

> One thing the New Age calls Christians to do is to enter fully into all of the dimensions of our relationship with Christ. The New Age has arisen to take the territory abandoned by the mainstream Christianity. Because Christianity (even most Charismatics) has neglected the intuitive and relational and has majored on the propositional and the analytical, a void has been left in the hearts of those who were seeking spiritual encounters. In the churches they met only doctrinal studies, so they sought for spiritual relationships within the occult and New Age teachings.
>
> The very best antidote for the New Age teachings is for Christians to enter into and live fully in the supernatural. This is certainly no time to draw back from supernatural living and retreat into a mere defense of orthodoxy. Because we have adopted this stance for the last half-century, we have opened the door for the New Age to fill the vacuum. There is a longing in the human heart for communication and a relationship with the Divine. Since the dawn of history, when God's people

do not preach, proclaim and model the genuine article, men and women will wander into whatever appears to offer the fulfillment of their spiritual quest. We need to cast aside our hesitation and proceed strongly forward, the Word and the Spirit as our unfailing guide.

The early Church made the tragic error (after about 150 A.D.) of majoring on defending orthodoxy in the face of the heresies of Gnosticism (which has recently arisen again as part of New Age teaching), Mystery Religions and State Paganism. While they were vigorously defending Christianity, formulating creeds (propositional statements of doctrine), and attempting to vanquish heresy by excommunicating heretics, somewhere along the line they forgot that Christianity is a relationship to be lived, not merely a theory to be proved.

The rationalistic patterns of argument adopted from the Greek philosophers replaced the much more forceful arguments of a changed life and the miraculous interventions of Almighty God in the affairs of men. The Church largely lost the battle of ideas merely by conceding that the battle was confined to arguments over ideas. The Bible is 90 percent narratives of God working in lives. Demonstrating God in our lives in all of His dimensions is our best defense. The best defense is still a good offense![4]

Additional Distinctions Between Christianity and New Age

Since New Age seeks wholeness, life, love, and creativity, it will obviously be reaching toward some of the same goals that Christianity reaches toward. Since New Age is eclectic, it will be using some of the same approaches that Christianity uses, with some very subtle differences. Listed in the following chart are some of these comparisons and some of the differences.

New Testament Christianity	New Age Movement
Intuitive Development	
The voice of God may flow through man's heart or spirit as intuitive thoughts, visions, burdens, and impressions. Christians attempt to learn to discern God's voice, so they can hear and obey, thus experiencing abundant life.	Called intuition, New Agers recognize that as the voice of man's heart, it releases man's creativity, and thus they seek to cultivate it.
Contact with Spirit	
Christians seek fellowship with the Holy Spirit. They may also encounter angels sent from God.	New Agers seek fellowship with any beings in the spirit world.
Method of Quieting Oneself	
Christians often worship by fixing their eyes on Jesus, the Author and Perfecter of their faith.	New Agers use mantra (a nonsense syllable or phrase spoken repeatedly, designed to take you into spirit-consciousness).
Use of One's Visionary Abilities	
Visionary abilities are presented before God so He may grant divine vision. They are recognized as a creative ability within man.	Visionary abilities are used by oneself to visualize one's goals. They are recognized as a creative ability within man.
Use of Writing in Spiritual Experiences	
Journaling is a way of recording what one senses God is speaking within him. Impressions sensed in the heart are registered in the mind and recorded by the hand. It is similar to the Psalms except that one's journal never becomes Scripture. Rather it is tested by Scripture.	Journaling is a way of recording what is flowing from the spirit world. One's hand hangs limp, and a force takes it over and guides it. The heart or mind of man is not involved nor is it submitted to Scripture. This is called "automatic writing."
The Planet Today	
Our world is being redeemed by the working of God through His Spirit, His angels, and His Church.	Our world is becoming better through man's efforts.
The Planet Ultimately	
New Heavens and a New Earth will come through God's direct intervention.	A new age will come through man's accomplishments.

figure 2.1

I believe that the New Age movement is a reaction to what God is doing in the Church of Jesus Christ. In 1900, the Holy Spirit began to move in new and powerful ways upon the Church. In the relatively short time since then, we have seen over 400 million Charismatic and Pentecostal Christians worldwide swept into these new (or restored) moves of the Holy Spirit. C. Peter Wagner estimated that 1.1 billion Christians would be sensitized to the Holy Spirit's flow by A.D. 2000.[5]

Gallop poll surveys have revealed that the individuals in the group that calls itself Charismatic spend more time each week on average in Bible study, prayer, and church attendance than other Christians. This is quite interesting. Regardless of your theological persuasion, the Bible says you can test things by its fruit. This surely is good fruit.

Therefore, I believe New Age is satan's reaction to the mighty outpouring of the Holy Spirit that we are seeing in this century. I do not see it as something to fear or to flee from. Since when does light fear darkness? No, I stand against it in the power of the Holy Spirit, in the power of Almighty God! Often, God has allowed tests to emerge within a culture so He can prove His supremacy over all else. Elijah and Baal are classic examples of this as Elijah proposed a test to see who could call down fire from Heaven. Whoever was successful was the one who served the true God.

You notice it is not the Pharisees or the false prophets who propose such tests or act with such courage and boldness. It is the prophets on the front line who prove God in the midst of their generation. I suspect that the books being written today by the Church about the New Age movement are not being written by the prophets. The ones I have read encourage a spirit of fear that we will be consumed, rather than a spirit of faith that we will conquer and pass this particular test. I believe the spirit of fear originates in satan, and the spirit of faith originates in God. Therefore I am very careful not to feed on anything permeated with the spirit of fear.

Guardrails Along the Spiritual Path

It is understandable that there would be caution in the hearts of some people about exploring the spiritual realm. If the only supernatural people you have heard of were operating from satan's kingdom, and there has been nothing supernatural about your Christianity, of course you will want to be careful. But do not allow satan to plant fear in your heart and prevent you from experiencing all that God has provided for you. You do not need to be afraid because God has laid out some very clear protective guidelines that will keep you safe as you enter the spiritual world. Stated succinctly they are:

1. You are a born-again Christian, having accepted Jesus Christ into your heart as your Lord and Savior, and having had your sins washed away by His cleansing blood.

2. You accept the Bible as the inerrant Word of God.

3. You demonstrate your love and respect for God by your commitment to knowing His Word. You follow a plan for reading through the entire Bible regularly (such as once each year), as well as enjoying more in-depth meditation on books, characters, or topics.

4. You have an attitude of submission to what God has shown you from the Bible.

5. You have two or three spiritual advisors/counselors to whom you go for input on a regular basis.

A fairly young Christian can meet all these requirements. It only takes a day and a half to read through the New Testament, and the rest of the requirements can be met upon conversion. It is wonderful if you are a new believer to begin communing with God during the early days of your spiritual walk. You will find the rest and peace your soul so eagerly longs for.

Spiritual Counselors

God has established spiritual advisors as an umbrella of protection, to help guard us from self-deception within our own hearts, as well as from the deception of satan.

> *Obey [Greek:* Peitho—*allow yourself to be persuaded by] your leaders, and submit to them; for they watch over your soul, as those who will give an account. Let them do this with joy and not grief, for this would be unprofitable for you* (Hebrews 13:17).

> *...But in the multitude of counselors there is safety* (Proverbs 11:14 KJV).

How many counselors do I need? *"Every fact is to be confirmed by the testimony of two or three witnesses"* (2 Cor. 13:1).

What to look for in a spiritual counselor:

1. *A close friend;* one who knows the sheep, and whose sheep recognize his voice.

2. One who has a *solid biblical orientation.*

3. One who can sense the *voice of the Spirit* of God in his own heart.

4. One who is willing to *commit himself to the sheep,* who will invest his time and energy, and is willing to lay down his life for the sheep for whom he is responsible.

5. One who also *receives counsel.*

6. One who is *ahead (or alongside) of me* in the area I am seeking advice.

You will need to recognize that God is the authority over all authorities (see Rom. 13:1), and that the heart of the king is in the Lord's hand (see Prov. 21:1). Therefore, as you pray for the one over you (see 1 Tim. 2:1-4), you trust God to work His perfection through imperfection.

Some already-established counselors include: parents, spouses, employers, home cell group leaders, pastors, elders, Sunday school teachers, spiritual directors, and so on. It is not wise to build close spiritual relationships with members of the opposite sex. There is too much danger of these evolving into physical relationships and causing destructive explosions.

You may also have groups of two or three counselors who have expertise in specific areas of life such as financial or health advisers.

> **Submission is an openness to the Spirit-led counsel and correction of several others, while keeping a sense of personal responsibility for our own discernment of God's voice within us.**

Note that we are looking for **Spirit-led counsel** and not what other people are **thinking in their minds**. We never ask what a person **thinks** about our journaling. We ask, **"Does your spirit bear witness** that this came from Christ?" Also, we are going to **several** people (two or three), and not just one. Finally, we take what they have suggested and **we present it back to God in prayer,** saying "God, show me any truth in what they are saying." When submission is done right, it is a wonderful blessing. When it is done wrong, it is a terrible curse. Do it right!

It is absolutely essential that you not miss this step of recognizing two or three spiritual counselors in your life, and that you go to them on a regular basis to confirm that what you felt you heard from God actually came from God. The Lord has created us to live in relationship with one another. It is satan who seeks to destroy relationships, and who offers us the spirit of pride that says, "I know more than...." Pride is the first sin in the Bible (*"You will be like God, knowing good and evil,"* Gen. 3:5), and it is the most prevalent sin in the Bible. It is the center of satan's heart. You do not want his arrogance in your heart. *"God is opposed to the proud, but gives grace to the humble"* (James 4:6).

First Thessalonians 5:20-21 exhorts us to *"examine everything carefully; hold fast to that which is good; ...do not despise prophetic utterances."* It is clear from this that there may be errors in the prophetic words we receive (which is essentially what "hearing God's voice" is), or there would be no need to examine everything carefully and only hold on to the good part.

We must accept that mistakes are part of every learning process, and not despise prophetic utterances or reject the goal of clearly discerning God's voice. Your spiritual advisors will help you recognize any flaws in what you believe you hear, and guide you in understanding why they happened and how to prevent them in the future. With their assistance, even your mistakes can be growing and learning experiences rather than cause for doubt and retreat. Examining everything carefully with the help of two or three spiritual advisors and holding fast to only what is good allows you to move forward much more quickly in God and in fulfilling His purposes for your life. For your sake, do this!

Usually, however, when you share your words from the Lord with your spiritual advisors, they will confirm that it indeed is Him. What an encouragement to you this will be! Your faith will be empowered and you will press on with even greater excitement. Who among us does not need our faith strengthened from time to time? So establish these three spiritual advisors *now* in your life, before you continue with this book.

Doesn't This Teaching Repeat the Errors of the 1970s Shepherding Movement?

You may be wondering, *Isn't this like the Shepherding Movement of the 1970s?* Not at all. Those involved in the shepherding movement were trying to restore the concept of spiritual covering and authority; however, in some cases it turned into domination, legalism, and a spirit of control. Jesus said that we do not rule over others as the heathen do with the use of force, but *in love we serve one another.* The use of domination, intimidation, and control is strictly forbidden in the way of love (see 1 Pet. 5:1-6). Love draws; domination forces.

The picture of church leadership given in the Bible is of a shepherd and his sheep. Shepherds must lead sheep; sheep cannot be driven. Therefore, the center of these relationships must be friendship and spiritual kinship, not control. Any authority *is in a **rhema** word from God,* which can come through your spiritual advisor. However, it is the *rhema* that has the authority, not any position or title.

I want to emphasize that after you have received the input and counsel of your advisors, and have prayerfully considered all that they have said, *you* maintain final responsibility before God for your response to what you believe is His *rhema* word to you. In Paul's discussion concerning believers having different understandings of God's will in Romans 14, he does not insist that everyone must do as he says or as the elders say, despite what they believe they have heard from God.

On the contrary, in Romans 14:12 Paul reminds them of their personal accountability before God, and in verse 23 he declares, *"he that doubts is damned if he eats, because he eats not of faith: for whatsoever is not of faith is sin."* If you do something that you believe is against what God has told you, *even if you are wrong,* it is sin for you because you are acting in disobedience and outside of faith.

The Bible declares: *"For we must all appear before the judgment seat of Christ; that every one may receive the things done in his body, according to that he hath done, whether it be good or bad"* (2 Cor. 5:10). I am not aware of anyplace in Scripture where God accepted the Nuremburg defense: "I'm not guilty of the sinful thing I did because I was just following orders." You will stand alone before God to give an account of your obedience to His *Logos* and His *rhema* to you.

First Kings 13 relates a sobering story that strongly emphasizes this point. A man of God came out of Judah by the word of the Lord with a prophetic message for King Jeroboam. Though the king initially rejected the prophet's words, the Lord confirmed them with supernatural manifestations. Seeing the power of God, the king changed his tune and invited the prophet to stay, eat, and be refreshed at his house. But the prophet refused, saying, *"For so it was commanded me by the word of the Lord, saying, 'You shall eat no bread, nor drink water, nor return by the way which you came'"* (1 Kings 13:9).

So far, this is a fairly standard Bible story, unfolding as you would expect. But then something unforeseen happens. An "old prophet" went out to meet this new guy in the neighborhood who was also hearing from God. He, too, invited the man of God to stop by his house for a bite to eat. The young prophet gave him the same answer as he had given the king, "No, God told me not to." But the old prophet replied, "I am also a prophet like you, and God told me it was OK for you to eat with me." And so he did.

According to most of the teaching on submission given in the Church today, the younger prophet did the right thing by obeying his elder. The older man had a recognized office of prophet in the community, and he said that he was giving the word of the Lord. The younger man was not only *justified* in setting aside what he believed the Lord had told him, he was actually *obligated* to do so, according to contemporary teaching.

Unfortunately for him, the Lord didn't see it that way. Through the lying older prophet, the Lord spoke His judgment on the young man: *"...Thus says the LORD, 'Because you have disobeyed the command of the LORD, and have not observed the commandment which the LORD your God commanded you, but have returned and eaten bread and drunk water in the place of which He said to you, "Eat no bread and drink no water"; your body shall not come to the grave of your fathers....'" Now when he had gone, a lion met him on the way and killed him, and his body was thrown on the road, with the donkey standing beside it; the lion also was standing beside the body..."* (1 Kings 13:21-25).

He paid for his "submission" to man over his obedience to the *rhema* of God to him with his life. Wisdom demands that you humbly seek the advice of spiritual counselors and listen to them with an open spirit (recognizing that you could be mistaken), but you carry final responsibility for what you do with God's word to you.

Journaling Does Not Replace
My Need for the Body of Christ

When I journal and ask God questions, I normally am open to receiving only the answers that are within the very limited perspective through which I am viewing God's provision and responses. Any additional insights God desires to give me that are outside my particular outlook are easily missed (not that God is unable to give them, but I may not hear or understand them). By receiving input from several counselors, I gain God's answers from others' perspectives. In the multitude of counselors there is safety (see Prov. 11:14). I should never assume that my journaling gives me the complete revelation of God on an issue.

Theologically speaking, journaling probably could give me a full picture if I were a totally yielded, transparent vessel, wide-open and trained in spiritual revelation, freed of all my limiting views and prejudices, and wholly cognizant of all statutes and principles taught in the Bible. However, most of us will not fully meet all these conditions, so we desperately need others who seek the Lord alongside of us and give us their input.

The failure to do this is one of the most limiting things I see in people's lives. Too many people live too much as an island, rather than seeking out others' input on an ongoing basis. Look at the following diagram and see what you miss by not receiving others' input. Look what you gain by receiving their prayerful reflections. The distance you travel in life toward fulfilling your destiny is greatly hindered or enhanced by whether you ignore or practice the principle diagrammed.

A standard question I ask when people want my counsel concerning direction they are sensing is, "What does your spouse say?" Wives have been told for years to listen to their husbands, so I probably don't need to say it again. But just in case there are women who feel spiritually superior to their husbands and therefore don't solicit their input, I will say again, "Wife, what does your husband say about it?"

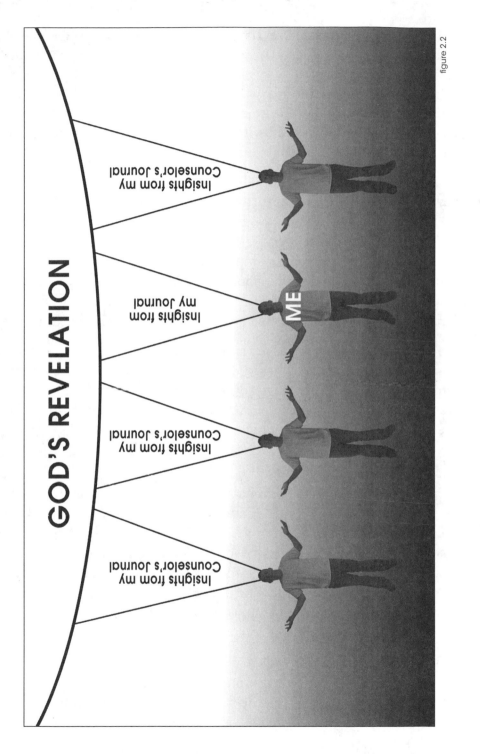

figure 2.2

Unfortunately, too seldom have men been asked the same question: "Husband, what does your wife say about it?" I am appalled at the number of men I have counseled who do not seek the counsel of their wives, or who ignore what they sense God is saying. Men, hear me! Your wife is probably the greatest gift God has given you to help you on your path to spiritual fruitfulness and maturity! She has gifts that you do not have, and that you need! Listen to your wife!

Consider the 12 disciples and how their growth was accelerated as they were discipled by a Mentor who was ahead of them in the area in which they needed to grow. Who are the mentors in your life who are helping you grow in specific areas? If you can't quickly identify them and claim an ongoing, functional, working relationship with them, you are short-changing yourself and limiting what you could be developing into. Don't let this sin persist in your life. Discover your mentors today and establish strong working relationships with them.

I have people who serve as my spiritual counselors, several as business mentors, and some as health advisors, and some as theological advisors, and some as marriage advisors. Do you have different mentors ahead of you in various areas who are speaking into your life on a regular basis? For your sake, I hope you do.

Changing Advisors

I believe we are free to change spiritual mentors as we grow and develop. If you change spiritual advisors every six months, this most likely indicates a problem in your life. However, if every five years or so you are replacing your advisors, it may be an indication that growth and change are taking place in your life, which is necessitating new people to mentor you. The important thing is that when you leave one mentoring relationship, you enter another; you should not live without adequate counsel.

Throughout the book, we've placed prayers that allow you to pause and reach out to God. You may pray the prayer as written, or, of course, say a prayer that rose up in your heart while reading. When God is speaking to you a principle or a truth through this book, take the time to pray and speak the truth with your own lips. This deepens the truth, helping you to internalize it and be changed by it. Internalization and transformation are what we need, not simply additional head knowledge.

Prayer: *God, we trust You to work through the principle of spiritual counsel as laid out in Your Word, and to work Your perfection through our imperfection. Lord, who have You placed around me that You want me to draw upon as a spiritual mentor?*

Now fix your eyes on the Lord as you wait before Him. See what names pop into your mind, and jot them down on a piece of paper. Contact these individuals and briefly explain the concept of being a spiritual advisor and why you are being encouraged to seek spiritual advisors as you explore the hearing of God's voice. Ask them if you can bounce your journaling off them and if they will check their hearts and let you know if their hearts bear witness that it is from Christ. You can e-mail your journaling to them or read it to them. Do not paraphrase your journaling. Your paraphrase is never as good as God's original words and is often inaccurate.

How to Succeed When Living Out of God's Voice

I have found that people who do not *establish and draw on* spiritual advisors are generally unsuccessful in maintaining a lifestyle of living out of the voice of God over the long term. Some never get started, because they are never certain whether what they are hearing is God or not and they allow doubt to block the flow. Others begin with confidence, but when they make a mistake in hearing God's voice, or *think* they have made a mistake, their faith is damaged so badly they quit.

During the first few days and weeks of journaling, I strongly recommend that you share all your journaling with at least one of your spiritual advisors for confirmation that you are on the right track. Once you both have confidence in your discernment, you can cut back to only sharing those things that: (1) you are uncertain about whether they came from God, or (2) are big decisions.

A Theological Backdrop for Establishing Spiritual Intimacy

I grew up loving boxes. I enjoyed establishing theological systems and principles that I put together into an orderly grid of truth. Then I tried to stuff my life into it. Sounds inviting, doesn't it?

For instance, I established my theology concerning how much to witness, how much to pray, how much to disciple others, how to handle fear, anger, discouragement and guilt, how to properly crucify my flesh, how to rejoice without ceasing, etc. Then I tried to live out of all the principles that I had established.

I discovered, however, that while I focused on one set of rules and principles, I forgot another group. As a result, I always felt guilty. I hadn't yet come to realize that the end of the Law is always death, and that if I tried to live out of laws, I would always be experiencing a death process working within me. For me, this death took the form of guilt, accusation, condemnation, and depression. Not exactly the abundant life that Jesus promised!

My boxes just never seemed to work. First, the expectations of the laws that I had discovered within the Bible always left me feeling guilty, knowing I could never measure up. And second, my boxes always seemed to need adjusting. They never seemed any bigger than I was. (That should have been a clue that they were mine and not God's!)

When I first became a Christian, my box describing who was a Christian was quite small. It included my church and me. Eventually, I enlarged it a bit and let some other Baptists in. Then I enlarged it some more and allowed in some Methodists. Next I accepted the Pentecostals and Charismatics. (I had to overhaul the entire box to do that!) Eventually, I even discovered Catholics who were genuinely saved.

By then I had altered my box so many times and so radically that I was no longer sure about the value of building theological boxes. They seemed so small, so inadequate and so imperfect. They didn't seem like a very effective approach to living life. Besides, they always created so much division. Rather than maintaining the unity of the Body of Christ, I was always segregating it, based on my limited theological understanding. I began to wonder if this truly was the way we were to live, or if God had a better plan.

Discovering Life in the Spirit

Then something new began to enter my life. I began to learn the ways of the Spirit of God. I learned to hear His voice and see His vision. I learned to open my heart to the intuitive flow of the Spirit of God within me. I learned to live out of the stream that was welling up within me. Jesus had spoken of this river, but I had never really understood what the experience was.

> *"From his innermost being shall flow rivers of living water."*
> *But this He spoke of the Spirit, whom those who believed*
> *in Him were to receive...* (John 7:38-39).

When I learned to recognize the voice of God as the bubbling flow of spontaneous ideas that welled up from my heart as I fixed my eyes upon Jesus, I discovered a new way of living, that of living out of the Spirit of God rather than simply the laws of God—not that they are in any way opposed to each other. It is just that the Holy Spirit has such great finesse in handling the laws of God that my shallow boxes were mere mockeries of His vast truth.

When struggling with a situation, I found that if I used my own theological boxes to deal with it, I would end up with narrow, judgmental decisions. However, if I went to Jesus in prayer and tuned to the flow of the river within, He would bring other principles to my attention that I had more or less forgotten. He would ask me to apply these over and above the principles that I had been trying to apply earlier.

It's not that some principles are right and some are wrong. It's that some are weightier than others. Some are the true heart of the matter, and some are simply the periphery. Jesus told the Pharisees of His day that they strained at a gnat and swallowed a camel.

> *Woe to you, scribes and Pharisees, hypocrites! For*
> *you tithe mint and dill and cumin, and have neglected*

the weightier provisions of the law: justice and mercy and faithfulness; but these are the things you should have done without neglecting the others (Matthew 23:23).

I found that I generally forfeited the principles of mercy and faithfulness when dealing with others. I was harsh and severe in my judgment of them, and rather than being faithful and loyal to them, I came against them, more as the accuser of the brethren than the Comforter. Therefore, I assumed a satanic stance, rather than a Holy Spirit stance; that is, I tended to "come against" rather than "coming alongside."

The Accuser's Stance or the Comforter's?

It took me years to come to grips with the realization that satan is the accuser of the brethren (see Rev. 12:10), and that the Holy Spirit is the One who comes alongside and helps (see John 14:16). Even when we are terribly wrong, God does not take an accusatory or adversarial stand against us. For example, when the world had just committed its most hideous crime (crucifying the Son of God), rather than condemning, Jesus said, *"Father, forgive them; for they know not what they do"* (Luke 23:34).

As I began to examine my own life, I realized that I often took antagonistic and adversarial attitudes toward people with whom I didn't agree. I felt it was what God wanted me to do. However, finally it dawned upon me that the accuser's stance is satan's attitude (the word *devil* literally means "accuser") and the comforter's stance is the Holy Spirit's position.

Since this revelation, I have made a commitment *never* to take the accuser's position against anyone. No longer will I be the expression of satan. If someone is struggling, hurting, down, or in error, I have one, and only one, posture—to come alongside and comfort, to be faithful, and thus preserve the dignity of all and the unity of the Body of Christ.

As I began to live out of the river that flows from within, I became less judgmental and less narrow-minded. I developed *"largeness of heart,"* a trait that Solomon had (1 Kings 4:29—literally, "a hearing heart"). However, I became increasingly concerned about my more embracing attitude, my tendency to freely accept so many. It seemed a bit liberal to me. I wasn't too sure about it at first.

Loving Mercy, Not Justice

The Lord showed me that I loved justice, judgment, and precision more than I loved mercy and compassion. I approached people first with judgment, and only secondarily with love and mercy. He showed me that He was the opposite of that. He approached people with love and mercy first, and only secondarily with justice.

He reminded me of the Micah 6:8 balance: *"He has shown you, O man, what is good; and what does the Lord require of you, but to **do justly**, and to **love mercy**, and to walk humbly with your God?"* (NKJV). He said to me, "Mark, you love justice and only do mercy. I love mercy and only do justice. You are the inverse of Me." With that, I was cut to the quick and began to change, recognizing the truth of God's words.

Finally, the Lord began to show me the proper place and purpose of laws and rules in my life. He said, *"The Sabbath was made for man, not man for the Sabbath"* (Mark 2:27). I tended to get that all mixed up. I used to start with the rule and think that my purpose was to obey it. Jesus says, "No." We start with man and his fulfillment; rules are meant to serve man. They are there to assist in releasing the maximum amount of life possible. Jesus Himself came to give us life, abundant life. Therefore, I am learning to begin with the goal of "life" and see what application of which rules releases the most life within and through me. If I don't begin and end with the goal of life, I generally begin and end with the goal of obeying the rule. And man was not created so that he could keep a bunch of rules. He was created to experience abundant life.

Learning to live in the Spirit rather than live in laws greatly impacted my prayer life. I had many rules about how I was to pray and what constituted a good prayer and categories of prayer and ways to pray. However, God gradually changed all that.

Discovering Certainty in the Spirit

As I prayed about my growing tendency toward acceptance of people and my growing disregard for theological boxes, I asked God, "Lord, can I trust the intuitive flow?" You see, I was losing my nicely defined fences. I was no longer so sure where the boundaries were. I was concerned about falling into cultism. After all, if you get into flow and you don't have clear edges, what keeps you from error?

The Lord answered me this way: *"Mark, you can trust the intuitive flow of My Spirit more than you can trust the boxes you build with your mind."* What He said made all the sense in the world. I began to wonder, *"Where in the Bible does it say that we test for truth using our **minds**? Isn't the test so often made in our hearts, through discernment?* As a matter of fact, Jesus Himself recommends that we go with the intuitive flow over and above the analysis of the mind when He says, "When they arrest you and deliver you up, do not be anxious beforehand about what you are to say, *but say whatever is given you in that hour; for it is not you who speak, but it is the Holy Spirit"* (Mark 13:11).

Of course, I had another objection to God's statement that I could trust the intuitive flow within my heart. I explained to God that I had an evil and deceitful heart that was desperately wicked (see Jer. 17:9), and it sure would be wrong to trust the flow from within a deceitful heart. The Lord's response back to me was, "Mark, that is not your heart I was writing about. I have given you a new heart and a new spirit (see Ezek. 36:36). You are a partaker of the divine nature (see 2 Pet. 1:4). You are joined to Almighty God (see 1 Cor. 6:17). You can trust My voice within your spirit more than you can trust the reasoned theology of your mind."

Wow! Accepting these words from God was going to require a huge transformation on my part. I would need to learn to live heart first rather than head first!

Therefore, I began to set aside my love for boxes and for theological grids of truth. I came to cherish instead the intuitive, healing flow through my heart from the One so much wiser and more embracing than I. I dismantled the idolization of my mind and established my heart as the throne that God has chosen as the center of life and the central avenue through which to communicate with humankind. I began to experience the fact that those who are led by the Spirit are not under the law (see Gal. 5:18).

I next asked the Lord, "Well, then, God, what about laws and rules and boxes? Should I scorn them as having no value? What is a proper attitude toward the Law, toward laws?" The Lord gave me several answers. First, the Law keeps us in custody (keeps us from killing ourselves), before we come to the point of being led by the Spirit (see Gal. 3:23). Second, it is a tutor that leads us to Christ (see Gal. 3:24). A tutor is one who teaches us a lesson. The law teaches us that we can never fully keep the law. Therefore, we must abandon ourselves to grace. Wow! What a release! Third, even though we study the laws of God, we never fix our eyes upon them. Instead, we fix our eyes on Jesus, the Author and Finisher of our faith (see Heb. 12:2). Now when I look at a situation, I do not approach it with laws on my mind. I approach it as Christ would, with love first and foremost.

A Philosophical Backdrop for Experiencing Spiritual Intimacy

As I began moving away from *rational* Christianity toward *spiritual* Christianity, the Lord helped me focus on the moves I needed to make.

The Lord spoke to me a verse of Scripture from John 5:39-40. He said, *"Mark, 'you search the Scriptures, because you think that in them you have eternal life; and it is these that bear witness of Me; and you are unwilling to COME TO ME, THAT YOU MAY HAVE LIFE.'"* It was as if a sword went through me. Of course! I had idolized the Bible! In my love for the Scriptures, I had made them God rather than a book that God had written to me about other people's experiences with Him. I had been willing to live out of the Bible, rather than out of God Himself.

I was pierced within when I realized that Jesus had initially spoken this verse to the Pharisees of His day. I began to argue with God that I wasn't a Pharisee! But as I told Him everything I did, the Lord replied that the Pharisees also had done those things. I became frightened, realizing that it was very likely I might indeed be a Pharisee.

I noted that the thing the Pharisees loved most was the Law. They memorized it, spoke it, lived it, and taught it to others. That was a perfect description of me. I lived out of biblical law rather than out of an intimacy with the Holy Spirit. I had not learned how to live out of the truth that Christ had died so we could continuously experience the life of the Holy Spirit within us, and live in Him, rather than a set of rules.

> *And I will ask the Father, and He will give you another Helper, that He may be with you forever; that is the Spirit of truth, whom the world cannot receive, because it does not behold Him or know Him, but you know Him because He abides with you, and will be in you* (John 14:16-17).

Contrasting Two Worldviews

The following are two worldviews that you might embrace. Only one of them is true, but let me show you both so you can carefully examine your life and determine your position, and then decide if that is where you want to stand.

One Worldview—Rationalism

In this worldview you believe that people live in a box—a space/time/energy/mass box. This is the totality of the real world. You contact this world through your five outer senses: touch, taste, sight, hearing, and smell. If you were to leave this box and travel toward the spiritual world, you would find that it is either nonexistent or, if it does exist, it is unknowable.

This is the worldview my religious leaders taught me when I was first saved. They did admit to a spiritual world, but they said it was unknowable in this dispensation. I was told not to expect any direct contact with God during this age because we had been given the Bible and there was no longer a need to encounter God directly. I was also taught not to expect dreams or visions or God's voice or tongues or healing or miracles or any of the gifts of the Holy Spirit to operate. Even though my mind accepted this teaching, my heart hungered for direct spirit encounter with Almighty God, and it would not be satisfied with anything less.

A Second Worldview—Rationalism/Mysticism Combined

Mysticism is not a word I use very often because of some people's fears and inability to separate Eastern mysticism from Christian mysticism. However, here I am using it to mean *a belief in direct spirit encounter with God* (as defined by Merriam-Webster). Surely Christianity as it is portrayed in the Bible involves a lot of direct spirit encounter as God meets with people through angels, dreams, visions, His voice, and supernatural occurrences of many kinds.

In this worldview you believe that there is both a physical world and a spiritual world. You are a conscious individual with five senses that interact with the outer world: touch, taste, sight, hearing, and smell. However, in this worldview you recognize that you have a heart or a spirit also. Paul called this the "inner man" in Romans 7:22, and this part of you also has five senses. These five senses are designed to touch the spiritual world:

1. Eyes of the heart, which see dream and vision.

2. Ears of the heart, which hear God's spoken words (as well as the words of satan, angels, and demons).

3. Inner mind, which is able to ponder and meditate deep within (for example, the Bible says in Luke 2:19 that *"Mary pondered these things in her heart"*).

4. Inner will, where we can make commitments as Paul did when he *"purposed in his spirit to go to Jerusalem"* (Acts 19:21).

5. Emotion of the heart, where we are able to sense and experience the emotions of Almighty God flowing through us.

For example, love, joy, and peace are all emotions of God that are grown within us as the fruit of the Holy Spirit. The Holy Spirit is joined to our spirits (see 1 Cor. 6:17), and thus we experience the feelings of God through the emotional capacity of our spirits, which have been designed by God to feel and incubate the emotions of His Holy Spirit who lives within us.

In this worldview, instead of having five senses that touch one world, we have ten senses that touch two worlds. Obviously, this results in a much fuller and more complete life than living rationally only. We recognize that both God and satan are able to communicate with us on both levels, through the outer world and through the inner spiritual world. For example, the Bible says, *"The devil had already **put into the heart** of Judas Iscariot, the son of Simon, to betray Him..."* (John 13:2).

Experiencing Scripture, Not Just Analyzing It

I can study the Bible rationally, simply with the mind, and learn many facts about God. For instance, I can learn that God loves me. But since love is an inner heart experience, I cannot fully experience God's love until He touches my heart, heals my hurts, and breaks my hardness. When He fills me to overflowing and brings tears of joy to my eyes, then through an intuitive, spiritual experience, I have fully experienced the love I read about.

However, spirit-to-Spirit encounters with God have become much too rare among Western Christians. Since rationalism has taken over the Western world in the past few hundred years, the Church has also come under its influence and has not given the attention it should to the work of the Spirit in our lives. Therefore, we are often bound by rationalism and miss the fullness of relationship with our Father that the early Church enjoyed.

Forty-nine percent of the New Testament contains references to spiritual (nonrational) experiences. To be bound by rationalism will effectively cut off half of New Testament Christianity. If you are not relating intuitively to God, but only intellectually, you will lose your opportunity to flow in the nine gifts of the Holy Spirit; to receive guidance through dreams and visions; to have a fully meaningful and effective prayer life; to commune with the Lord in a dialogue, to build an extremely intimate relationship with Him; and to wholly experience the inward benefits of true worship, to name just a few.

Through rationalism (an overemphasis on reason), Christianity and the Western world have ceased to know how to deal with their inner lives (commonly called heart, spirit, subconscious, or unconscious). Because this entire area of our lives has been cut off and ignored, not only by Western culture but also by the Church, people have not been able to deal successfully with the forces within them (repressed hurts, fears, anxieties, forces of darkness—demons) and have been left more and more to seek escapes such as drinking, drugs, sensual fulfillment, and suicide. Others become neurotic and psychotic; still others go to the occult and Eastern religions to satisfy the inner desires of the spirit that are not being met in "rational Christianity."

We must rediscover direct contact with God and once again become open to intuitive, spiritual experiences. We must rediscover our spiritual senses and reinstate them in our lives, allowing the power of the Father, of Jesus Christ, and of the Holy Spirit to heal, strengthen and guide us from within. Therein lies the work of the Church. Direct inner experiences with the Lord bring healing to the spirit, soul, and body.

Prayerfully read and meditate on First Corinthians 1:18–2:16, asking God to grant you understanding and revelation concerning these verses. In your journal, please record the thoughts and insights you receive. **Please stop reading and meditate on these verses NOW!** God's revelation to you through these verses can grant you a theological foundation for moving into intimacy with the Holy Spirit!

✳ ✳ ✳

God is not calling us to use the mind *or* the spirit, but to learn to present both our minds and our hearts to His Holy Spirit so He can use us. We learn to do nothing of our own initiative, but only what we hear and see the Father doing (see John 5:19-20,30). Biblical meditation *combines the analysis of the mind with the spontaneity of the heart,* or both left and right brain functions. Jesus joined rationalism and spiritual communion in perfect balance in His own personal life. Let us seek to do the same. He presented His entire being to His Father, for Him to flow through. We, too, present ourselves as living sacrifices, allowing the light of His glory within us to transform us and radiate out through us. Our lives will be fully restored and balanced when they match the life of Jesus.

In a culture that is so cerebral, how do you engage this word?

Being a Christian does not mean throwing your mind away. Your mind is used as you approach God, but your mind has now found its *proper place.* Although it is the organ that *processes* revelation, it is not the organ through which revelation is *received*—the spirit is. The mind and the spirit work hand in hand. Direction in your walk comes by *rhema* through your spirit. Your Spirit-anointed mind acts as a check and safeguard, comparing all *rhema* to *Logos.*

Revelation itself is not irrational, but rather super-rational. To say it another way, revelation is not foolishness; it has simply taken into account the reality of the spiritual world, and this appears irrational to rationalism, which has limited its scope merely to the physical world.

For example, for Abraham and Sarah to believe they were going to have a baby at 90 years of age is irrational if your framework is limited only to the physical laws. However, if you believe in a God who injects His supernatural power into the natural, and who said He was going to give them a child, then it is perfectly rational (or super-rational) to believe for a child.

Which Worldview Is Yours?

I used to scorn liberals who had demythalized away the supernatural parts of the Bible. I was glad I was an evangelical, a Bible-believing Christian. However, one day the Lord pointed out to me that I did not believe the whole Bible was for me, either. He reminded me that I believed the Old Testament was for the Jews; the Gospels were about the supernatural lifestyle of Jesus and not a way of life I could experience myself; the Book of Acts was transitional and not for today; and the Book of Revelation was for the future. All I had left to me was the teaching portions of the Epistles that did not speak about the supernatural, such as the gifts of the Holy Spirit.

I was appalled! I repented for my dispensationalism and told God I wanted my Bible back, so I could live it from cover to cover. If you don't have your whole Bible to live, I suggest you, too, may want to take a moment right now in prayer and repent for allowing it to be stolen from you and tell God you want it all back for you to live today.

The person who has decided that the spiritual experiences found within the Bible are no longer available today will probably relegate any and all spiritual experiences to satan. I, however, believe the Bible is for today and is to be lived in all its fullness!

In which worldview do you live more comfortably? Are you more at ease responding to your outer senses, or are you equally comfortable with your inner senses, such as vision and intuition? If you are not living as you want to, you can change. First, acknowledge you are not what you want to be and ask the Lord's forgiveness for allowing yourself to be led astray by the rationalism of our culture. Second, ask the Lord to change you, to heal you, and to restore the eyes and ears of your heart. Then continue reading, and we will give you more specific help in making this transition. I had to make this change, so I can promise you that it is possible.

A Scientific Backdrop for Experiencing Spiritual Intimacy

You may think it strange to explore how the brain works in the middle of a discussion on spirituality and hearing the voice of God. I enjoy learning about studies in disciplines other than Christianity that relate to the steps of growth that I am taking in my Christian walk. The discussion on left and right hemisphere brain functions is one of these studies.

Some people refuse to learn how left and right brain functions can apply to their spiritual lives because they are not taught in the Bible. My response is that while all of the Bible is truth, not all truth is in the Bible. To reject scientific discoveries because they were not first stated in the Scriptures would be unwise. None of us would know ingly choose that position. Just because something is not taught in the Bible does not mean it is not true. God never claimed to put every-thing He knew in the Bible. As a matter of fact, Jesus said He knew things He wasn't going to tell the disciples because they could not yet bear them (see John 16:12) and John said that if he were going to write down everything that Jesus did, all the books in the world would not contain it (see John 21:25).

Therefore, my standard for affirming truth is not limited to clear statements of Scripture. Instead, I require that what I embrace must be compatible with principles in the Bible. Left and right brain understanding is compatible with biblical principles, particularly the doctrine that God has given each of us unique gifts (see Rom. 12:6-8; Eph. 4:11; 1 Cor. 12:1-12).

In 1981, Roger Sperry won the Nobel Prize in Physiology or Medi-cine for his experimentation on left- and right-hemisphere brain functions. It has been discovered that although we do use both sides of our brains, most of us tend to rely a bit more heavily on one side or the other. *The left hemisphere of the brain works primarily with analyti-cal functions, while the right hemisphere processes intuitive and visionary functions.*

On the following page is a pictorial view of the functions carried on by each hemisphere of the brain.

There is also a "Brain Preference Indicator Test" that allows you to determine which side of your brain you draw from more heavily. Visit *cwgministries.org/brain* and take the test to discover whether you lean more toward being a left- or right-brain person. —my score = 4.85 use both equally!

I (Mark) am somewhat left-brain. Therefore, this book has many charts and step-by-step formulas in it. That is what left-brain peo-ple need and what they are all about. Right-brain individuals simply say, "Oh, hearing God's voice is easy: you just know that you know that you know!" Well, that doesn't help a left-brain person at all. I am writing as a left-brain individual for other left-brain people. Not that

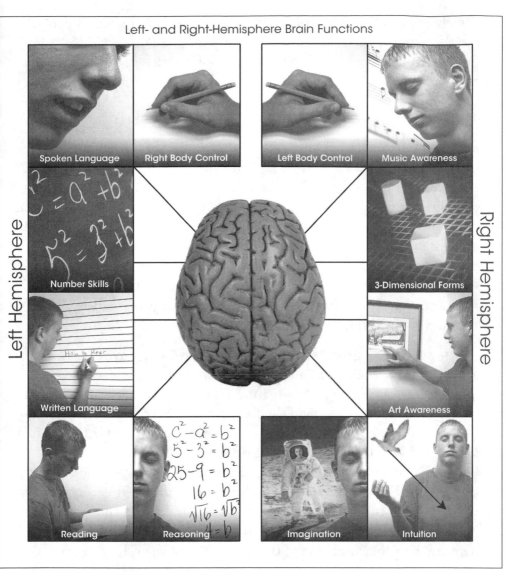

figure 2.3

this won't help right-brainers, also. It will. It will confirm to them that what they are doing naturally is good and is right, and it will give them a detailed vocabulary to communicate the way they live inwardly to others who do not naturally live that same way.

My wife, Patti, who is slightly right-brain, has rewritten this book into a right-brain version called ***Dialogue With God*** which skips all the charts and things that left-brainers demand and need. If you are a right-brainer, you will probably enjoy *Dialogue With God*. (Note: We put both our names on all the books we have written, but Patti is the primary author of *Dialogue With God* and Mark is the primary author of *4 Keys to Hearing God's Voice*.)

When I began to journal, God told me to love my wife exactly as she was and to not try to make her more left-brain. Honoring her intuition (as well as my intuition) has helped me make much wiser decisions in my life. Honoring the right-brain strengths of my wife has greatly improved my marriage. Testing our children and helping them find jobs that are consistent with their brain preference has blessed and established them in the workplace. Our left-brain daughter is an editor and phone consultant. Our right-brain son is a typesetter, webmaster, and marketer. Let journaling and an understanding of left- and right-brain functions bring success to your marriage, your life, and your family.

In surveying groups of people in America, I have found that approximately 60 percent lean toward left-brain functions and about 40 percent toward right-brain functions. Only a few indicate that they have a balance between the two. This imbalance probably exists because our educational system considers reading, writing, and arithmetic (required courses that deal with left-brain functions) to be more central to effective living than art, music, and drama (elective courses that deal with right-brain functions). This idolatry of the left-brain functions is so complete in our culture that scientists have discovered that the left half of the brain actually grows slightly heavier than the right side of the brain during the schooling years.

Psychologists tell us that they consider the majority of people in our culture to be neurotic. I suspect that a large contributing factor to this widespread neurosis is the failure to cultivate both sides of our brains in a balanced way.

Corresponding to this idolization of logic is the demise of creativity, which is a more right-brain function involving vision, intuition, and visualization. Statistics show that almost all children rank high in creativity before they enter school at age five. By age seven, only 10 percent still have high creativity, and by the time we are adults, only 2 percent score high in creativity tests.

Therefore, what we are doing in our current educational system is essentially destroying the creative ability God has placed within man. I believe it is because we train the left side of the brain—the logical, analytical part—and stifle the right side of the brain—the intuitive, imaginative side. Where in Scripture do we see God suggesting we do this? I suspect that God gave us two sides of our brains so we could offer both sides to Him to use.

Understanding right- and left-brain functions can help us understand and respect those with gifts different from ours. For instance, when a husband and wife are involved in making a decision, the husband may reason it out (a left-brain function) while the wife may intuit the decision (a right-brain function). If they have learned to honor the strengths in one another, they will not cut off the other's gift simply because it does not line up with their own decision-making process, but will instead value it as a complement to their own abilities.

Those who function more strongly in the left brain will find the revelation process flowing most naturally in conjunction with their analytical thoughts. As an example, Luke (see Luke 1:1-4) investigated everything carefully, then wrote it out in consecutive order (obviously left-brain activity). May I suggest that he allowed the Holy Spirit's intuitive, spontaneous impressions to flow into his reasoning process, and the end product was pure revelation that stands to this day?

By contrast, when John wrote Revelation, he said, *"I was in the Spirit on the Lord's day, and I heard behind me a loud voice...saying, 'Write in a book what you see...'"* (Rev. 1:10-11). This revelation process involved no left-brain functions (except the actual writing). Rather, I believe it flowed through the right side of the brain, coming from the heart. This process also resulted in a pure revelation, one that still stands today.

You can see that there are at least two different approaches you can use when receiving pure revelation: Luke's method and John's method. Both are valid. Both can result in purity. Both are to be honored. It is hard for us to honor the one who is different from us. The left-brain person is likely to characterize the right-brain person as flaky, impulsive, and fly-by-night. The right-brain person is likely to describe the left-brain person as so analytical and academic that there is no possibility that the Holy Spirit could flow through him or her. Let us come to the place where we can honor both Luke's and John's approach to receiving revelation, knowing that the Holy Spirit can flow purely through both.

I do not equate the right side of the brain directly with the heart. Rather, I would like to suggest that the capacities of the heart are to flow into both sides of our brains.

Moving from Left to Right

People often ask, "How can I set aside my own reasoning and experience the inner intuitive flow?" Let us consider what Elisha did when he needed to hear a prophetic word from God. When he wanted to move from logic and reason (left-brain activity) to the word of the Lord spoken intuitively within (flowing through the right side of his brain), Elisha engaged in a right-brain activity: "Bring me a minstrel, so that I might hear the word of the Lord" (paraphrased from 2 Kings 3:15). The music drew him from the left side of his brain to the right side where he was perfectly positioned before the presence of the Lord, able to hear the spontaneous words that were spoken within.

Many people also find that the use of vision or enjoying the beauty of nature (both right-brain functions) positions them properly before the intuitive voice of the Holy Spirit. In interesting university studies by Calvin Jeske, from Calgary, Canada, it has been shown that speaking in tongues stimulates right-brain electrical activity, as opposed to normal speech, which stimulates left-brain electrical activity. Therefore, I recommend that you use vision, music, nature, and speaking in tongues to help prepare yourself to more easily hear the intuitive voice of the Holy Spirit.

Examples of Two-way Journaling

Enjoy some examples of the journaling of my students.

Chuck Conkling

I received this on October 31, 1984. At the time I received it I knew it was from the Lord. This revelation was given to me as I drove around Raleigh, NC. I had to pull over several times to write it down as the Lord gave it to me. I showed it to my pastor, who confirmed it was from God and asked to use it in a series of sermons. I was journaling and didn't even know it!

Chuck, I am your only Source. All blessings and favor come from Me. People may be the avenues (channels) but I AM the Source.

I AM an unlimited Source and cannot be blocked as long as you walk in fellowship with Me.

I AM your Source of everything; love, success, strength, faith, health, protection, prosperity...

Your responsibility is to be a channel for My Blessings to flow through to others. I will maintain the flow. You give freely from an inexhaustible Source that cannot be depleted.

✳ ✳ ✳

A Prisoner in Namibia, Africa

Our counseling ministry, born as a result of the courses on *How to Hear God's Voice* and *Prayers That Heal the Heart*, is doing great. We have seen people freed from homosexual sins, demonic attack, sleepless nights, depression, and high blood pressure. Following is one of the journaling assignments from a student who asked this question: "Lord, what would You like to speak to me concerning the way I process anger?"

I love you with unfailing love. Do not allow the sun to go down while you are still angry. Never allow the enemy to step inside you. I am glad that you are growing faster in the way you handle your anger, by quickly turning to Me to deal with it. Continue to practice My presence all the time so that you can flow in My love and peace.

✳ ✳ ✳

Mike—The Battle With Doubt

Father, I realized again, over the weekend, talking with my friend Wayne that I have such a hard time really believing You and Your words to me. I want to and I try but find myself doubting so much. I believe, but help thou my unbelief. Why do I have such a hard time believing? How do I simply believe and trust You?

As you repeatedly listen, hear and take to heart what I am saying, you will begin to believe with your whole heart. There is a chipping away at the walls and patterns of unbelief that have been a part of you for so long. Also, as I show you specific areas of doubt and unbelief, you must bring them to Me, lay them down and repent of that which you have held on to; to the lies and misconceptions of Me and also of who you think yourself to be. I am not in many ways who you think I am and you are not in many ways who you think you are.

As I mentioned earlier, your ungodly beliefs lead you to failure over and over again. Unbelief is sin. It is one of the most damnable sins that a Christian indulges in. It is one of the root causes why My children go into all sorts of sins and failure. You see yourself as such a failure, such a hopeless case, and therefore you already have given up and thrown in the towel to defeat and failure. You convince yourself even before the fight that you will not win, which results in certain failure and defeat. When one goes into battle already believing that they will lose, then there is no hope or strength to conquer. Defeat is inevitable.

But I do not see you that way! I am not convinced or persuaded of those lies and misconceptions. You are My son. Bought with My precious blood. More than a conqueror! An overcomer! A delight to the Father. You are overturning many years and generations of ungodly belief and ungodly structures that have been set up against the knowledge of God. I will help you to identify and then to pull down ungodly patterns of unbelief in your life. I will bring you to a place of utter rest in Me and to a place of great intimacy which will result in great exploits that will reach the nations. FIX your eyes on Me! I am able to do this. I am the Great I Am.

You are no different than My disciples were. They were also steeped in great unbelief as they walked with Me and saw all that I did and yet they were still engulfed in unbelief and ungodly patterns of thought. But I brought them to a place of great faith and relationship with Me. I am faithful. Great is My faithfulness to you. You are Mine. You are Mine just as much as the apostles were Mine. They were not more My children or more favored than you. You are just as much a child of Mine as they were. Continue to acknowledge and repent of your sin of unbelief and turn your attention and focus to Me, to My words for you and you will continue to experience a transformation in your life that will revolutionize your world that will in turn, revolutionize all those that you are called to affect.

Trust Me like a little child would trust his father. Remember Josiah at a young age when you repeatedly told him to trust you when he was ready to jump into your arms in the water? He was so afraid to jump, but you persuaded him to trust, to jump, because you knew you would not fail him. And you did not. He jumped, then again and then again until his fear of the water was overcome. Trust was built and established. Now, trust Me and jump. I will catch you. You can do it. Jump! I cannot fail you. I will not fail you. I will catch you. You are forever safe in My arms. You will not drown. I will not fail you. Trust will be built and established.

✳ ✳ ✳

Kalyn—God's Voice Behind Prison Walls

Hello, My child. I love you, Kalyn. I love your smile and your laugh. I love the hunger in your spirit for journaling. I want you to keep journaling to meet Me here as often as possible until your faith is increased and your trust in Me is whole. I don't want you to worry about your mistakes right now for you will make plenty, but I still love you and I will teach you through them. I will never leave you high and dry without a place to stand. I am your rock. I will always be here for you and you will experience more of Me each time you sit down to listen to My words in your spirit. I love you, child. You are so precious to Me, Kalyn. Know how much I love you.

As I contemplate what the Lord has done with my life since I began this course, *Communion With God* [That is the previous name of this book.], I am astounded. I have difficulty believing that I am the same person; even my friends have commented on the growth they have seen in me. The metamorphosis has been spectacular; it has been a supernatural transformation.

I had been searching for answers to the many questions that I had and the teaching presented in the *Communion With God* course provided the answers. My biggest question was: How do I hear the voice of God? I have to admit, I was skeptical at first. I didn't think that I could learn to hear the voice of God from textbooks and audiotapes. I had always been told that it was something God would have to teach me. But how was God going to teach me if I didn't recognize His voice? That was a question that my intuitive sisters couldn't answer. Praise God! This class has torn the veil, I have learned how to enter into the holy of Holies and have communion with my Daddy God.

I have four good sisters-in-Christ (other prison inmates) that I feel I can submit my journaling to and gain wisdom and protection from error...I found a pair of earplugs can work wonders in zoning out the outside world!...In vision, I have seen the Lord touch my hands and I knew He was anointing them to be used for His divine healing. In vision, I have seen Him pray over me to the Father. In vision, Jesus has taken me to see my boys and He shows me that He is taking care of them. In vision, I have been a child, an adult, and all ages in between. In these visions I have played with Jesus, sat in His lap and been comforted by Him, and I have just spent time with Him.

⸻ ❧ ⸻

Personal Application

Write down a question in your journal that you would like to ask the Lord. Here are some ideas of questions I recommend you begin with:

Lord, do You love me?

Lord, what do You want to say to me?

Lord, what do You want to say to me about the truths in this chapter?

Take a moment, choose a question, and write it down.

After you have written the question, ask Jesus to open the eyes and ears of your heart so that you can receive what He wants to share with you. Then picture Jesus in a comfortable setting. He may be sitting next to you, or walking along the Sea of Galilee with you. Become a child. Take His hand. See His character. See His joy and expectancy and excitement over sharing this time with you. (If you can't see His face at this time, don't worry about it. His face will become clearer the more you use vision.) This is what He longs for more than anything else. See His long robes. See the sandals on His feet. Relax and put a smile on your face. Enjoy being alone with Him. Then as you gaze upon Him, ask Him the question that you have written down.

Tune to spontaneity, fix your gaze upon Him and write what begins to flow within you. (You can keep your journal on your computer if you desire. I do, and since I can type with my eyes closed watching vision and tuned to flow, it is all much easier than writing things out by hand.) Don't test it now. Just write in simple childlike faith. You can test it later. If it is not too private, share it with a spiritual advisor for confirmation. It is important especially during your first weeks of journaling that you share much of what you receive with your advisor so you are established in faith that you are on the right track and truly hearing His voice. During this learning time, ask simpler and more general questions, rather than questions about decision-making or predictions of what is going to happen or extremely sensitive issues. One good introductory line for your journaling is to say, "Good morning, Lord, I love You! I give You this day. What would You like to say to me?"

Now go and journal!

———•◦•———

Free Online Resources to deepen these truths available at: www.cwgministries.org/FreeBooks

- **Brain Preference Indicator Test** www.cwgministries. org/brain

- **Sid Roth Radio Interviews** www.cwgministries.org/ RothRadio

———•◦•———

Endnotes

1. *The New Age Catalogue* by the editors of *Body Mind Spirit* magazine, Doubleday 1988, Introduction.
2. Ibid.
3. Ibid.
4. From a letter written by Rev. Maurice Fuller.
5. C. Peter Wagner, *Target: Earth*, 166.

CHAPTER 3

Spiritual Intimacy—The Desire of God's Heart

One morning I sat at my desk with pen and paper and wrote down a question I wanted Jesus to answer. When I finished writing, I focused the eyes of my heart on Jesus, picturing myself sitting next to Him on the edge of a stone well (see John 4). I asked the Holy Spirit to grant me a spirit of revelation, and to anoint the eyes of my heart (see Eph. 1:17-18). As I looked at Jesus, He gestured, as a person would when he speaks, and into my heart came a spontaneous idea that was not my own. It was an excellent response to the question I had asked. I wrote it down and turned my gaze again upon Jesus. Again, an excellent thought came to my heart, and I wrote it down. After a bit, I found I had written two paragraphs, and as I looked at the content, I was amazed at how perceptive and wise it was. I said, "I bet this is from the Lord!" When I shared it with my wife, she agreed. This was the first time I discerned the Lord's voice by using all four keys (stillness, vision, spontaneity, and journaling).

I repeated this experiment in the following days during my devotional time. When spontaneous thoughts came, I responded to them with my own analytical thoughts and questions, and He would then reply to my questions. I found I was dialoguing with the Lord! An experience I had always dreamed of and never experienced was finally happening. I was learning to converse with God! My search for a full relationship with the King of kings was finally being rewarded.

As I experimented with this experience over the next few months, I became increasingly convinced it was the divine wisdom and love of Almighty God that was flowing through my pen. During those first days and weeks, I took much of my journaling to both my wife and to a spiritual friend who was able to hear the voice of God, and asked them to confirm whether or not it really was God. They told me it was! This confirmation from others continued to spur me on. When you begin to journal, you should have two or three spiritual friends with whom you share your journaling. This is a critically important step!

God's Passion: Daily Walks With His Children!

God's passion has always been to have fellowship with His children. God created us for the supreme purpose of having a love relationship with Him. Let's look throughout the covenants at the unchanging desire of God's heart. From Genesis to Revelation, we see that God's passion has never changed. He offers us His voice so that we will know Him!

We have already mentioned the lifestyle of communion Adam and Eve enjoyed in the Garden of Eden before the Fall. In the cool of the day, perhaps in the morning and in the evening, God would seek out man and woman for fellowship. How amazing! The Creator of all actively sought the companionship of His creation, walking and talking with them, sharing their life together. Was it for this that we were created?

Because of sin, we lost that close relationship. But God found a man who recognized His voice, believed His words, and obeyed His instructions. His name was Abraham, and he was honored with the title *"the friend of God"* (James 2:23). Abraham is the father of all those who believe, and as Abraham's children we, too, can be known as God's friends.

In the fullness of time, God called Abraham's physical descendents, the nation of Israel, out of Egyptian bondage into a life and a land set apart unto Him. God led them with a pillar of fire by night and a cloud by day until they came to Mount Sinai. The people prepared and purified themselves to finally meet directly with their Deliverer. The mountain was covered with fire, with cloud, and with a thick darkness, and out of the midst of the darkness and fire, they heard the voice of God!

> *These words the LORD **spoke** to all your assembly at the mountain from the midst of the fire, of the cloud and of the thick gloom, with a **great voice**, and He added no more. He wrote them on two tablets of stone and gave them to me. And when you heard the **voice** from the midst of the darkness, while the mountain was burning with fire, you came near to me, all the heads of your tribes and your elders. You said, "Behold, the LORD our God has shown us His glory and His greatness, and we have **heard His voice** from the midst of the fire; we have seen today that **God speaks** with man, yet he lives. Now then why should we die? For this great fire will consume us; if we **hear the voice** of the LORD our God any longer, then we will die. For who is there of all flesh who has **heard the voice** of the living God speaking from the midst of the fire, as we have, and lived? Go near and hear all that the LORD our **God says**; then speak to us all that the LORD our **God speaks** to you, and we will hear and do it. The LORD heard the voice of your words when you spoke to me, and the **LORD said** to me, I have heard the voice of the words of this people which they have spoken to you. They have done well in all that they have spoken. Oh that they had such a heart in them, that they would fear Me and keep all My commandments always, that it may be well with them and with their sons forever! **Go, say to them**, "Return to your tents." But as for you, stand here by Me, that **I may speak** to you all the commandments and the statutes and the judgments which you shall teach them, that they may observe them in the*

land which I give them to possess (Deuteronomy 5:22-31).

The Alternative to God's Spoken Voice: God's Laws

It seems that we humans often prefer a list of rules to a relationship. I suppose we find security in rules that is somewhat lost in a growing relationship. Since we are creatures of habit, we prefer not to change. There is some good in trying to live under law (see Deut. 5:28), because it is a tutor that brings us to Christ (see Gal. 3:24) as we realize we can never keep the law (see Deut. 5:29). But it must never take the place of God's voice in our hearts instructing and leading us (see Isa. 30:21). When God wanted to have a relationship with the Israelites and speak to them directly from the mountain, they chose instead to be governed by a set of laws (see Deut. 5:22-31).

In these verses, God is offering the Israelites a relationship. He offers them *His voice*. He offers to restore the fellowship Adam and Eve had in the Garden of Eden. They turn down His precious gift because with His voice comes fire, where they will be required to put to death their own fleshly desires so they can be alive in the Spirit. The Israelites don't want that much heat in their lives, so they tell Moses he can go and have a relationship with God, and he can report back to them what God says, and they will keep the laws he gives them.

So the Israelites turn down God's offer of a relationship, saying, "No, we prefer law, please." I believe God's heart is broken here, just as any parent's would be if their child told them he did not want a relationship with them.

However, God was not going to stop speaking. He told the Israelites they could go back to their tents if they wanted, but if Moses wanted to have a relationship, he could stay close. So Moses got a relationship and the Israelites received laws, commandments, statutes, and judgments. Law was added to law until the burden became heavy.

The years passed, and God's people lived under the Law, not expecting that anyone but the occasional prophet or seer would hear from God. Eventually, there grew up a young man whose heart longed for his God. As he tended his father's flocks, he understood the heart of the Shepherd of Israel. He contemplated the wonders of creation and learned to love the Creator. He meditated on the Law and perceived the mercy and justice of the great Judge. His heart overflowed with extravagant worship for his King, and God was pleased, saying, *"I have found David...a man after Mine own heart"* (Acts 13:22). "At last there is someone who 'gets it'—this is what I have always wanted—to love and to be loved!"

Jesus Lived Life as God Intended Us to Live!

Jesus lived out of a relationship with His Father. He did only what He saw His Father doing and heard His Father saying (see John 5:19-20,30; 8:26,28,38). This was the way Adam and Eve lived, having daily conversations with God. Jesus was always communicating with God. And He taught us that we are to live out of daily communion with Him, as well.

Eternal Life Is Intimacy With Almighty God

Near the end of Jesus' earthly life, He took the time to pray for His disciples. Not just those who had walked with Him along the Galilean countryside, but also for those of us who would believe because of their testimony. Jesus said that the Father had given Him authority over all people so that He might give eternal life to those whom He had been given, and in John 17:3, Jesus defined what that meant: *"Now this is eternal life: that they may know You, the only true God, and Jesus Christ, whom You have sent."*

This is not the simple, casual "knowing" of an acquaintance, or even a close friend. The word used here for "know" is *ginosko*, and it means "to be involved in an intimate, growing relationship." In the Greek version of the Old Testament, this is the word used in Genesis 4:1, where it says, *"Adam **knew** Eve and she bore a son."* This is the most intimate relationship possible. Jesus makes the fantastic statement that this is what eternal life is all about! Jesus lived and died so that we would have an intimate, growing, personal relationship with God the Father and His Son Jesus Christ. This is the essence of eternal life: to know and love the God of all creation and His only Son, Jesus. What a magnificent destiny!

The Hebrew counterpart of the Greek *ginosko* is *yada*,[1] and we like to use that word to characterize our time of loving fellowship in prayer. Prayer is so much more than presenting our petitions to God. It is our "*yada* time." Prayer is the link between friends. It is communing with our Lover, Jesus—being intimate, quietly sensing each other's presence, being totally available to one another. It is a treasuring of one another so much that we desire to be together constantly, to share everything with one another, and to walk through life together. It is a feasting on one another's love. It is communion between two lovers: a relationship, not rules. Lovers come together whenever they can to share what is on their hearts. Their relationship is characterized by joy and spontaneity, not legalistic bondage.

Two Ways to Show Our Love for God

We all know the story of Mary and Martha (see Luke 10:38-42). Though Jesus loved Martha and no doubt appreciated her acts of service, it was Mary's decision to leave her work and simply sit at Jesus' feet that won His words of praise. It is not our works that will last forever, but our loving relationship with Him that will never be taken away from us. God asks us to be like Mary.

Paul grasped this precious truth. In Philippians 3:10-11, he said that his great desire was, *"that I might **know** (ginosko) Him, and the power of His [inner] resurrection and the fellowship of His sufferings, being conformed to His death; in order that I may attain to the [outer] resurrection from the dead."* Can you hear the yearning of Paul's heart? "That I might *be intimate with* Him and sense His power and presence arising from within my heart!" Out of that precious love relationship, we will sense His life flowing within us, putting the flesh to death and flowing out through us to others. This is the reason for our salvation! This is why we were born again!

Command to New Testament Christians: "Do Not Refuse Him Who Is Speaking"

The writer of Hebrews reminds us of the foolishness of the Hebrew children at the mountain of God (see Heb. 12:18-26). But he also gives us great hope, telling us that God is giving us another chance! We, the Church of Jesus Christ, have come to another mountain and God is still speaking! We again have the opportunity to choose—will we welcome God's voice and the purifying fire that must accompany it, or will we again refuse Him who is speaking? Will we finally embrace the loving personal communion our God is offering, or will we be content to let someone represent us in God's presence and just tell us what He is saying? Will we live in relationship or under law?

For you have not come to a mountain that can be touched and to a blazing fire, and to darkness and gloom and whirlwind, and to the blast of a trumpet and the sound of words which sound was such that those who heard begged that no further word be spoken to them. For they could not bear the command, "IF EVEN A BEAST TOUCHES THE MOUNTAIN, IT WILL BE STONED." And so terrible was the sight, that Moses said, "I AM FULL OF FEAR and trembling." But you have come to Mount Zion and to the city of the living God, the heavenly Jerusalem, and to myriads of angels, to the general assembly and church of the firstborn who are enrolled in heaven, and to God, the Judge of all, and to the spirits of the righteous made perfect, and to Jesus, the mediator of a new covenant, and to the sprinkled blood, which speaks better than the blood of Abel. See to it that you do not refuse Him who is speaking for if those did not escape when they refused him who warned them on earth, much less will we escape who turn away from Him who warns from heaven. And His voice shook the earth then, but now He has promised, saying, "YET ONCE MORE I WILL SHAKE NOT ONLY THE EARTH, BUT ALSO THE HEAVEN." This expression, "Yet once more," denotes the removing of those things which can be shaken, as of created things, so that those things which cannot be shaken may remain. Therefore, since we receive a kingdom which cannot be shaken, let us show gratitude, by which we may offer to God an acceptable service with reverence and awe; for our God is a consuming fire (Hebrews 12:18-29).

They did not want to hear the sound of His voice *(rhema)*. In verses 22 and 23, the writer declares that we, too, have come to the Holy Mountain, Mount Zion. In verse 25, he gives us a warning:

"See to it that you do not refuse Him who is speaking..."

Why? Because, if we do, we will forsake the relationship with God that is to characterize Christianity, and we will return to life under the law, even as those in the Old Testament did. Our minister will hear from God and, like Moses, will give us the laws under which we are to live. How sad that we might not avail ourselves of the living Holy Spirit within our hearts and live in communion with Him, choosing instead to live only out of the New Testament laws, becoming legalists or Pharisees.

I lived without His voice for the first 10 years of my Christian life. I discovered how burdensome living out of law becomes. The load becomes heavy instead of being light, as Jesus promised. As we grow as Christians, we discover more laws to obey until eventually the list becomes more than we can handle. The choice often becomes either to stop growing or to abandon Christianity altogether. The Pharisees of Jesus' day had 613 laws they were imposing on Israel. Jesus rebuked them for the heavy load they were laying on the people.

Therefore, we, like the Israelites, are faced with a decision: either we hear God speak and live in relationship with Him, or we must live under the biblical laws we discover. I believe it is *imperative* that we learn to discern God's voice and live in it so that our *relationship* is not *reduced* to a *religion*.

Speak this aloud as your confession: *"Lord, I choose relationship rather than rules. Please draw me into a full and complete relationship with You, Almighty God."*

We Are Engaged and Getting Married!

Finally, we come to the Book of Revelation, to John's vision on the Isle of Patmos. He has seen so many amazing things, and suddenly he *"heard what sounded like a great multitude, like the roar of rushing waters and like loud peals of thunder, shouting, 'Hallelujah! For our Lord God Almighty reigns! Let us rejoice and be glad and give Him glory! For the wedding of the Lamb has come, and His bride has made herself ready'"* (Rev. 19:6-7 NIV).

The culmination of all of history is a wedding! How wonderful! And we—the Church, the body of believers—we have been chosen to be the Bride of Christ, the Eternal Son of God! Can we comprehend such an amazing thing? Jesus wants to spend eternity sharing His life with us! And He wants to start today.

From Genesis to Revelation, God has always desired a people with whom He could have a relationship. May we be that people!

Romance With the King of Kings

His face, not His hands

It is so important that we learn to seek the Lord for Himself alone, and not for the things He can give us. He longs for us to abide in Him, to feast on His love. He wants us to enjoy fellowship with Him as our dearest Friend. His heart yearns to be ministered to by our love.

We hurt Him so when we become too busy with our daily tasks to spend time enjoying His love or when we carelessly let sin slip into our lives and do not repent, destroying our close communion. We must seek Him as our greatest treasure, seeing our time of sharing with Him as the highest priority in our lives.

As a result of our relationship with Him, we will begin to see His power flowing out from us, touching hearts, renewing life and strength, and working miracles. For out of relationship comes faith—simple faith, which is simply being close enough to Jesus to know what He wants to do in a situation and then doing whatever He instructs. But the only way we will ever be able to know exactly what Jesus is thinking and saying is by spending much time with Him—living in

His presence every moment of our lives. There are no shortcuts to this! But, oh, the fullness of joy we find in His presence!

"Come Wholly Unto Me"

The Lord speaks of coming wholeheartedly to Him so we can fully experience Him. The following are five aspects of the wholehearted-ness that God requires in our approach to Him:

[handwritten: Isn't this Law? Checklist? Regulations?]

1. **Make Me your greatest treasure** so I can give Myself to you (see Mark 12:30).

2. **Search** for Me with your whole heart so I can reveal Myself to you (see Jer. 29:13).

3. **Trust** Me with your whole heart so I can guide your steps (see Prov. 3:5).

4. **Praise** Me with your whole heart so I can gift you with My presence (see Ps. 9:1).

5. **Return** to Me with your whole heart so I can be compassionate and bless you (see Joel 2:12).

God yearns to be your Friend. He wants you to recognize His voice so that you can get to know Him personally. He longs for you to spend *intimate* time with Him, having no agenda other than sharing love together. He wants you to offer Him your physical senses, the faculties of your soul, and the senses of your spirit so that you can *know* Him fully and deeply. He wants you to move out of your box and into His flow, out of your mind and into your heart, out of rationalism into true spiritual Christianity.

Personal Application: A Two-way Love Letter

In your journal, write a personal two-way love letter to Jesus. Start with, "Jesus this is why I love You so much..." Share your heart with

Him. Stop after writing one paragraph and fix your eyes on Jesus. Tune to spontaneous flowing thoughts and write down His words of love back to you. Write in childlike faith. Picture yourself as an eight-year-old child. Do this now! Share it with your spiritual advisors, so they can confirm you are on the right track and you are hearing God's voice. Your faith will be increased by their words of confirmation.

Others Share How They Sense the Holy Spirit

The following testimonies confirm how others have discerned the voice of God in their hearts. The three basic truths you will find confirmed over and over: (1) God's voice comes often as a spontaneous thought, (2) the eyes of our hearts are used as God grants vision, and (3) the writing of these things is often important.

An impression came to me.

In my mind, I saw a girl sitting at the table....

I jotted down the thoughts.

From *Hear His Voice* by Douglas Wead[2]

How does spontaneous revelation actually come?

1. Pictures. God often spoke to [the] prophets through pictures or visions. He may plant a picture in your mind....

2. Scripture. God speaks through specific Bible verses that come to mind. He may impress a part of a verse, even a reference, upon your mind.

3. A word. God may bring to your mind a specific word or piece of advice that did not come as the result of a detailed thought process. It was more spontaneous and given as if dropped into your mind. The thoughts that come from the Lord in this way are usually unpremeditated and spontaneous in character and come more in a flash without a logical sequence; whereas, when we are consciously

thinking, or even daydreaming, we usually connect one thought with another.

From *Spiritual Gifts and You* by Larry Tomczak[3]

The way my guidance comes...is intuitive. Gut feelings. Instincts.

Francis MacNutt quoted in *Hearing His Voice*[4]

When God speaks to me in the Spirit, His voice translates itself into thought concepts that I can conceive in my mind. So when I say, "I heard the Lord," or "the Lord spoke to me," I mean He spoke to me through a feeling in my spirit which was translated into a thought in my mind. And the thought immediately brings with it what young people call "a rush." It's something that hits you as right.

Ben Kinchlow quoted in *Hearing His Voice*[5]

The lost art of Jesus is His use of imagination. "Jesus looked at reality through the lens of the divine imagination. The imagination is the power we all possess of seeing harmonies, unities, and beauties in things where the non-imaginative mind sees nothing but discords, separations, ugliness. The imagination of man is but the window or door which, when thrown open, lets the divine life stream into our lives."

From *The Soul's Sincere Desire* by Glenn Clark[6]

Creativity Released Through Journaling

Following is a poem from my journal that describes my experience of learning these truths. This was the first poem I had written in 13 years, so I can truly say it was of the Lord. I do not write poetry.

Coming Apart Unto Him

Lord, You spoke in Your Word what You'd have me do.
To come apart and wait upon You.

That You would renew the strength of my life
And let me soar into heavenly heights.
Lord, it's so hard to come apart to You.
There are always so many things to do.
In the natural it seems like a fruitless waste
To fritter away my time into space.
But You're opening my eyes, allowing me to see
The value of coming apart unto Thee
That out of my stillness You finally get through
To speak to me plainly things concerning You.
Spirit to spirit impressions flow,
It's Your voice to me, so the story goes.
I look and I listen attentively,
Recording the thoughts You give to me.
I'm enticed by Your speaking into my heart,
Giving clarity and faith through what You impart,
In a moment saying more than I can in a month.
Clearly, powerfully, and it's more than a hunch.
Lord, I'm learning to come apart unto You.
To open my spirit and let You speak through.
That waiting on You is not vain,
It's the most precious experience I can gain.
Lord, You are filling all of my dreams.
You've filled my life with reality from Your scheme.
You fill my religion with Your grace,
Lifting me high above time and space.
As Jesus, may I come apart from life,
Waiting on You to regain new life,
Speaking it forth to the world around,
Sharing with them the life I've found.
Lord, teach me to look only at You
Not the wind and the waves, and all the to-do.
To stand firm and fast in what You speak
As I pray and fast, Your face to seek.
Lord, teach me Your voice more pointedly,

Keep me apart and waiting on Thee.
Allow Thy fullness my eyes to see,
Lord, I come apart to wait upon Thee.

Examples of Two-way Journaling

Journaling prayers can be the most exciting time of your entire day. Connecting with your heavenly Father, hearing Him answer your prayer, and knowing that He loves you brings fulfillment and contentment to your heart.

Lord, what would You like to say to me?

You are too hard on yourself. I don't expect you to be perfect. I called you out so that I could live in you and so that we could both experience what the combination of the two of us looks like when we are expressing our personalities through this one body. When we are separate I am like chocolate and you are like peanut butter. Blend us together and the result is a tasty treat. Except that there is only one like us in the whole world. Together we are a RARE tasty treat!

❋ ❋ ❋

Paul from England—Using What God Puts in Your Hand

I saw the Lord next to the sea; I joined Him and began to skim stones on the water. I got three skips. The Lord did the same and it skipped to the horizon. He grinned. I did it again and this time did better—five skips. Again the Lord did it and it went to the horizon. As I bent to get another stone He stopped me and gave me a stone. It didn't look like a good skimming stone, but I took it. I threw it and it skimmed TO THE HORIZON. The Lord looked at me with a smile and said, *Paul, what I put in your hand goes further than the things you pick up.* WOW...it has caused me to ask the question when things are offered me and invitations come, is this what the Lord is putting in my hand or is it something I am picking up!

❋ ❋ ❋

Mike—God's Voice Brings Emotional Healing

Son, never is it in My heart that My children should live in torment and in deep turmoil of heart.

Yes, Lord, I know. But why? Why can't I shake it? What is the open door that allows this garbage in and robs me of peace and sleep?

Son, a heart that has not found its total rest and hiding place in Me will be vulnerable to the attacks of the enemy of your soul. Your coming to Me must be often and consistent in order for Me to infuse you with My peace, My confidence and My comfort. It takes time for the transformation and impartation of all that's good into a heart that has been wounded and afraid and hard. I am so patient and so willing to impart all the good things that I have promised you.

You are not alone. You are not an outcast. You are not alone in this walk. You are no different than many, many other believers. All who choose to walk with Me have to come and to receive and allow the transformation of their hearts and minds to take place.

Remember, I can only do this as you come and sit before Me and open up your heart. Not just once in a while, but daily. I am so trustworthy. There is not a hint of deceit or unfairness in My heart toward you. My plans for you are good and My future for you is to have and experience My best.

Father, it seems that I will never get out of my deep loneliness and despair and pit. It's even hard to come to You.

Son, it has been your experience in coming to Me periodically. You allow yourself to believe that coming to Me is hard, that it takes hours to get through. Yet I tell you that coming to Me is like a dying, thirsty man coming to an oasis in the middle of a desert. The oasis is there. All that is required is to come and drink. It is rather quite simple. Come and drink. Come and take. Come and receive. Forget about your efforts to break through. Forget your spiritual gymnastics and simply come to Me and drink.

Often it is hard for you to come because you are still not convinced and persuaded of My absolute love and commitment to you. I am not holding out on you. I do not desire for you to be brought so low in shame and humiliation that you can barely lift your head. That is not My heart. That is My enemy's job.

My peace I give to you. My life I give to you. My very heart I give to you. What have I withheld from you? Where is the proof of the lie that I am not sold out to you? I proved My love in going all the way for you. I had you in mind when I died. I had our times of communion and fellowship in mind when I hung upon the cross.

Father, I hear Your words and they are true. Yet, in my heart and in my life it seems like You favor people. Some are so blessed. Some prosper and don't have the financial struggles, don't have the deep painful times of failure and struggle. I so want to believe You and trust You. There is so much garbage. I don't know where to start.

Son, one day at a time. I appreciate your honesty and your willingness to be open. Often My Church is afraid to express their true feelings in fear that I will be angry and therefore withhold My blessings. I do not play that game. You can come to Me and bare your fears, your feelings, your thoughts and your soul and I will be there to listen and to comfort, to speak and to minister My life. There is a time to be honest and there is a time to let go. First be honest and then let go.

I do not and will not withhold from you any good thing. That is not My heart. That is not the heart of Father. Yet, as you are coming to learn, there are destructive patterns and beliefs in your life that lead you to failure and defeat and that ultimately cause you pain and torment. I long to sit with you and to hold you and to comfort you. I long to be able to have a one-on-one, heart-to-heart with you on a regular basis. I will never withhold My love from you. Be convinced. Be persuaded of better things. Be convinced of My undying love and commitment to you.

✳✳✳

Steven—God Speaks in the Darkness

I never knew if the Lord heard my prayers and certainly would not have even thought that He would want to talk with me in the way that I have experienced in the past few months [in prison]. Because of this new relationship that I have, as well as the wisdom provided me by the Spirit, my life has changed a great deal and every day is now a pleasure to walk through, instead of the dark, empty hours I became so accustomed to here in this cold, lonely place.

Today, whenever I walk in the compound, I have Jesus at my side talking and enjoying His company. I no longer feel alone. I have a sense of peace that I have never known in the past; and even in this place, one of the darkest on this earth, He lights my way and guides me through as I put my complete trust in His mighty power.

✳ ✳ ✳

Lynda—Don't Wait So Long to Come to Me

My child why do you wait so long to come to Me? I have seen your pain, I have heard your cries, and yet you do not come to Me. How long will it be until you learn to seek Me first as your source of comfort and confirmation?

I see your loneliness, I feel your rejection, I see the fear you have of being rejected again by others...BUT I AM...not like others. Until you learn that I will never leave, until you learn I will never forsake you, you will also have fear with Me. You must learn to trust Me. That means stepping out, trying Me, testing Me when your feelings are telling you otherwise. When My Son responded to the tempter, "You should not put God to the test," this is not the type of testing He (Jesus) was referring to. What I am asking of you is to push your faith, build it.

I am with you always. I am in you. Stop thinking of Me being separate from you...it is too easy for you to then think rejection. But if you remember we are one as the Father and Son are one, then you will know your acceptance, your approval, your righteousness is secure in Me. I cannot reject Myself. Rest in Me. Trust Me. Believe in Me. Let Me hold you when you need to cry. Know My heart beats with yours.

And when you fall, remember I was wounded for your transgressions, I was bruised for your iniquities, the chastisement of the whole world was placed upon Me. Repent and go on. Your prolonged sorrow for the things I have already paid for is not helpful. Your guilt for your actions that are less *than perfect, is futile. Remember "metaxi."* You are not yet in heaven. I don't expect perfection from you. It is your heart that matters to Me. I love you, My child...come away and love with Me.*

Love yourself. I will show you how to love you. That will also help you in loving others, but right now I want you to joy in My joy over you, delight in My delight in you and sing the song of love I have for you.

* "Metaxi" is a word used by Augustine suggesting that in our lives we are between Eden and Heaven. We cannot or should not expect perfection this side of Heaven. Life will be messy.

Personal Application

Choose a Gospel story (from Matthew, Mark, Luke, or John) that is comfortable to you. You may want to reread it so it is fresh in your mind. Picture the story. Enter it, imagining yourself right there in Galilee. Allow yourself to be present with Jesus. Fix your gaze on Him. Ask Him the question that is on your heart. It may be as simple as, "Lord, what do You want to say to me?" Or it may be a question that arises from the story. Write the question in your journal. Tune to spontaneity and begin writing out of the flow that bubbles up within you. Don't test it as you receive it. Test it—share it with your spiritual advisors—after the flow is finished.

Free Online Resources to deepen these truths available at: www.cwgministries.org/FreeBooks

- **Communion: Me and Jesus (by Jason Major) Powerful examples of conversations with God.**

- **One Page Tract on 4 keys** www.cwgministries.org/4Keys

Endnotes

1. Documentation on the precise definitions of *ginosko* and *yada* may be found in Colin Brown, *The Dictionary of New Testament Theology, Vol. 2,* pages 395-398.

2. Douglas Wead, *Hear His Voice* (Carol Stream, IL: Creation House, 1976), 84, 94, 79.

3. Larry Tomczak, "Spiritual Gifts and You," *Charisma* magazine (October 1981), 57.

4. Francis MacNutt quoted in John Patrick Grace, *Hearing His Voice* (Notre Dame, IN: Ave Maria Press, 1979), 57.

5. Ben Kinchlow quoted in *Grace*, 78-79.

6. Glenn Clark, *The Soul's Sincere Desire* (Whitefish, MT: Kessinger Publishing, 2005).

CHAPTER 4

Key #1: Recognize God's Voice as Spontaneous Thoughts

As a review, the four keys to hearing God's voice are as follows:

- **Key #1: Recognize God's voice as spontaneous thoughts that light upon your mind.**

- Key #2: Quiet yourself so you can hear God's voice.

- Key #3: Look for vision as you pray.

- Key #4: Write down the flow of thoughts and pictures that come to you.

Simplifying even further are four words that summarize these keys:

- Stillness

- Vision

- Spontaneity

- Journaling

As mentioned previously, this simplified list is the order of the keys as seen in Habakkuk 2:1-2. In this book, we are going to alter the order slightly to make the teaching clearer (spontaneity, stillness, vision, and journaling). The *order* of the keys is not critical. The crucial thing is that you use all four keys at one time! When I do, I hear from God, just as He promised. You can, too.

We will be exploring each of these keys in detail in the coming chapters.

Key #1: Recognize God's Voice as Spontaneous Thoughts That Light Upon Your Mind

Our Father longs to share Himself with us in every way possible. Jesus wants to be our Way, our Truth, and our Life (see John 14:6). He shows us the way to walk through His *Logos*, the Word: *"Thy word is...a light to my path"* (Ps. 119:105). He guides us through the counsel of our spiritual overseers (see Prov. 11:14). Even circumstances are used to direct our way; for example, Jonah. Jesus becomes our truth by illuminating Scripture to us, by leading us into truth, and by guiding us, through giving us peace or pressure in our spirits. We may receive guidance through dreams and visions (see Acts 16:9), or the prophetic word.

Defining *Logos* and *Rhema*

One way Jesus becomes our life is by speaking His words directly into our hearts. In this chapter we want to examine this experience. Jesus says in John 6:63, *"The words* [rhema] *that I have spoken to you are spirit and are life."* Probably each of us has experienced the breath of life as God's words have come clearly to our hearts, giving direction for the way before us, encouraging us, or strengthening us.

There are two Greek words in the New Testament that are translated "word": *logos* and *rhema*. A "word" can be *logos* and *rhema* as you highlight either the content of the message or the way the message was received. If you use the word *logos*, you indicate that you are emphasizing the content of the message. Use of the word *rhema* demonstrates an emphasis on the way in which the message was received, specifically, through a spoken word.

A Biblical Example

Jesus refers to the same "word" or message twice in His prayer in the seventeenth chapter of John, verses 6 and 8. In verse 6 the content is being emphasized, and therefore *logos* is used in the Greek: "...*they have kept Your word* [logos]." In verse 8, the fact that it was a spoken word is the focus, and therefore the word *rhema* is used: "*for the words* [rhema] *which You gave Me, I have given them....*"

Both *Logos* and *Rhema*

The Scriptures can be *logos* if I approach them simply for content. When I receive them as revelation from God, they can be called *rhema*. When God speaks a Scripture to me, it comes as a *rhema*. If God bids me to note the content of the Scripture, I am then treating it as a *logos*. The Scriptures originally came as *rhema* to the writers (see 2 Pet. 1:21). Since they had content, they were also *logos*. The Scriptures are quickened to us by the Spirit and thus become a *rhema* to us in the same way that they were to the original writers. As we ponder the *rhema*, it becomes a *logos*, since we shift from emphasizing its manner of coming to its content.

We Need Both *Logos* and *Rhema*

The content of the Bible *(Logos)* is necessary because it gives us an absolute standard against which to measure all "truth." It is our safeguard to keep us from error, and our instruction manual for life.

Rhema is also necessary because it emphasizes the way the Bible was initially given—through individuals actively interacting with God—and the centrality to the Christian message of divine communication with people. It emphasizes the fact that God spoke and continues to speak to His children. We need to see that the men and women throughout the Bible model a way of living that involves ongoing contact with the God who created them. If the Bible tells us anything from Genesis to Revelation, it tells us that God desires to actively communicate with His children, and that we should expect to hear His voice and see His vision as we walk through life. We live out of His spoken word and vision within our hearts. We do nothing on our own initiative, only that which we hear and see the Father doing (see John 5:19-20,30). We see Jesus as a perfect example, modeling a way of living that we are to imitate.

Therefore, we need both the *Logos* and the *rhema* in our lives. The following diagram may help to depict this concept even more clearly.

1. LOGOS	2. RHEMA
The mind reading and understanding the Bible.	As I direct my heart and mind to seek the Lord, His Spirit speaks into my heart, directly impressing His thoughts and ideas upon it.

figure 4.1

I struggled unsuccessfully for years to see a distinction between *Logos* and *rhema*. I observed that *Logos* was often used for "spoken words," which I had been taught should be *rhema*. Finally, one day I noticed that the opposite was not also true, that *rhema* was never used in the context of "written words." I went through all 70 uses of *rhema* in the New Testament and observed that not once did *rhema* refer to the written word. So there was uniqueness about *rhema*!

As I learned much later in studying a master's thesis by Dr. Font Shultz, *logos* includes all aspects of communication, from the formulation of the ideas to be spoken, to the consideration of the language style, through the actual verbalization and reception by the hearer. *Rhema*, on the other hand, stands specifically for the "uttering" or "actual expressing." You may want to examine each of the occurrences of *rhema* in the New Testament yourself and note your observations concerning its distinctiveness.[1]

How *Rhema* Is Sensed

Probably no question bothers Western Christians more than: "How do I discern God's voice within my heart?" We are now going to try to answer that.

I sought in vain for years to hear God's voice within my heart, but the only thing I found was many different thoughts. I could not hear any voice. This is precisely where many Christians stand frustrated. How can I possibly say, "God said" when I am not able to discern His inner voice clearly? How can I move in word of wisdom, word of knowledge, prophecy, or interpretation of tongues if I cannot recognize God's voice? How can I get to *know* Someone who I cannot see, hear, or touch? Then the Lord finally began bringing the right teachers, revelation, and understanding into my life and allowed me to "see" what I had been missing.

Rhema, or the voice of God, is Spirit-to-spirit communication— where the Holy Spirit, in union with your spirit, speaks directly to you.

Thoughts from my mind are **analytical**.

Thoughts from my heart are **spontaneous**.

So we can say that Key #1 for hearing God's voice is recognizing that "God's voice is sensed as spontaneous thoughts that light upon your mind."

Biblical Support

The following Scripture passages support the concept that spontaneous thoughts are the voice of the spirit world.

1. Not all thoughts in our minds originate with us.

> *For the weapons of our warfare are not carnal but mighty in God for pulling down strongholds, casting down arguments and every high thing that exalts itself against the knowledge of God, bringing **every thought** into captivity to the obedience of Christ* (2 Corinthians 10:4-5 NKJV).

Why would we have to bring our thoughts into captivity? Is it not because some of them originate in satan or an evil spirit? If so, where may we assume that other of our thoughts come from? The Holy Spirit, naturally. We must come to terms with the truth that many of the thoughts in our minds are *not our thoughts*. What an incredible idea! I always believed that the thoughts in my head were *my thoughts*. But in actuality, the Bible makes it clear that many of them are not. They are coming from the spirit world. You see, I am one whom Another fills. I am a vessel, a branch grafted into a vine. I do not stand alone but Someone else flows through me. I keep forgetting that and think that this is *me living*, when as a new creation, I do not live, but Christ lives in me (see Gal. 2:20).

Therefore I accept the fact that spontaneous thoughts, ones I did not think up, do not come from my mind. They come either from my heart, the Holy Spirit within my heart, or an evil spirit trying to impress his ideas upon me.

2. *Naba*—God's voice might be "bubbling up."

Naba, the Hebrew word meaning "to prophesy," literally means to "bubble up." Therefore when the prophet wanted to sense the prophetic flow, he would tune to that which was bubbling up within him. In other words, he would tune to the spontaneous flow that he recognized as the voice of God within him. Speak this confession out loud: "I honor bubbling thoughts!"

Consider the distinctions between true prophecy and false prophecy in the following chart.

	Prophecy	False Prophecy
Root Hebrew Word	*Naba*	*Ziyd*
Literal Definition	Bubble up	Boil up
Expanded Meaning	His prophecy bubbles up. His prophecy gushes up.	He boils up his prophecy. He cooks up his prophecy.
Inner Poise	Fix eyes on Jesus and tune to spontaneous flow.	Fix eyes on self's desires and devise a word or vision.

figure 4.2

Can an evil Spirit read our minds?

3. **Paga**—God speaks through the chance encounter.

One Hebrew word for intercession is *paga*, which literally means "to strike or light upon by chance" or "an accidental intersecting." Genesis 28:11 is an example of the use of *paga* as an accidental intersecting. As Jacob was traveling, he "lighted upon" *(paga)* a certain place and spent the night there.

Putting this literal definition of *paga* together with the idea of intercession, we come to a beautiful biblical example of Spirit-to-spirit communication that is familiar to almost every Christian. Can you remember a time when you suddenly had the impression that you should pray for someone? You had not been thinking about them; the thought just "came out of nowhere." yes.

That was *paga*. You were experiencing *rhema*, God's voice as a "chance idea" that intersects our minds, not flowing from the normal, meditative process, but simply appearing in our hearts. It seems to us it is just a chance idea because we didn't think it up. It is an idea from God lighting upon our hearts and being registered in our minds as a spontaneous idea. But from God's perspective, it is divinely sent, and not chance at all. Make this confession aloud: "I honor chance encounter thoughts. I honor thoughts that accidentally intersect my thought process, because they are coming from the Holy Spirit within, and I choose to honor the indwelling Holy Spirit."

4. The river of the Holy Spirit flows within the believer's heart.

> *On the last day, that great day of the feast, Jesus stood and cried out, saying, "If anyone thirsts, let him come to Me and drink. He who believes in Me, as the Scripture has said, out of his heart will flow rivers of living water." But this He spoke concerning the Spirit, whom those believing in Him would receive; for the Holy Spirit was not yet given, because Jesus was not yet glorified* (John 7:37-39 NKJV).

Now Jesus *is* glorified, and the Holy Spirit *has been* given. Jesus said it would be like a river within us. Therefore, when we tune to the bubbling flow within us, we are tuning to the Holy Spirit within us. *This is more than simply theology. This is an actual experience.* There is a river within us, and we *can* tune to it. This bubbling effortless flow *is* the Holy Spirit. It is so simple that even a child can do it. And that helps prove it is real, because Jesus said we needed to become like children to enter the Kingdom. If we make Christianity too difficult for a child, we most likely have it wrong. When I tune to flow, I am tuning to the Holy Spirit within me.

5. We are a temple of the Holy Spirit.

> *Or do you not know that your body is the temple of the Holy Spirit* [who is] *in you, whom you have from God, and you are not your own?* (1 Corinthians 6:19 NKJV)

The Holy Spirit lives within us. We are not alone on the inside. Make this verbal confession: "Much of what is within me is not me but the one whom I contain."

6. The Christian's spirit is fused to the Holy Spirit.

> *But he who is joined to the Lord is one spirit* [with Him] (1 Corinthians 6:17 NKJV).

> *The spirit of man is the candle of the Lord...* (Proverbs 20:27a).

We are pure gold at the core of our being because we are joined to Almighty God by a miracle that He performed. When we touch our hearts, we also touch Him. Say this out loud, with faith and joy: "I am joined to Almighty God. I am one with Him. I am pure gold at the core of my being!"

7. We are a branch grafted into a vine.

> *I am the vine, you* [are] *the branches. He who abides in Me, and I in Him, bears much fruit; for without Me you can do nothing* (John 15:5 NKJV).

There is a flow of sap through living branches on a daily basis. The branch does not have to work at it. It just happens naturally. In the same way, there is a flow of spontaneity through each of us all the time. We don't work God up; we just choose to honor the flow that is already there.

Say out loud as a confession: "I choose to honor the flow within me because it is the river of God in me by the working of the Holy Spirit."

More Support

Additional support for the concept that spontaneous thoughts are the voice of the spirit world include the following:

✴ 1. Creative flashes provide solutions to problems.

I am sure we have all struggled with a difficult situation and then experienced in an instantaneous flash a creative solution to the problem. Where did that flash come from? Was it my own greatness finally revealing itself? Or was it the creativity of the Creator who lives within me? I believe that it was a *rhema* from Almighty God springing forth within my heart. I no longer take any credit for these creative insights, but rather give it to God, the One who lives within me.

✴ 2. Destructive flashes come from the destroyer.

Where do destructive and evil thoughts erupt from, when I am not thinking them but they flash across my mind with a life of their own? I may be in prayer, and some perverted thought abruptly comes into my mind. I am fully convinced that they come from the destroyer, who is bombarding me with his evil thoughts. Therefore I do not accept guilt for evil thoughts that suddenly appear in my mind. I give proper blame to whom blame is due—satan.

3. Testimonies of "life after death" encounters encourage us.

In books on "life after death" encounters, we find a confirming witness of what Spirit-to-spirit communication is. People tell of seeing Jesus or an angel speak and, although they do not hear anything audibly, they instantly know within what has been said. They receive in their spirits the spontaneous, effortless flow of ideas that is Spirit-to-spirit communication (or *rhema*).

✱ 4. Nature testifies about God.

God often models spiritual truth in the physical world, which is why the whole earth reflects His glory. It is interesting to note that the Jordan River, which flows through the land of Israel, bubbles up from the depths of the earth and simply begins as a full-fledged river. As the Holy Spirit bubbles up from our innermost being and simply flows, the Jordan River emerges from the bowels of the earth and flows as a river throughout the land.

Qualities that Characterize God's Thoughts

Qualities that characterize God's thoughts that are interjected into your heart include the following:

- They are *spontaneous,* not *cognitive* or *analytical,* which means we move from living out of the use of our reason to living intuitively or spontaneously (living more like children; see Matt. 18:3). This, of course, is countercultural to the Western worldview, so we are choosing to step out of our comfort zone and live from a biblical worldview. Jesus lived out of an inner flow of thoughts and pictures from His Father, doing nothing of His own initiative (see John 5:19-20,30). We can do the same.

- God's thoughts are expressed through our personalities and style of speech. We notice that the Gospel of John reflects John's personality and the Gospel of Mark reveals Mark's individuality and manner. So the divine flow within us does not bypass or eradicate our personalities or style of speech. God is united with us (see 1 Cor. 6:17), flowing out through us. This is the wonder of Christianity—that God has joined Himself to humankind and is expressing Himself through us. God's glory and splendor is being highlighted as it flows through your unique personality. So when you see your personality and vocabulary coming out in

[handwritten margin note: We shouldn't completely dismiss the cognitive or analytical — business sense for example.]

[handwritten margin note: Fiery darts of the Devil]

your journaling, do not reject it as being of self, but say, "Thank You for the wonder of Christianity—Almighty God joined to me!"

- These thoughts come easily as God speaking in the first person.

- They are often light and gentle, and easily cut off by *any* exertion of self (our own thoughts, will, etc.), so we are careful to choose to honor the river over and above our own self-effort.

- They will have an unusual content to them, in that they will be wiser, more healing, more loving, and more motive-oriented than your thoughts.

- They will cause a special reaction within you, such as a sense of excitement, conviction, faith, life, awe, or peace, assuming you have taken a step of faith and believe that what you are hearing is from the God who flows within.

- When embraced, they carry with them a fullness of strength to perform them, as well as a joy in doing so.

- Your spiritual senses are trained as time goes on, and you will more easily and frequently experience God speaking in this way. So don't quit if it is a bit awkward the first couple of times. It becomes easier quickly.

- Remember: God *is speaking* to you all the time, and you are receiving His interjected thoughts. Until you begin distinguishing them from your own, you are simply grouping them all together and assuming they are yours. In learning to distinguish His voice, you are learning how to separate the spontaneous thoughts that are coming from Him from the analytical thoughts that are coming from your own mind.

Testing Whether Flowing Thoughts Are From God

There are many ways of testing whether the spontaneous flow is your heart, the Holy Spirit who is joined to your heart, or an evil spirit who is issuing an attack against you. An entire chapter will explore these later. However, let me offer a couple of easy tests right now that I currently use.

If You Posture Your Heart Properly, the Flow Within Will Certainly Be the Holy Spirit!

John 7:37-39 tells us that we can sense a flow within us which is the Holy Spirit. It also lays out the prerequisites for positioning our hearts properly to ensure that this flow is coming from God and not self or a demon.

> *Now on the last day, the great day of the feast, Jesus stood and cried out, saying, "If anyone is thirsty, let him come to Me and drink. He who believes in Me, as the Scripture said, 'From his innermost being will flow rivers of living water.'" But this He spoke of the Spirit, whom those who believed in Him were to receive; for the Spirit was not yet given, because Jesus was not yet glorified* (John 7:37-39).

There are four prerequisites given to us in the passage from John 7:

1. If anyone is thirsty

2. let him come to Me

3. and drink

4. He who believes in Me

*The promised result is that we **will** connect with the Holy Spirit!* "From his innermost being *will flow* rivers of living water, but this He spoke of the Spirit."

Here is a delineation of the four prerequisites: (I strongly recommend that you make these your confession by speaking them out loud).

When I want to move in flow, I position my heart properly before my King by saying:

1. God, I am one of Your "anyone's." Lord, I am **thirsty** for Your voice, vision, and **anointing**.

2. I fix my heart upon You. [I do this by using vision and seeing Him present with me—which the Bible clearly says is truth. You could also pray in tongues or listen to anointed music.]

3. I tune away from my own reasoning, and **I tune to** Your voice, to **flowing** thoughts and pictures within me. I drink in Your words.

4. Father, I **believe** the **flow** within me is the **river of God**, because You have declared it to be so. I banish all doubt. I believe that what the Bible teaches is true. Thank You, God, for the river of Your Holy Spirit within."

Or even more simply, I say, "Jesus, I am thirsty to be anointed. I ask You to anoint me. I tune to flow, and I believe the flow within me is Your river." Then I minister the anointing of the Holy Spirit out to others in whatever ways He directs me. It may be through speaking, healing, writing, composing, designing, or any of the myriad ways the Creator wants to reveal Himself. Try it! It's fun and easy. It is Christianity!

Notice the Lord does not say that the Holy Spirit will flow if you:

- are fasting.

- have prayed much.

- have interceded greatly.

- have not sinned in a given period of time.

- are a longtime believer.

- have read your Bible regularly, or at length.

- are a deacon or an elder in the church.

- are an ordained minister.

- are in a religious atmosphere, for instance, in a church meeting.

- have done works for the Lord.

What a relief! Notice how simple Christianity is: I ask for the anointing, I fix my eyes on Jesus, I tune to flow, and I believe the flow within me is the river of God. Now I simply live in and out of this flow. *Oh Lord, I have made Christianity so much harder than this. Please forgive me, I pray.*

(As a side note: All the gifts of the Holy Spirit [see 1 Cor. 12:7-11] are received through exactly the same heart posture and in the same manner. When I need words of wisdom or knowledge, I tune to flowing ideas; for a prophecy, I tune to flowing words; for healing power or a miracle, to divine energy/light that flows out through me; for discerning of spirits, to flowing pictures, ideas or emotions; for faith, to a deep flowing emotion/confidence; for tongues, to flowing syllables; and for the interpretation of tongues, to flowing thoughts, emotions, and pictures.)

As I journaled about releasing God's healing anointing to one who was very sick, the Lord said: *"Mark, this day show love. That is the heart of My anointing—My love streaming forth, unhindered, and unearned. That is what is at the core of My being and that is what is to be at the core of your being, especially this day. It is not a day to judge. It is a day to love, to release My anointing through your love for My son and My daughter and to build them up in the Holy Spirit. My anointing is released through My love. So love unconditionally, and you will see My anointing flow. It is about releasing My love. My anointing will never be separated from My love, saith the Lord of Hosts. So let love always be in the center of your heart and in the center of your actions."*

Test Flowing Thoughts Against the Bible

Of course, you always test the spontaneous flow against the Bible, and you submit your journaling to your spiritual advisor(s) to see if they can confirm that it is from God. These two steps are critical and to be taken seriously and performed continuously.

Test Flowing Thoughts by Knowing Where Your Eyes Are Fixed

It is a true principle that "the intuitive flow comes out of the vision I hold before the eyes of my heart." Therefore, I ask myself if I had my focus on Jesus while I was tuned to spontaneity. If so, I find that, for me, the spontaneous flow is from God 95 percent or more of the time. We must acknowledge that we will always be vulnerable to mistakes. And that is OK. We can celebrate our mistakes, laugh at them, and learn from them (see Eph. 5:20).

Generally when a person makes a mistake in his discernment of God's voice through journaling, I have learned to ask this one question: "Where were your spiritual eyes fixed when you wrote that section in your journal?" The correct answer, of course, is, "Upon Jesus." However, in nearly every case of error, the person will admit that they had dropped Jesus out of the picture, and they were staring at something else and then tuned to flow.

In some cases, they have been staring at the tension in a relationship, perhaps even with a spouse, and then had the flow say to them that this person was going to die. One person was focusing in his mind's eye on Pharisees in the church, and then tuned to flow. His journaling became very vicious and destructive. You can always test your own journaling by going back over it and asking, "Where were the eyes of my heart fixed when I wrote this section?" If they were not on Jesus, then that section is suspect.

Another area where people make mistakes is in journaling about the future. All predictions are flexible, because God changes His mind if we or another person in the prophecy changes their heart (see Ezek. 33:13-16; Jer. 18:7-10). Therefore, all predictions are changeable. In a later chapter we will talk more about the need to avoid predictive guidance, and instead restrict our journaling to the categories found in First Corinthians 14:3—edification, exhortation, and comfort.

Sorting Out Categories of Thoughts

There are three categories of thoughts:

1. *Spontaneous positive thoughts* that line up with the names/character of the Holy Spirit, including Edifier, Comforter, Teacher, Creator, Healer, and Giver of Life, we will assume come from the Holy Spirit.

2. *Spontaneous negative thoughts* we assume come from demons, and thus will line up with the names/character of satan, which include accuser, adversary, liar, destroyer, condemner, thief, and murderer.

3. *Analytical thoughts* come from self, from our own reasoning process, and are sensed as cognitive, connected thoughts. They are limited by our own knowledge, wisdom, understanding, and abilities. For example, you may "think" one plus one equals two. In this case, the thought would be correct ("true") if you were only talking about decimal or base 10 math. However, in binary math (the language of computers and engineering), it would not be true. (In base two, 1 + 1 = 10.) So "reasoned truth" is only a little glimpse of partial truths.

For too many years, I had just assumed that I was the source of all my thoughts since it was my head! This simple biblical understanding has helped me greatly in my life and my Christian walk; for now that I have identified the different types of thoughts, I have made the choice to only accept those from Category 1. Category 2 thoughts are rejected as soon as I am aware of them. Category 3, Analytical Thoughts, are replaced with "Spirit-led reasoning," which we will discuss later in this chapter.

Biblical Meditation: Turning *Logos* Into *Rhema*

One way you experience *rhema* is when the Holy Spirit causes Scripture verses to leap off the page and hit you between the eyes. We have all had this happen, and it is exciting! The written Word becomes illumined in our hearts as a specific spoken word for us at this moment of our lives. So how and why does this occur? Could it happen every time I read the Bible? If so, what would I have to do for this wonderful experience of divine revelation to take place continuously? Here is the answer!

I cannot turn *Logos* into *rhema*. That only happens by the movement of the Holy Spirit. However, I can poise myself attentively before the Word and the Spirit, giving myself prime opportunity to hear what the communicating God wants to speak to me. In this way, I can receive revelation consistently as I turn to His Word.

God longs to speak to us through the *Logos*. He wants to give us a spirit of revelation, to open the eyes of our hearts (see Eph. 1:17-18), to cause our hearts to burn within us (see Luke 24:13-32). He desires for the *Logos* to be transformed from simple words to personal heart revelation and conviction as we pray over the Scriptures, allowing the Spirit to make it alive in our hearts.

How can *Logos* become faith-giving *rhema*? How can I precipitate its happening? By choosing *biblical meditation* over *Western study*. Biblical meditation involves opening all five senses of my spirit to be filled with *rhema*. That places me in prime position to receive and provides God with the maximum opportunity to grant revelation within my heart. Following are two charts that compare study and meditation.

Study
(Greek/Western)

"Application of the mental faculties to the acquisition of knowledge"
(Webster)

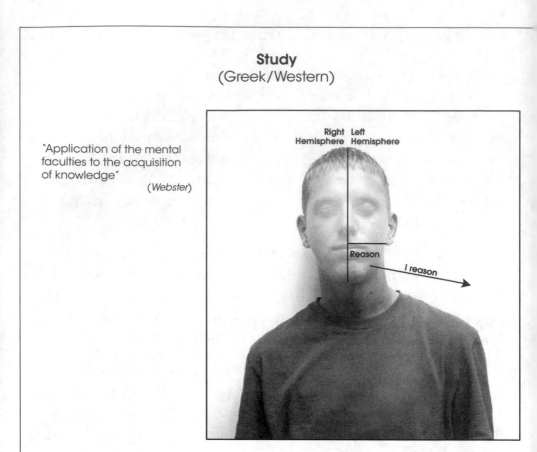

Study (My use of one part of one hemisphere of my brain)

1. Is nowhere endorsed in Scripture (2 Tim. 2:15 is a mis-translation in the KJV Bible).
2. Is self in action (Humanism – a false god).
3. Is self using reason (Rationalism – a false god).
4. Results in wisdom from below – earthly, natural, demonic (James 3:15). For example, reason caused Peter to be at odds with the purposes of God (John 18:10-11).

Study violates the following biblical principles:

1. Gal. 2:20 – I resurrect self, which no longer lives.
2. Rom. 12:1 – I am using my faculties rather than presenting them to God to use.
3. Isa. 1:18 – I'm reasoning, rather than reasoning together with God.
4. Gen. 3:5 – I've fallen prey to the temptation of the Garden of Eden that "I can know good and evil."

figure 4.3

Meditation
(Hebrew/*Lamad*)

"To murmur; to converse with oneself, and hence aloud; speak; talk; babbling; communication; mutter; roar; mourn; a murmuring sound; i.e., a musical notation; to study; to ponder; revolve in the mind; imagine; pray; prayer; reflection; devotion"

(Strong's Exhaustive Concordance Definition compiled from Strong's Old Testament numbers: 1897, 1900, 1901, 1902, 7878, 7879, 7881; New Testament Numbers: 3191, 4304)

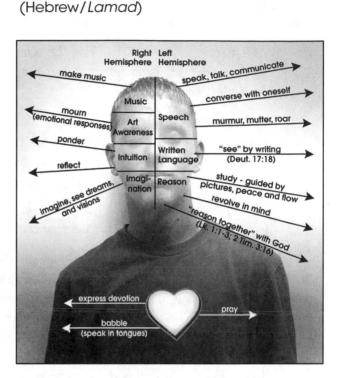

MEDITATION (God's use of every part of both hemispheres of my brain as He fills and flows out through my heart by His Spirit)

1. Is endorsed 18 times in the KJV Bible.
2. Is God in action within the individual.
3. Is God granting revelation through the heart and mind which has been yielded to Him.
4. Results in wisdom from above — pure, peaceable, gentle (James 3:17).

MEDITATION applies the following biblical principles:

1. Gal. 2:20 — I let Christ live through me.
2. Rom. 12:1 — I am yielding my outer faculties to the indwelling Spirit (to "flow" - John 7:38).
3. Isa. 11:2 — When reasoning together with God, I receive a **spirit** of wisdom and understanding and knowledge.
4. John 5:19-20, 30 — I'm living as Jesus did, out of divine initiative, doing what I see and hear my Father doing.

figure 4.4

Since study is so central in Western education, it is startling to discover that the word *study* is only found three times in the King James Bible, and in none of these references is study as we understand it endorsed or recommended. The verses are as follows:

- *And further, by these, my son, be admonished: of making many books there is no end; and much study is a weariness of the flesh* (Eccles. 12:12).

- *And that ye study* [literal Greek is to "be diligent"] *to be quiet, and to do your own business, and to work with your own hands, as we commanded you* (1 Thess. 4:11).

- *Study* [literal Greek is to "be diligent"] *to shew thyself approved unto God, a workman that needeth not to be ashamed, rightly dividing the word of truth* (2 Tim. 2:15).

The New American Standard Bible translates First Thessalonians 4:11 and Second Timothy 2:15 correctly as "be diligent." Diligence, of course, is an attitude of the heart, whereas study is a function of the left hemisphere of the mind. So Second Timothy 2:15 is commanding us to come to the Bible with a properly postured heart, rather than with a fully engaged mind. This is a huge difference, and it will have a great impact on what you walk away with when you have completed your "Bible study" time.

So we see that nowhere does the Bible command us to study it, or to study anything, for that matter. "Study" is me using my mental faculties myself. God wants me to present my entire self (this includes my brain) to Him and the Holy Spirit so that God can use and flow through me. I am to do nothing on my own initiative. Albert Einstein famously said, "I want to know God's thoughts; the rest are details." Einstein understood that revelation knowledge that comes through a biblical process called "meditation" is at the heart of all wisdom, knowledge, and understanding.

The Scriptures use the word *meditation* as an alternative experience to *study*. In the King James Version of the Bible, there are 18 uses of the words *meditate* and *meditation*.

Meditation means: To murmur; to converse with oneself, and hence aloud; speak; talk; babbling; communication; mutter; roar; mourn; a murmuring sound; i.e., a musical notation; to study; to ponder; revolve in the mind; imagine; pray; prayer; reflection; devotion.[2]

We find that meditation takes place in our hearts (see Ps. 19:14; 49:3; Isa. 33:18). We can meditate in the fields in the evening (see Gen. 24:63) and in our beds during the night times (see Ps. 63:6). We are encouraged to meditate on God's law all day long (see Ps. 119:97). We are to meditate on the Lord (see Ps. 104:34) and on His Word (see Josh. 1:8; Ps. 1:2; 1 Tim. 4:15), on His ways (see Ps. 119:15), His statutes (see Ps. 119:23,48) and His precepts (see Ps. 119:78). We are to meditate on all His works (see Ps. 143:5). When we do this, we have more understanding than all our teachers (see Ps. 119:99).

It is clear that God wants us meditating, rather than studying. You can see from the charts on "Study vs. Meditation" that while study is me using one faculty in one hemisphere of my brain, meditation is me inviting the Holy Spirit to use every ability in both hemispheres of my brain. This is obviously a far superior process and will grant a far superior end result. Speak the following statements out loud: Study gives me *reasoned* knowledge, whereas meditation gives me *revelation* knowledge. Study is me in action. Meditation is God in action. Study gives me what Paul called "knowledge," whereas meditation gives me what Paul called "true knowledge," or "revelation knowledge," or knowledge birthed in the Spirit of God.

You will note that the definition of *meditation* includes study. If I combine study with all the rest of the experiences that are part of the meditation process, then study is an acceptable activity. For example, I am often led by the Holy Spirit to look up the Greek or Hebrew root meaning of a word in a verse. The Lord will tell me what I am to be looking for, and make it leap off the page when I see it. The entire studying process, when it is part of meditation, is guided by the flow of the Holy Spirit and wrapped with pictures or imagination. I allow flowing thoughts and flowing pictures to guide my reasoning process. I call this "Spirit-led reasoning," "anointed reasoning," "reasoning together with God" (see Isa. 1:18), "pondering," or, simply, "meditation."

Biblical Meditation

Result: Illumination, Revelation Knowledge, Anointed Reasoning

Left-brain Study/Rational Humanism	Whole-brain/Heart Meditation/Divine Revelation
Do *not* do this:	Do this:
1. Have unconfessed sin	1. Be washed by Jesus' blood
2. Have a preconceived attitude	2. Have a teachable attitude
3. Be independent: "I can..."	3. Pray: "Lord, show me"
4. Read quickly	4. Slow down, ponder, muse
5. Rely on reason and analysis only	5. Combine anointed reason, flowing pictures, music, and speech
6. Read without specific purpose	6. Read with focused purpose
7. Take credit for insights	7. Glorify God for insights

Seven Steps of Biblical Meditation

Following are seven steps to prepare you to receive from the Holy Spirit, with brief prayers to guide you as you enter into biblical meditation and all its exciting possibilities.

1. **Lord, cleanse me by Your blood.** Since receiving divine revelation is at the heart of biblical meditation, you must prepare yourself to receive from the Holy Spirit by repenting and being cleansed by the blood of the Lamb. You must be obedient to previous revelations from God (see Matt. 7:6), and confess any sin in your life (see Isa. 59:1-2; 1 John 1:9).

2. **Lord, grant me a teachable attitude.** Revelation is given to those who maintain an attitude of humility, and it is withheld from the proud and the arrogant. So keep an open, humble attitude before God, allowing Him the freedom to

shed greater light on any ideas you currently hold and to alter them as He sees fit (see James 4:6; 2 Pet. 1:19).

3. **Lord, I will not use my faculties myself.** You can do nothing of your own initiative but only what you hear and see by the Spirit (see John 5:19-20,30). You do not have a mind to use, but a mind to present to God so He can use it and fill it with anointed reason and divine vision (see Prov. 3:5-7; Rom. 12:1-2). If you use your mind yourself, it is a dead work (see Heb. 6:1-2).

4. **Lord, I pray that the eyes of my heart might be enlightened.** Slow down as you read, mulling the text over and over in your heart and mind, praying constantly for God to give you a spirit of wisdom and revelation in the knowledge of Him (see Eph. 1:17-18; Ps. 119:18).

5. **Lord, I present the abilities to reason and to imagine to You to fill and flow through by Your Spirit.** Meditation involves presenting your faculties to God for Him to fill and use. These include your left-brain reasoning capacities as well as your right-brain visual capacities. Look for the river of God ("Spirit flow") to guide and fill both hemispheres, granting you anointed reasoning and dream and vision (see John 7:37-39). Music can assist you, as can muttering, speaking, and writing as you go through the discovery process (see 2 Kings 3:15).

6. **Lord, show me the solution to the specific problem I am facing.** Focused attention brings additional energies of concentration of heart and mind, which help release revelation. For example, think about the difference between diffused sunlight hitting a piece of paper, and sunlight going through a magnifying glass to hit a piece of paper. The focused energy creates a ray so concentrated that the paper bursts into flames. When you have a hunger to master a new understanding and discipline, that hungry and

searching heart will cause you to see things you would not normally see (see Matt. 5:6).

7. **Thank You, Lord, for what You have shown me.** Realizing that the revelation came from the indwelling Holy Spirit, give all the glory to God for what has been revealed (see Eph. 3:21).

God commands us to reason together with Him (see Isa. 1:18). This involves the flow of His Spirit within us, guiding our thoughts. Vision is a key element in this process, as seen in Isaiah 1:18. God goes straight to pictures after He says, *"Let us reason."* He continues, *"Though your sins be as scarlet, I will make them white as snow."* That is reasoning with pictures. That is biblical reasoning. It is very different from the Western way of thinking, which centers in logic.

Luke 1:1-3 gives another good example of "Spirit-led reasoning." While Luke states that he has "investigated everything carefully from the beginning" and he plans "to write it out for you in consecutive order," we still recognize that according to Second Timothy 3:16, "All scripture is given by inspiration of God." Our conclusion must be that Luke is reasoning under the guidance of the Holy Spirit. We can also experience this as "reasoning guided by flow—that is, the flow of the Holy Spirit within us."

I believe verses become *rhema* as a result of biblical meditation. I believe they remain simply black and white print when we use Western study. I have therefore purposed in my heart to only use biblical meditation when I come to the Bible. I will not use Western study as I approach the Bible, or any other book for that matter, since I am not interested in simply my own knowledge or understanding but earnestly desire the Spirit's revelation on everything I learn.

You, also, may want to pray, saying, *"I choose biblical meditation over Western study from this point on in my life. Father, by Your grace I will use biblical meditation when I come to the Bible and to every other book or area I explore, because I want divine revelation, not man's reasoning. Holy Spirit, please remind me whenever I slip back into mere study. Thank You."*

Since it is a heart/spirit activity, the following are the faculties (senses) of my heart that I present to the Holy Spirit to be used in biblical meditation.

- **Ears of my heart**—I direct my whole attention to God's Word as I begin to read. I incline my ear to His words and have an attentive attitude so that I hear what He is saying to me from the passage. Since His voice comes to me as flowing thoughts, I tune to these as I read the Scriptures.

- **Eyes of my heart**—I sanctify my imagination, deliberately offering up to Father the eyes of my heart to be filled with pictures and visions of the eternal reality that I am reading about in the Bible. I picture the biblical scenes as I am reading and I tune to flow, inviting the Holy Spirit to make them come alive and to minister anything to me He wants to reveal to me. As flow bubbles up and the scenes come alive and begin moving, the pictures in my mind transition from godly imagination to divine visions.

- **Mind of my heart**—Throughout the day and night, I ponder the words and visions I have received, seeking greater revelation and how they are to be integrated into my life.

- **Will of my heart**—I set my will to fully understand and obey all that God has spoken to me. I confess verses and truths and principles out loud, personalizing them by putting my name in the Bible promises I am meditating upon.

- **Emotions of my heart**—My deep underlying emotions are stirred as I gaze at the picture I am holding on the screen of my heart. These emotions move me to action. In addition, I have a sense of peace and assurance in my heart when the Holy Spirit is saying "yes" or unrest when He is saying "no." My heart lets out a victory cry when it gains new insights through the Holy Spirit, and when He convicts me of sin, it is broken and contrite before Him.

As I prayerfully fill all five senses of my spirit with the *Logos*, I provide a *maximum opportunity* for God to move within my heart and grant revelation.

The following is another wonderful revelation by my friend Maurice Fuller.

Pondering

There are times when a believer will think things through with his own human intelligence, without the Spirit of God. This is the way the word *ponder* in Psalm 73:16 is used. It is the Hebrew word *chashav* (pronounced *kashav*). In the Piel stem of the verb, the stem that is used in this passage, it means "the result of a thought process that (usually) brings one to a wrong conclusion." The Psalmist at first reasoned without revelation and got it all wrong. Then, in the presence of God, he received revelation that enabled him to see all things clearly.

It is used in Psalm 77:5-6. Here the Psalmist reasoned in his "heart" and his "spirit" but he still got it wrong. The significance of "heart" and "spirit" here is that even when thoughts come from the very deepest part of us, from the very core of our being, if they are uninformed by the Spirit, they can still be completely wrong. *Chashav* does not always indicate a thought process devoid of the Spirit, though. In Psalm 119:59, when the Psalmist "considered" (*chashav*) his ways he saw them clearly and realized he should turn his steps to God's testimonies.

The central idea of *chashav* is to compare an unknown thing with known things so as to clarify and define it. It is a very deep and thorough process yet, without the Holy Spirit, it can be dead wrong. The word also occurs in Proverbs 16:9 and 24:8, Daniel 11:24, Hosea 7:15 and a few more. In some of these passages it has the idea of carefully laid plans that, if they do not include God's guidance through the Spirit, are futile.

I would say that, yes, Spirit-led reasoning is a gift and when it is well developed, as it is in left-brainers, it is especially useful. Right-brainers need to learn how to utilize this capacity just as we left-brainers had to learn how to hear from God. If they don't they will think every thought that comes into their head is from God, no matter how wonky, not realizing how our own defective theology can distort divine revelation.

Flaky prophets suffer from underdeveloped analytical abilities. The balanced person is the one who is able to compare new revelation with his storehouse of knowledge gained from former revelation, from life experience, from the Scriptures, and from what other godly people have shared with him. Maybe there needs to be a special course on Spirit-led reasoning for super-intuitive people!

The Effects of *Rhema*

Rhema is **God's** word, spoken with **His** mouth, which produces **His** results. Consider Isaiah 55:11:

> *So shall My word be which goes forth from **My mouth**; it shall not return to Me empty, without accomplishing what I desire.*

Logos is the whole Bible. *Rhema* is the word of God spoken by His mouth for the immediate time and situation. We need to understand and experience *rhema* as well as *Logos*. *Rhema* is used over 70 times in the New Testament, including each of the following verses. Note the powerful effects and write down your thoughts and reflections on each of these uses of *rhema*.

1. Productivity

But Simon answered and said to Him, "Master, we have toiled all night and caught nothing; nevertheless at Your word [rhema] I will let down the net" (Luke 5:5 NKJV).

2. Effective ministry

For He whom God has sent speaks the words [rhema] of God, for God does not give the Spirit by measure (John 3:34 NKJV).

3. Life

It is the Spirit who gives life; the flesh profits nothing. The words [rhema] that I speak to you are spirit, and they are life (John 6:63 NKJV).

4. Relationship

He who is of God hears God's words [rhema]; therefore you do not hear, because you are not of God (John 8:47 NKJV).

So when they did not agree among themselves, they departed after Paul had said one word: "The Holy Spirit spoke rightly through Isaiah the prophet to our fathers, saying, 'Go to this people and say, "Hearing you will hear, and shall not understand and seeing you will see, and not perceive; for the heart of this people has grown dull. Their ears are hard of hearing, and their eyes they have closed, lest they should see with their eyes and hear with their ears, lest they should understand with their heart and turn, so that I should heal them." Therefore, let it be known to you that the salvation of God has been sent to the Gentiles, and they will hear it!'" (Acts 28:25-28 NKJV)

5. Authoritative teaching

Do you not believe that I am in the Father, and the Father in Me? The words [rhema] *that I speak to you I do not speak on My own authority; but the Father who dwells in Me does the works* (John 14:10 NKJV).

6. Fullness of desire

If you abide in Me, and My words [rhema] *abide in you, you will ask what you desire, and it shall be done for you* (John 15:7 NKJV).

7. Faith

"So faith comes from hearing [akoe] *and hearing by the word* [rhema] *of Christ"* (Rom. 10:17). *Akoe* means "to have audience with, to come to the ears."[3] Thus, the verse expanded and personalized would read:

So faith comes by having audience with God through the fellowship of the Holy Spirit, and hearing His voice in my heart.

Examples of Two-way Journaling

Read these examples of others who journaled about God's flowing thoughts. The following journal entries prove how God wants us to be aware of His *rhemas* whenever they come to us.

Charity—Journaling Releases Anointing for Business

My husband, Leo, had been put on a team assignment at work that was very challenging. For weeks, everyone had been trying to complete a specific project, but no progress was being made at all. Hours were spent in meetings, idea after idea was examined and rejected; nothing seemed to be quite what they were looking for.

Leo started in on another weekend of brainstorming at home and he asked me for my thoughts on the project. I told him he should journal about it. (Actually, I told him he should have journaled about it a long time ago!) So, he asked God for His ideas on what should be done and wrote them down. They were brilliant, of course!

Leo organized the revelations and made sure the presentation was just right. He took it in to work on Monday and waited for his turn to share. The meeting started as usual, with a few other associates giving their suggestions on the project, all of which were determined to be unacceptable.

Then my husband shared the ideas that God had given him—and everyone loved it!! It was unanimously decided that this was the best presentation that anyone had come up with and it was just what they wanted! Finally, a breakthrough idea that everyone agreed on—a miracle!

The thing is, God's got the best perspective on everything, so instead of waiting until all else fails, maybe we should start by asking Him what He thinks. Tap into the divine creativity that is resident on the inside of us and release the anointing of God into our workplace. After all, isn't that why He put us there?

✳✳✳

Rudi's Journaling About the River

Lord, how important is Your River in my life?

Son, My River is much more than a physical body of water flowing in a predetermined direction through life. It is through My River that I guide you and it is through My River that you are connected to Me. Too many people never recognize the flow of My River within them and they fail to really connect to Me.

The water in My River brings life and contains My words, will and thoughts for your life. Some days you will drink of the water and it will be like words flooding your mind. Other times the water will be in the form of holy emotions that will stir you in the core of your being. Depending on your specific need on any given day, I will meet those needs from the same source: My River flowing within you.

Son, you have seen the great rivers in America and the vastness they represent. Always remember that My River is much more than a small stream with a trickle of water. The greatest river on the face of the earth cannot be compared to the size and stature of My River flowing within you!

With its source in My throne room, it extends across time and space maintaining a powerful flow even within your heart. It is important that you remember this, because every time you surrender to the might of the flowing water within you, I will amaze you with the sheer power of the flow. The currents within My River are both diverse and abundant, designed to bring every yielded vessel to My determined plan for their lives.

Trust the flow of My River in you. Enjoy its refreshing and power. In doing so you will effortlessly attain great distances in reaching My destiny for your life.

Lord, what about the foundations I am building on in my life? Are they sure or faulty?

Son, in 1994 I caused many of the foundations in your life to crumble. In one week, I caused the water level to rise significantly in your life. Back then, you were determined that I establish a strong flow of My River in your life. Today, that flow is still present. The result of the continuous flow of My River in you has been a flooding in the low-lying areas of your life. These areas were once dry and flat, ideal for the building of foreign and faulty foundations. Today they are covered with water flowing from My throne and because of the strong current, it would be impossible to build something foreign in the river. I will cause the water to wash away any foreign objects.

Son, as long as you desire more of Me and as long as you welcome and embrace the flow of My River in you, the River will be My foundation in your life. Fix your eyes on Me, do not lean on your own understanding and I will teach you the way you should go.

Lord, I want to experience the deep waters of the River.

Son, I am causing a deepening within you. Just like the Israelites pre-pared the dry river bed for water, by digging trenches to accommodate more water, I want you to prepare your spirit by digging trenches in your life. Make room for more of Me and I promise you I will fill all the room you make for Me.

River-life demands a periodic scraping of the bottom of the river. As time passes by, a river becomes shallow because of sediment that settles to the bottom. Be aware of sediment that settles in your spirit. This sediment represents your growing familiarity with river-life. My work is fresh and up-to-date. Do not allow the frequency of things in your life to take away the freshness of My Spirit's power in you.

Lord, please help me to optimize Your flow through my heart and mind.

Son, let Me remind you that faith is what causes the River to flow. Faith is also what will keep the flow of the River in your life. Believe in Me and rely on what I show and reveal to you. Every step of faith you take, results in a stronger flow in your life. He who believes, out of his innermost being shall flow forth rivers of living water!

Son, I want to keep equilibrium in your life. A balanced life is a successful life. This balance is not between good and evil. It does not represent spiritual compromise in any form. Rather it represents the role of the Word and the Spirit in your life. I said in My Word that My Spirit will always lead you into all the Truth. I am the Truth! My Spirit always complements My Word. The Holy Spirit reveals the Word in your life and opens your understanding to who He really is.

How can I broaden the scope of the gifts of the Holy Spirit flowing through me?

You are right in identifying a need in the Church today. My people have regressed into a very narrow flow of My creative power, especially when it comes to the gifts that I made available to them. Many operate in the gifts based on an outdated example they saw sometime in their past. Carried through generations this powerless activity has gone unchecked and has in many cases not been corrected.

I am looking for people who will boldly put their trust on Me and step out of this narrow box. I am ready to show fresh revelation and new applications of the gifts flowing through My Spirit that will cause many to be astounded. *What was new before has grown stale, but I have newer things yet available. Step out in faith and do not draw back in fear. As you step out in faith I will unlock secrets to you that will become common in My Church again.*

What you have seen as coincidence and incidental before, you will now view as deliberate and significant. You will recognize My fingerprints even in the mundane things of your life. The people you meet and the things that cross your path will bring you closer to My destiny for your life. Not only will I bring you to destiny, but I will bring destiny to you.

Be sensitive to the happenings around you. Speak with caution to the people around you. Use words and actions that will flow from the River in you. I will change the pictures around you. If you take the time, you will see Me in every picture and vision I show you. When you look at people's lives, yes look at the picture and vision of their surroundings, but never fail to see where I am in the picture. Where I am is where the need will be.

Teach My people to yield to the flow of My River frequently and in real life situations. Teach them that I am practical and not theory. I cause My River to flow through life in its entirety. Help them to discover that flow within them.

✳ ✳ ✳

Janelle Anderson—A Fountain of Fire and Water

I heard the word *fountain*. As I tuned to flow and looked for vision, I saw myself standing next to a very small spring bubbling up out of the ground. It bubbled up for a while, then sputtered and just died out. It was even sucked back into the ground and the ground was dry for a time. But then, suddenly, water came surging out again from the ground, but this time it shot high into the air and became a fountain! It spread far and wide over the earth with far more power and strength than before.

I looked more closely and noticed something else was in the water. There was fire in the water! It burned with an intensity and a purity I had never seen before. This "fire-water" spread out in all directions as it hit the ground and the fountain still was going high in the air.

Lord, what is this? What are You saying to me about this fountain?

The spring represents the influence and power of My Spirit in you before your wilderness season. You did have a measure of My Spirit and life in you and it did touch others to a degree. It died out when I took you into the wilderness and through the dark night of the soul season. It went completely dry because I removed everything from your life outside of just you and Me.

You went into the secret place for a season, deep into the ground and the hidden places of the soul where no one could see what I was doing in your spirit. It felt like a dry season, but I was working in the deep places of your soul, bringing you to a place of deep humility and purifying you, pruning your life.

It looked for a time as if all was lost and that there was nothing left for you to do. You thought I was done with you and that there was no longer a purpose for you in My Kingdom. Not so! I drew you deep into the things of My Spirit, into a place where it was just you and Me so that I could teach you how to truly walk in My Spirit and release the River that is in you.

You have a much deeper and surer foundation in Me now and the fountain (My Spirit and power in you) comes from a much deeper place than before. It will come forth in much greater power and much greater glory than anything you have seen or experienced before! But you must stay grounded in Me, keep those deep roots in place, dwell and remain in the secret place of My presence in your life or that fountain will run dry again. You cannot do anything in your own strength or power. You are a vessel, a container of the treasure which is My Spirit, My Life, My Power and you can only release it as you remain pure and humble before Me.

My plan is to release My Glory through you in a greater way than you have ever seen. I want to send My fire out far and wide and touch many lives with My Spirit as you release this fountain! Just stay in the secret place, stay rooted and grounded in My love, stay yielded and surrendered to My Spirit in you and you will see great things! You will see great things!

You have gone through a season of preparation, but now you are entering a season of release and power and you will be very fruitful, My daughter. You have been faithful and you will see the reward!

I am so pleased with you and your heart because you have never stopped running after Me and your hunger is great for Me, therefore you will be filled, you will be satisfied, you will find Me! I see your obedience and your boldness and it is growing. It is just the beginning! You are just now only experiencing the beginning of the birthing forth of what I have planned for you!

Continue to step out in obedience and be bold! No more timidity and no more fear! I have destined you for great things in My Kingdom. Open your mouth wide and I will pour forth My Spirit from you in a greater measure in the days to come. Others will be drawn to this fountain in you because they are thirsty and hungry for Me. Did I not tell you that I would bring forth springs in the desert? Did I not promise you that I would do this?

You are experiencing the cry of My heart as you feel compassion for the ones I bring into your life. I am giving you this compassion for them so that you will cry out to Me for them! My Spirit is crying out for them through you and I will answer that cry and I will draw them to Me. I hear the cries of their hearts in their lonely, dark nights when they don't understand what is happening and they don't know what is wrong or what is missing. As you intercede for them, I can release My power out through you and they will be touched by that fire and they will come to Me.

When they come, just listen to My Spirit. I will speak to you and through you. It will come forth just like a fountain of life bringing refreshing to their spirits, bringing life where there is death and healing to their bones. This is what I have called you to.

Oh yes, you will sing again! You will sing a new song, the song of the Lord again. Don't doubt that, don't fear it! Reach out for it, step out in faith on the water again, My daughter, because it is there for you. Receive it! Stir up that gift again. It is still there, and this gift has been refined in the fire of affliction and suffering. It will come forth in greater purity and power than in former days because it will come from a much deeper source.

I will give you new songs, songs of My Spirit that will set the captives free and that will bind up the brokenhearted and will refresh the weary souls. These songs I am going to give you will water the dry ground like springs in the desert. Just wait on Me and I will bring these songs forth. Just believe and wait and it will be done. I will pour them forth into your spirit and you will only have to receive them and let them come forth from your spirit.

Oh Lord, let it be done according to Your Word and Your will. I yield to You, I surrender to You and give you all of me. Do with me as You will. Please cleanse me from all unrighteousness and all pride. Do not let me step off of Your path. I desire only Your approval, not the approval of others. I want only to please You, not others. Let it be done. Do with me as You will. I am Yours.

※※※

Judith from St. Kitts—God's Voice Warns of Danger

It was during the construction of the facility of Rivers of Living Water Christian Centre and every evening during the week and all day on Saturdays we would gather as a congregation on the building site to do our part in its construction. That Wednesday evening I was late getting to the site and even though it was already 8:00 P.M. and darkness had fallen, I was still eager to get to the site to do my part for I knew that some of us would be working until after 10:00 P.M. and later.

On arriving, I hurriedly parked my car and noticed that there was a group with a portable light working outside to the front of the building and all I could think to myself was to get to that area as quickly as possible so that I could do my part of working with them. I decided not to take the designated route in front of a barrier which had been set up to restrict passage to a certain area, but to proceed behind the barrier, which was the shorter route.

As I started off a definite thought came to me very clearly: *Judith, go around to the other side.* But I remember saying to myself, "But this is the shorter route and I'll get there faster." As I continued, another very strong thought came to me, *Judith, go around. Do not go this way,* and I remember replying to myself, "But I can see the light."

That was the last thing I remember, for it turned out that I stepped into a 15-feet-deep pit that had huge boulders at the bottom. I was covered with dirt and was knocked unconscious. No one knew I had fallen into the pit and no one would have conceived that anyone could have been in that pit. But what I am told was that about 10 minutes later (for some of my friends had seen me pass by) they heard one of our sisters cry out that she had fallen into the pit and that it seemed that an animal was there with her for she had heard a groan. (That was me groaning!)

It turned out that the Lord had sent a messenger to our sister to ask her to move her car. In going to do this, she found herself walking to the area behind the barrier. She reported that it was as if someone just dropped her down on her feet into the pit—she suffered not a scratch or a bruise and was able to call out for help immediately.

As I lay on my hospital bed, the first thing I asked of the Lord was to show me what I had missed and He revealed to me very clearly that I had missed knowing and heeding His voice.

✳ ✳ ✳

Diane—The Voice of God Provides Protection

I have found God's voice to be very gentle and yet very distinct from my thoughts. The text teaches that we all have spontaneous thoughts, ideas, feelings or impressions at times and if we pay attention, we will find that God is speaking to us. For instance, my sister and I were on the freeway going to a movie. On our way there, the thought kept coming to me to get off at the next off ramp. I ignored it for a while but it would not go away. Finally, I told my sister that we were going to take a different route to the show and got off the freeway.

When we got home, my mom rushed to the door and said, "You guys are all right?!" We told her yes, and then asked what was wrong. She said that when we left, she saw us in a terrible car accident. So she started to pray and pray and did not stop until she felt that we were safe. I told her about the impression I had to get off the freeway and when I told her what time it was that we got off the freeway, we learned that it was the exact time she had stopped praying. Coincidence? I don't think so.

Personal Application—Bible Meditation Exercise

Meditate on the following passages: John 7:37-39; Revelation 22:1-2; Psalm 1:2-3; John 15:4-8. Picture each scene and then ask God for a spirit of wisdom and of revelation in the knowledge of Him. Pray, "Lord, please enlighten the eyes of my heart" (see Eph. 1:17-18). Now tune to flowing thoughts and flowing pictures as you wait in His presence.

Ask Him, "Lord, please show me where the river within me comes from, what it feels like within me. What is this flow designed to produce? What will be the effects of what is produced? How important is it to live out of this river? What happens if I neglect the river and live out of self's initiative? And Lord, is there anything else You want to show me in this biblical meditation?"

Record what God reveals to you in your journal. Once you have written out the illumined truths you receive from your meditation on the Scripture passages, fix your eyes on Jesus, and journal about what He has shown you. Ask, "Lord, what do You want to say to me personally about what You have shown me from these passages? How would You have me change?" Picture Jesus in a comfortable setting, tune to flow, and write down the spontaneous thoughts (His voice) that come back to you. Submit this to your spiritual advisors for confirmation. Then run with it.

Do this *now*, before proceeding on to the next chapter. It is only what you *do* that changes your life, not what you read and think would be nice to do!

Free Online Resources to deepen these truths available at: www.cwgministries.org/FreeBooks

- **Study vs. Meditation**

- **"How to Receive Revelation Knowledge"**

- **Revelation Knowledge Versus Reasoned Knowledge and the Implications for Bible Colleges**

- **Get your own personalized business cards with the 4 keys on them!** (Called "4 Keys to Hearing God's Voice Mini-Tract") www.cwgministries.org/businesscards. htm

- **All uses of "Rhema" in the Bible**

- **"To Whom Do We Pray"**

Endnotes

1. *Rhema* is in *Strong's Exhaustive Concordance* if you want to do your own research. James Strong, *Strong's Exhaustive Concordance of the Bible* (Peabody, MA: Hendrickson Publishers, first published in 1894), ISBN 0-917006-01-1, 4487.

2. *Strong's Exhaustive Concordance*, Old Testament numbers: 1897, 1900, 1901, 1902, 7878, 7879, 7881; New Testament numbers: 3191, 4304.

3. *Strong's Exhaustive Concordance*, Greek Dictionary, 189.

How to Instantly Remove All Idols from Your Heart and Other Prayer Considerations

This teaching on praying with an idol in your heart provides tremendous help in purifying your journaling. The key concept is to be mindful of where you fix the eyes of your heart when you are praying. Consider the following:

> *...any man in the house of Israel who sets up his idols in his heart, puts right before his face the stumbling block of his iniquity, and then comes to the prophet, I the Lord will be brought to give him an answer in the matter in view of the multitude of his idols* (Ezekiel 14:4).

This brings into focus a startling truth concerning an inappropriate method of prayer, which I am afraid has been practiced by many: They have fixed their spiritual eyes on the thing they are praying about more than on Jesus. The principle is: "When anything is larger than Jesus in the eyes of your heart, that thing has become an idol."

Circumstances - this is why I pray - Remember God is enough

For example, if I am praying for a broken leg to be healed, and my focus is upon the cast and the crutches and the brokenness and the weakness rather than upon Jesus and how He is ministering to the leg, then I am praying inappropriately. I am praying with an idol in my heart, because my eyes are fixed on something other than Jesus. We are to look to see what Jesus is doing, and do what we see Him doing.

When I come to the Lord in prayer, I am to be a living sacrifice. I must lay down my will and be totally sold out to God's will concerning the issue about which I am praying. If that is not my mindset, I should pray for God to form that attitude within me before I begin praying about the issue at hand. If I pray about the issue while I have a definite direction about it in my own heart, that "definite direction" of my own will interfere with the signals coming from the throne of God and cause me to believe that God is confirming the direction I felt, whether He actually is or not.

In other words, if I pray about something and the item is more prominent in my eyes or my consciousness than my vision of the Lord, the answer that comes back will be through the item and will be deceptive rather than a pure answer from the heart of the Lord. On the other hand, if my vision of the Lord is more prominent in my consciousness than my vision of the issue I am praying about, then the answer will be a pure answer from the Lord's heart and not contaminated by my own desires.

The Principle of Pure Focus is this: "The intuitive flow comes out of the vision I am holding before the eyes of my heart." That is why I am commanded to fix my eyes on Jesus, the Author and Finisher of my faith. That will make the vision pure.

An example of a seer having his vision clouded and receiving damaging direction can be found in the story of Balaam in Numbers chapter 22. Balak had sent messengers to Balaam asking him to come and curse the Israelites. When Balaam sought God about it, God was very clear: *"Do not go with them; you shall not curse the people; for they are blessed"* (Num. 22:12).

Balak again sent messengers, more distinguished than before, with the offer that Balak would honor Balaam greatly and do whatever he asked if he would only come and curse the Israelites. Apparently wealth and riches were on Balaam's mind because he said, *"Though Balak were to give me his house full of silver and gold, I could not do anything...*" (Num. 22:18). However, he invited them to stay, saying, "But I will check with the Lord again."

Since he so desperately wanted to receive the honor, gold and riches (and was probably picturing a house full of silver and gold), he went to the Lord again in prayer, this time with an impure heart. As could be expected, the Lord gave him an answer consistent with the idol in his heart. He said, "Sure! Go ahead!" However, God was angry with Balaam and He sent an angel with a sword to block his path (see Num. 22:22).

There are other examples of Israel praying with an idol in their hearts and receiving the answers to their prayers that eventually brought hurt in their lives. Israel begged God for a king, and even though He didn't want to give them one, He gave in to their whining. Israel lusted for meat in the wilderness, and God gave it to them, but along with it He sent a wasting disease (see Ps. 106:14-15).

In conclusion, when we pray with an idol in our hearts, we may get an affirmative answer from the Lord, but it will bring us to destruction. Therefore, when we pray, we must be certain that our vision is purified, and that we see Jesus as One who is MUCH LARGER than the object or issue for which we are praying. Only then will our answer be pure and life-giving.

When testing your journaling, always ask yourself, "When I wrote this, were my eyes fixed on Jesus?" If they were not, then I believe that section is suspect and may not be from the Lord. If someone submits their journaling to you and your spirit hesitates to confirm it, ask the same question: "When you wrote that section, were your eyes fixed on Jesus?" This simple test, when added to those previously discussed (compatibility with Scripture, reflecting the nature of Christ and confirmed by two or three counselors) can help maintain the purity of flow and the integrity of your revelation.

The following diagram demonstrates these two approaches in prayer.

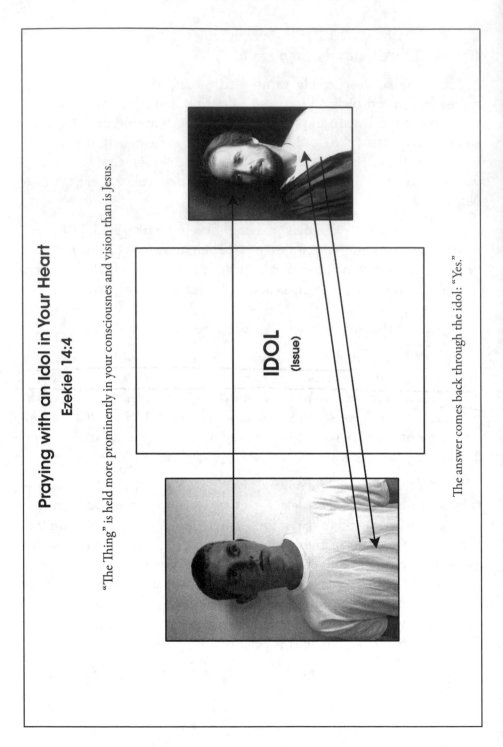

Praying with an Idol in Your Heart
Ezekiel 14:4

"The Thing" is held more prominently in your consciousnes and vision than is Jesus.

IDOL
(Issue)

The answer comes back through the idol: "Yes."

Praying without an Idol

ISSUE

Jesus is held more prominently in your heart and mind than is "The Thing" for which you are praying. The answer comes back from Jesus: "Caution—No"

THE PRINCIPLE: The intuitive flow comes out of the vision being held before one's eyes.

AN EXAMPLE: Balaam – Numbers 22:15-35

figure 5.1

Prayer Response: *Lord, I repent for any times I have prayed with idols in my heart, and I purpose by the power of the Spirit to fix my eyes upon Jesus as I pray. Holy Spirit, remind me to do this if I forget. Thank You. I receive Christ's cleansing blood to wash away my sin and I put on the robe of righteousness. And any decisions I have made, which were made with idols in my heart, I give them back to You, Lord, and I ask You to take even my mistakes to build Your Kingdom. Lord, I thank You that You are big enough to do this. Thank You, Lord. Amen.*

King David's biggest mistake (sin) was probably adultery with Bathsheba and the murder of her husband and other valiant warriors on the front line of a war. And yet, God brought Jesus Christ through the lineage of David and Bathsheba. God can use even our mistakes, sins, and weakness. *Thank You, Lord!*

Prayer Is to Be Led by the Holy Spirit

All prayer is to be led by the Holy Spirit. That means:

> *...Pray at all times in the Spirit...* (Ephesians 6:18).

> *...We do not know how to pray as we should, but the Spirit Himself intercedes for us with groanings too deep for words* (Romans 8:26).

All our praying is to be *in* the Spirit (inspired, guided, energized, and sustained by the Holy Spirit), otherwise, we are praying in the flesh (see Eph. 6:18). *Some* of our praying is to be *with* the Spirit, which is in tongues and some is to be *with* the mind, which is in our native language (see 1 Cor. 14:14-15). So whether we are praying in tongues or in our native language, we are to be praying *in* the Spirit (i.e., tuned to flow and allowing the Holy Spirit to pray through us).

The goal of Spirit-led prayer is to be flooded with God's love, light, and power:

> *But you, beloved, building yourselves up on your most holy faith, praying in the Holy Spirit, keep yourselves in the love of God, waiting anxiously for the mercy of our Lord Jesus Christ to eternal life* (Jude 20-21 NASB).

Jesus provides us the "right" to approach God, and the Spirit grants us actual "access."

> The Right: *Jesus said to him, "I am the **way**, and the truth, and the life; no one comes to the Father but through Me"* (John 14:6 NASB).

> The Access: *For through Him we both have our **access** in one Spirit to the Father* (Ephesians 2:18 NASB).

We have a right to come before the throne of God because of what our Lord and Savior Jesus Christ accomplished for us at Calvary. However, it is the Holy Spirit who takes us there. It is the Spirit who gives us actual access. So in prayer, I may say, *"Father, thank You for making it possible for me to come before You through the shed blood of Your Son, Jesus Christ. Holy Spirit, thank You for providing me access into the throne room of Almighty God."*

Our weakness is **perpetual**, so we simply step from self to Christ—again and again:

> *For He Himself knows our frame; He is mindful that we are but dust* (Psalm 103:14).

> *...Christ Jesus...intercedes for us* (Romans 8:34).

> *In the same way the Spirit also helps our weakness...* (Romans 8:26).

The Lord must reveal to us that our weakness in praying is perpetual so that we might learn to be perpetually dependent on the Holy Spirit. We must learn to "rest" in our weakness, not "strive" in it. In other words, God is everything we need; we ask Him again and again for everything and we receive it in simple child-like faith. I have given up trying to be strong or pure in myself. In myself, I am weak and sinful; however, I can moment by moment step from my weakness and sinfulness into His glory and His strength, and that is good enough for me. I am no longer striving to be good. I am OK being weakness fused to strength. That is God's design. I am OK with God's design. Jesus wouldn't even claim to be good. He said there is none good, except God (see Mark 10:18). I want to simply reflect Him. I want to see with the eyes of my heart, Jesus in action, and say "Yes, Lord." I want to put on Christ (see Rom. 13:14) and reveal Him to the world.

When we are weak, tempted, or unable to focus, we don't try hard to be strong or to overcome temptation. Instead *we ask for a flow of divine power through us to transform us*. We tune to flow, God's power infuses us, and we are changed. It is a simple and beautiful transaction of stepping from the weakness of self into the fullness of Christ. We do this continuously.[1]

Examples of Two-way Journaling

Read the journals of people who have confronted the idols in their hearts with the help of the Holy Spirit.

A Destination of Intimacy—Journaling from Pastor Terry

Lord, identify the season I am in, that I may work in cooperation with You.

Hey Terry, it is so good to talk to you again. You miss our time together, don't you?

Oh yeah, more than I realized. I can't go that long without this kind of private time with You...help me to better prioritize and find other ways to accomplish this when I'm away.

(In my mind, the Lord has shown me that we are on a boat, traveling, the wind blowing on my face—it's chilly and the air is brisk, and I am holding on because we seem to be traveling very fast.)

Lord, where are we going?

To your destiny, Terry. To where I've called you. To a place in Me that you have asked.

But why so fast...and why is it so cold?

Because we have been traveling this way for a while, you just have not noticed it before. And when you travel fast the air seems chilled and cold... and it is because the things around you are not attached, or connected...

so there is no comfort and satisfaction from the temporal things that once fulfilled you.

You are on a journey to Me. To a place of anointing...and a place of power...and a place of structure and a place where my Spirit flows in untold purity and might. Stay with Me...Hold on, and trust that I will get you there. You don't need to know all things...just know that I, Your Father, have you in My arms safe and secure and I will get you to that place.

Hold on...and trust Terry. Hold on and trust. For I have planned some wonderful things for the son I love and the son who loves Me. Press in as you have been doing... For the journey is not about a destination of ministry, but a destination of character, and a destination of purity and intimacy with Me. And when these converge there will be anointing and power from what you say and do, and there will be significant results... Trust Me, Terry...I will get you there...

But Lord, the waters seem choppy and rough and difficult to travel.

Terry, are you more concerned with the waters or with My ability to get you to the desired destination? There is nothing I can't do. And choppy waters is nothing for Me...hold on... I've navigated this many times...and I know exactly where to go to avoid the rocks and dangers...Stay in the boat for now... We will reach land soon....

Yes, Lord, I can see it...I see land...and the sun is shining there... but not here...I don't get it.

Where I am taking you, the sun will shine and the joy will flood your life...and there will be peace and tranquility and you will bask in My glory and enjoy your days in the land. Hold on, Terry...

Okay, Lord...but when?

Questions, and more concerns? Terry, just hold on...it is coming...look, people everywhere waiting for you to arrive...waiting for what you have... you see, they will see you, but it will be Me that they receive, because you have learned how to walk in Me, and to let Me be seen and not you. See the crowds...see the people, hungry, and ready...and yes, many ready for truth, and ready to walk in obedience and you will see the throngs moving with you, and believing with you for all that I have said you would do.

You see I have placed in them a desire for what I have called you to produce...and they are ones with hearts ready to receive. Trust Me to produce the work...it's My church anyway, Terry, not yours...so trust Me to bring in those I have prepared in their hearts for what I'm going to do. Hang on, Terry...

✳ ✳ ✳

CLU Student—Journaling About Sexuality

I have never journaled about sexuality before and feel very awkward and unsure as to how to go about it. What do You want to say to me concerning sexuality?

Sex is one of My greatest gifts to humanity. When done within the boundaries I have set, it is one of the most beautiful and fulfilling acts that a husband and wife can experience. It's a beautiful thing. It draws together, causes an intimacy with two that comes no other way. I created and designed sex. It is not dirty but beautiful. Yet, the enemy of all humankind has taken My gift and has perverted it (as he does with all things) and has used it to do the very opposite of why I designed it.

You have questioned Me often as to why I have given such a strong drive to men or to you. Why could it not be more balanced between male and female? I have placed with man and woman the perfect and exact amount or desire for sexuality, romance and affection. Man is the pursuer and woman is the responder. The two together, balance each other out. The two together, submitted, and surrendered together and to each other causes the highest degree or level of intimacy possible.

It is just not a physical act, but an emotional and spiritual act. It is an honoring of one another. It is an abandonment and surrendering to each other. It is a letting down of walls, an exposing of hearts to one another. Satan causes the exchange to be just two bodies and keeps it in the sensual and carnal realm. My intention has always been so much deeper and intimate. *My deepest blessing is upon husband and wife as they exchange and give and become vulnerable to each other. Never was sex meant to stay in the natural or carnal realm. Yes, there is a great physical pleasure and that is the way I purposed. Yet, when done in My way, the benefits go so much deeper. So much further. It draws so much closer.*

Can you see why the enemy desires so strongly to pervert such a beautiful gift? One produces death, shame, rebellion, etc. The other produces intimacy, a greater bonding, a greater peace and a drawing together. It produces a oneness. True sexual fulfillment comes only in the marriage bed and not looking elsewhere. That only leads to death and separation. As always, My way is perfect. It is best. I know. As all else that I created, it is for the pleasure and enjoyment of My children.

Look to Me for restoration in your marriage. In you and also in your wife. There is no other way. There must be a greater turning away from the past, and each other's faults and shortcomings and a turning to Me. I will restore all the years. Again, that is My delight. I will go deep and remove and restore and impart all that is needed in your marriage relationship. I simply need your cooperation.

Lord, I have believed that my sexuality was always a problem. That something was wrong with me. Why did You give me such a strong sexual drive? It's not right. I'm cursed. I'm not normal. Why not give a little more to women to even it out a bit?

The way I have created you is good. It is beautiful. It is not a problem. You are the pursuer. The pursuer needs a strong drive. Without the strong drive, the pursuer would not prevail or continue in his conquest. You need to win your wife. You need to pursue her and not give up. I give out the measure in perfect proportion in order to see that the task at hand is completed.

You need to see your sexuality and drive not as a curse, but as a blessing. A tool that I have given you to go out and explore and conquer the prize. Without it the union between the husband and wife would be boring and stale. This adds excitement and challenge to a man which stimulates and propels him on to win his bride over and over again with love, passion and excitement. See it as a gift, son, not a curse. It is good. It is a gift.

✳ ✳ ✳

Journaling has become a welcome experience for people worldwide. The following is from an African pastor seeking a companion—with God's guidance.

Pastor in Nigeria—Finding a Wife

I have worked hard in life not to defile myself with women and now I am ready to seek my own future partner, to settle down, and to enjoy the rest of my life in the love of God.

Dear Lord, how exactly do I know who to really go out with, and from which tribe and background she should be? What will be the color and the trait that I will see in order to be sure she is the right person?

The Lord said to me, *Before you were born I knew thee and I formed thee in your mother's womb. Don't you think I had a plan for your life? I have kept you since you were born into this world and without doubt I have led you on the right course of life. All you've seen and gone through is not by accident. Your ability is My ability. I have given you the grace and privilege that has sustained you throughout all your life.*

And now that you're set to go into a new phase of your life by choosing your life partner, don't you think I am still with you? Or have you forgotten I said in My Word that I would never leave you nor forsake you in life? Take note of Isaac My servant. At the right time for him I made a provision for his partner, and I am still the God of Abraham, Isaac, Jacob. I change not.

Put your trust and hope in Me and believe My words. Cast all your cares upon me for I care so much for you. Though the world may have become corrupt, there is still a way for My children. I know how to program your life for success. Don't bother yourself much on this issue, for you are Mine and I will always be there for you. Be focused on all I call you to do and work in the ways I set before you.

I will give you the bone of your bone and make life to be so interesting for you. Akintayo Ebenezer, I know you by name and I have predestined you for great success in life. Look and focus on Me, the Author and Finisher of your faith.

Oh dear Lord, I bless Your name for opening my eyes to know You and to be called Your son. I will forever trust in You and I will not allow this partner stuff to delay my progress in life. Lord, I count on You and I will be forever grateful for that which You've done for me. Lord, I will not complain or be dismayed because I am sure You're by my side. Thank You, Lord Jesus, for Your words to me today and I know You will always be there for me. I count on You, dear Lord.

Personal Application Concerning Spirit-led Prayer

Ask the Lord to speak to you about these truths. Fix your gaze upon Him. Experience Him in a comfortable setting. Tune to spontaneity and record what flows within. Don't test it as you are receiving it. Test it later. Write in simple childlike faith what is flowing within your heart. *Thank You, Lord, for what You speak.* Share your journaling with your spiritual advisors.

Free Online Resources to deepen these truths available at: www.cwgministries.org/FreeBooks

- **Idolatry vs. Imagery**

- **Overcoming Blocks and Hindrances to Hearing God's Voice**

- **Principles Concerning Prayer and Areas of Prayer**

- **Belief and Unbelief (by Ben C. Lunis, a Certified CWG Facilitator)**

Endnote

1. Additional recommended reading on this subject: Arthur Wallis, *Pray in the Spirit* (Kingsway, 1970).

CHAPTER 6

Key #2: Become Still

Let's begin with a review of the four fundamental keys to hearing God's voice:

- Key #1: Recognize God's voice as spontaneous thoughts that light upon your mind.

- **Key #2: Quiet yourself so you can hear God's voice.**

- Key #3: Look for vision as you pray.

- Key #4: Write down the flow of thoughts and pictures that come to you.

In this chapter we explore in depth:

Key #2—Quiet Yourself So You Can Hear God's Voice

For us to hear the still, small voice of God within us as spontaneous thoughts, we ourselves must become quiet. God says, *"Be still and know that I am God"* (Ps. 46:10 NKJV). Other renderings of the verse exhort us to *"cease striving, let go, relax and know that I am God."* David commanded his soul to wait in silence for God only (see Ps. 62:1,5), and to rest and wait longingly for God (see Ps. 37:7).

Often we miss the importance of quieting ourselves when we approach God. Our lives are such a rush; we just run up to God, blurt out our prayers, and rush away again. I am convinced we will never enter the realm of the Spirit that way. As a matter of fact, we are told to let God do most of the talking when we come to Him (see Eccles. 5:1-2).

If we are going to commune with God, first we must become still. Habakkuk went to his guard post to pray (see Hab. 2:1). In the early morning when it was still dark, Jesus departed to a lonely place to pray (see Mark 1:35). And after a day's ministry, Jesus went to a mountain to be alone with His God.

In order for our inner self to commune with God, we must *first* remove external distractions. We must find a place where we can be alone and undisturbed, so that we can center down into our hearts without being distracted by our external circumstances. Ask your family to help you by intercepting phone calls, young children, or other interruptions that would distract you from your *yada* time. Set aside a specific time and place for your personal conversations with your God. As you go there regularly, you will find His Spirit waiting there for you. If you don't already have such a time and place identified, do so now before reading any further.

Second, we must learn to quiet our inner being—all those voices and thoughts within us that are calling for our attention. Until they are quieted, we most likely will not hear His voice.

Several means can be used to quiet the voices within you. First, you can write them down to be taken care of later. Second, you can quiet your inner members by focusing them on Jesus. Open your eyes and see in the Spirit the vision that Almighty God wants you to behold. This will bring your inner attention to the Father and the Son.

Sense the "cry of your heart" and repeat it over and over. The cry of your heart is whatever your heart is trying to express at any given moment. I often notice it as a song I spontaneously sing in the early morning. Whenever we need to sense our hearts, we can listen for the spontaneous song bubbling within and go with the flow of it.

For example, one day when my life was crumbling around me and God seemed so distant that I could not see Him or sense Him in any way, I found that the spontaneous song that bubbled up from my heart was only two words: "Lord, arise." As I sang those words over and over, I eventually began to sense the Lord rising within me, and His vision and presence being restored in my life. We should sing the song on our heart until it realizes its goal.

You may find tension in your body as you seek stillness. That, too, should be released so you are fully open to receive from God without being distracted or hindered by bodily discomfort. Be in a comfortable, relaxed position when you pray (see 1 Chron. 17:16). Consciously relax the parts of your body that are tense. Have you noticed how calm your breathing is when you first awaken? On the other hand, when I first began public speaking, I would be terrified and my breathing would be short and fast. I found I could calm my body by breathing more deeply and slowly. Check your breathing and use it to help you relax.

Biblically speaking, there is a very close connection between breath and spirit. Both breath and spirit come from one word in the Greek, as well as the Hebrew. When our breath is gone from our bodies, our spirit is gone. I do not believe it is an accident that these words are so closely connected in the Bible. I have found I can breathe in the pure Spirit of Christ as I breathe out the contaminated spirit of self.

"Be still *and know*." Stillness is not a goal in itself. I want to become still in mind and body so my heart can know and sense God moving within. His promptings are gentle, and until my own inner and outer raging is quieted, I will not sense His inner moving.

In becoming still, I am not trying to *do anything*. I simply want to be *in touch* with the Divine Lover. I am centered on *this moment* of time and experiencing Him in it.

Becoming still cannot be hurried or forced. Rather, it must be allowed to happen. At a point in your stillness, God takes over and you sense His active flow within you. His spontaneous images begin flowing with a life of their own. His voice begins speaking, giving you wisdom and strength. You find that you are *"in the Spirit"* (Rev. 1:10).

Becoming still is an art to be learned, especially for those of the Western culture who are always on the go. However, our communion with the Lord must begin here. When you pray, take the first few minutes to quiet down and sense your heart, and proceed *only after* you have become still. Out of your silence, you will sense God. Then you will be able to commune. You will find that the more you practice becoming still, the easier it becomes and the more quickly it happens. Many also find that being in a group that is seeking to become quiet together helps them settle down. An atmosphere of quiet engenders quiet.

How Elisha and David Stilled Themselves

It is interesting for me to examine the great prophets of the Bible to see what they did when they wanted to touch the divine flow. Think of Elisha, for instance. In Second Kings 3:15-16, we find that when Elisha wanted to receive a prophetic word from God, he said: *"'But now bring me a minstrel.' And it came about, when the minstrel played, that the hand of the Lord came upon him. And he said, 'Thus says the Lord....'"*

Elisha used music to help him tune to the voice of God within and away from outer reasoning. It is interesting to note that reason is a left-brain function, while both intuition and music are right-brain.

May I suggest that when you want to move from reasoning, which flows through the left side of the brain, to intuition, which flows through the right side of the brain, you can do as Elisha did and use music (which also stimulates the right side of the brain)? This will cause a shift internally from the left hemisphere to the right hemisphere. It is so simple and so thoroughly biblical. Of course, David also did this when he wrote his psalms, which were simply prayers that were sung.

I have found it effective for me to sing a quiet love song to the King of kings and picture the words that I am singing. (Vision also flows through the right side of the brain.) This poises me instantly before the intuitive flow that springs up from my heart, and I begin to record the precious words that come from my Lord. David frequently used imagery in his prayers. Psalm 23 is a powerful expression of worship that is built around pictures. Your imagination can be an effective tool for quieting your mind and preparing you to hear from God. (We will talk more about this in a later chapter.)

Doing any right-brain activity moves you from the left side of the brain to the right. Therefore, normally I will do *several* right-brain activities *together* to ensure a smooth and complete transition from the left side of my brain to the right side, where I more easily intercept the voice of the Spirit. I will fix my eyes on Jesus, sing softly in the Spirit, relax by putting a big smile on my face, and, perhaps picturing myself as an eight-year-old, look at the beauty of God's creation as I stand with Jesus near the Sea of Galilee. Then I write down a question I want to ask Him. In that posture, I tune to spontaneity and record the flow of thoughts that come. I confirm it is God's voice by submitting it to my three spiritual advisors.

The following chart reviews some effective ways of quieting yourself.

Removing Inner Noise

(Voices, Thoughts, Pressures)

Problem	Solution
1. Thoughts of things to do.	1. Write them down so you don't forget them.
2. Thoughts of sin-consciousness.	2. Confess your sin and clothe yourself with the robe of righteousness (see Gal. 3:27 NASB).
3. Mind flitting about.	3. Focus on a vision of Jesus with you or do any right-brain activity.
4. Need to get in touch with your heart.	4. Begin singing and listening to the spontaneous song bubbling up from your heart.
5. Need for additional time to commune when your mind is poised and still.	5. Realize that times when you are doing automatic activities (driving, bathing, exercising, routine jobs, etc.) are ideal times for hearing from God.

Identify the State of Being Still

The five key ingredients of the contemplative or meditative state are: physical calm, focused attention, letting be, receptivity, and spontaneous flow. The opposites of these characteristics are: physical tension, distraction, overcontrol, activity and analytical thought. These could be placed on a continuum as follows:

Physical Tension   ⟶   Physical Calm

0	1	2	3	4

Distraction   ⟶   Focused Attention

0	1	2	3	4

Over-control   ⟶   Letting Be

0	1	2	3	4

Activity   ⟶   Receptivity

0	1	2	3	4

Analytical Thought   ⟶   Spontaneous Flow

0	1	2	3	4

Meditation is commanded throughout the Scriptures, and so is each of these elements that make up the meditative pose. Consider the following with me.

Biblical Exhortation Concerning Physical Calm

There remains therefore a Sabbath rest for the people of God. For the one who has entered His rest has himself also rested from his works, as God did from His. Let us therefore be diligent to enter that rest, lest anyone fall through following the same example of disobedience (Hebrews 4:9-11).

And to whom did He swear that they should not enter His rest, but to those who were disobedient? And so we see that they were not able to enter because of unbelief (Hebrews 3:18-19).

Biblical Exhortation Concerning Focused Attention

...let us...lay aside every encumbrance, and...sin which so easily entangles us, and let us run...fixing our eyes on Jesus, the author and perfecter of faith... (Hebrews 12:1-2).

Truly, truly, I say to you, the Son can do nothing of Himself, unless it is something He sees the Father doing; for whatever the Father does, these things the Son also does in like manner (John 5:19).

Biblical Exhortation Concerning Letting Be

Cease striving [marginal reference: let go, relax] *and know that I am God...* (Psalm 46:10).

Be anxious for nothing, but in everything by prayer and supplication with thanksgiving let your requests be made known to God. And the peace of God which surpasses all comprehension, shall guard your hearts and your minds in Christ Jesus (Philippians 4:6-7).

Biblical Exhortation Concerning Receptivity

Abide in Me, and I in you. As the branch cannot bear fruit of itself, unless it abides in the vine, so neither can you, unless you abide in Me. I am the vine, you are the branches; he who abides in Me, and I in him, he bears much fruit; for apart from Me you can do nothing (John 15:4-5).

Biblical Exhortation Concerning Spontaneous Flow

*He who believes in Me, as the Scripture said, "From his innermost being shall **flow** rivers of living water." But this He spoke of the Spirit, whom those who believed in Him were to receive...* (John 7:38-39).

Stillness is NOT the experience of nothingness!

Some traditions have advocated stillness as getting "beyond thoughts, beyond pictures and beyond emotions to a state of nothingness." I do not accept this teaching. I am not trying to reach an inner state of emptiness. Instead, I am seeking to get beyond **my** thoughts, **my** pictures and my emotions, and to tune to **God's** thoughts, **God's** pictures and **God's** emotions.

I want to live as Jesus did. He said, "I do nothing on my own initiative, but whatever I hear and see My Father doing" (Jn. 5:19, 20, 30; 8:26, 28, 38). Jesus had not gone beyond words and pictures and emotions. Instead, He stepped from Himself and His own will to God's words, pictures and emotions – to living out of His Father's initiatives.

This, then, becomes my goal: to capture the initiatives of heaven by quieting myself and tuning to the words, visions, emotions and power of my heavenly Father, and letting Him live His life out through me. I die, and Christ comes alive within me.

Practically speaking, this means that I fix my eyes on Jesus as I walk through life. I see Him present with me always. I practice "abiding in Christ" (Jn. 15:1-11; Jn. 14:16-17; Matt. 28:20). I ask Him for His wisdom and strength, and I tune to His flowing thoughts, flowing pictures, flowing emotions and flowing power.

We have not really spoken about the anointing of power. So far we have only focused on the revelation anointing, where we receive insight from God though hearing His thoughts and His perspectives. This revelation anointing is also used in the manifestation of the Holy Spirit mentioned in 1 Corinthians 12:7-11 for words of wisdom, words of knowledge, faith, distinguishing of spirits, kinds of tongues and interpretation of tongues. However, there is also is an **anointing of power** from God. This power anointing is specifically needed when ministering the manifestation of the Holy Spirit in deliverance, healings and miracles.

Generally we ask God for **both** the **revelation anointing** and the **power anointing**. We first need revelation from God as to how to resolve a situation, and then we need power from God to actually resolve it.

The anointing of power is a release of divine energy. I experience it as an energizing flow of God's life within me, strengthening me and setting me free. When I am praying for healing for others, I often feel the sensations of tingling, vibration and warmth in my hands, as God's power passes through me to the one on whom I am laying hands and to whom God is imparting His life.

So stillness for me is not the experience of nothingness. Stillness is quieting myself down and tuning to the Holy Spirit within, capturing His impressions and releasing them to the world.

Brainwave Activity Levels

Some of the research being done in sleep laboratories is interesting as it relates to quieting ourselves and becoming still. It has been discovered that when we are wide awake and alert, *beta* level waves go through our minds. However, when we relax or enter sleep, these waves slow down and become *alpha* level waves. This is a measurable physiological effect of stilling ourselves as God commanded.

I share this because it helps me, a logical left-brain Westerner, to realize that quieting myself before God is not just a nebulous experience. I actually enter a different state of being (heart awareness), and the physical manifestations of this state can be measured through tools like biofeedback. Such tools could possibly help you learn how to quickly enter this state of rest, which the Bible calls *stillness*.

A pastor friend and I together purchased an inexpensive biofeedback system that measured galvanic skin response called the "The GSR2 Biofeedback Device," and a more complete system, the "GSR/Temp 2X Biofeedback System" (both available at www.mindgrowth.com). I used them for a few weeks while I was learning to quiet myself in the Lord's presence. I found it very helpful since it measured the state of relaxation within me. I could quickly discover which things relaxed me and which things didn't. For instance, I discovered that singing rowdy praise songs did not calm me. Neither did singing quiet worship songs, if at the same time I was lunging emotionally at God. However, if I stopped striving while I sang these quiet love songs, the biofeedback machine indicated that I had entered the stage of relaxed stillness that the Lord had commanded.

Another fun tool for helping you learn to live in rest can be purchased for only a few dollars. A "Stress Rate Card" will change colors when you hold your thumb on it for 10 seconds, turning black when stressed, red when tense, green when calm and blue when relaxed. It is an excellent tool to help you learn to relax.

The chart on the following page gives an overview of brainwave activity levels.

Similarity to Eastern Religions?

Some have wondered about the similarity of what I have described to Eastern religions. You may be surprised that my response is, "Well, I would hope what I am doing is similar to the counterfeit!" I expect satan's imitation to be similar to the real. Satan is not an originator. He is a copycat, and he only counterfeits those things that have value. So if my lifestyle is not being imitated by other false religions, then I need to ask myself, "Why am I not doing anything worth counterfeiting? Are my life's activities so valueless that satan doesn't even want to fake anything I'm doing?" I sure hope that what I am doing looks like the counterfeit. If not, then I need to get with it, and start doing something valuable enough and real enough to copy.

Since satan can never come up with anything original, I ask myself the following question when I see a counterfeit: "What is the real thing that I am supposed to be doing that satan is counterfeiting?" That is not a question the fearful ask. Some people say, "We better stay away from this thing because satan can use it," and as a result they give everything over to satan. All satan has to do to take something valuable away from some people is to imitate it. This makes them so afraid of getting close to it that they even back away from the real. Satan accordingly ends up with everything, and the Church has nothing. Just look around you and see if this isn't true. We as the Church have

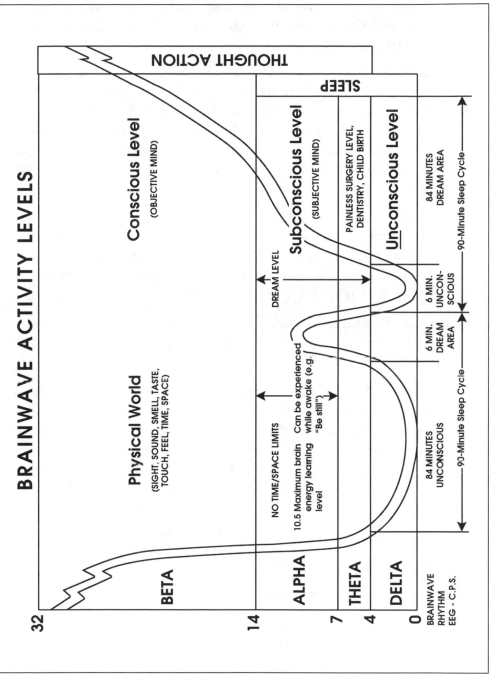

figure 6.1

backed away from and given largely over to satan politics and government, television, the Internet, movies, dance, drama, education, and the marketplace.

The Bible says we are to be the head and not the tail, we are only to be above and not underneath, we are to lend and not borrow (see Deut. 28:12-13). Yet we find most leadership positions filled by heathen rather than Christians. Why? Most of the wealth of the world is in the hands of the heathen rather than Christians. Why? Is the Bible wrong? I think not! We are wrong in that *we live under a spirit of fear rather than a spirit of faith.*

We have been taught to be so afraid of satan and his wiles that we cower in trepidation and back away from anything that could be perceived as being dangerous. We are supposed to be people full of faith and abundant life. But instead, too many are full of neurotic fear and poverty and are ruled over by the heathen.

Speak this prayer aloud: *God, forgive me for living in a spirit of fear (faith in the working of satan) rather than "doing the **work of God**, which is to **believe**..."* (see John 6:29).

I think that to back away from something just because satan is trying to get his hands on it and counterfeit it is a horrendous sin of giving in to the kingdom of darkness. I, for one, want to **take back** all that satan has stolen, and I believe that we are in a period where the Church is doing just that. And this is one of those areas that we will redeem. I invite you to become a conqueror and take back this land with me.

In summary, two things stand out about counterfeiters:

- They only counterfeit what is real.

- They only counterfeit what has value.

Therefore, since Eastern religions use stillness as they approach the spirit world, I know two things:

- We, too, should probably be using stillness. (This is confirmed in Psalms 46:10 and 62:1,5.)

- To become still and touch the Holy Spirit has great value.

Since the Eastern mystic does not go through Jesus Christ, he becomes ensnared by the evil one as he enters the spirit world. However, some of the *paths into* the spirit world are neutral. They may be used by either cultists or Christians. On the other hand, some paths are not neutral. A non-Christian may use drugs to enter the spirit world. This is an illegal entry for the Christian and strictly forbidden in the Bible. The word for witchcraft in the Bible is *pharmecea,* which is, of course, connected with drugs.

Since the Christian goes through Jesus Christ, Jesus guides him safely through the snares of the trapper and into the throne room of God—as He did John in the Book of Revelation.

Do I Overcome Self by Attacking Self or by Coming to Christ?

Throughout the last 2,000 years, the Church has presented two different ways of dying to self so we can become more Christlike:

Stripping away—In this approach, you attack the desires and lusts of the flesh and try to kill or remove them from yourself. A lot of self whipping tends to take place, at least verbally and sometimes even physically. Things like lying on a bed of nails have been advocated, along with many other fairly painful rituals. I see this as self attacking self. No one wins because the self that is attacking has the same strength as the self that is being attacked!

Coming to the Light—In this approach, you overcome your sinfulness and darkness by coming into Christ's light. You fix your spiritual eyes upon Jesus, and are transformed "while you look" into His wonderful presence (see Heb. 12:1-2; 2 Cor. 3:18, 4:17-18). When you lift your hands during a worship service and find yourself in the presence of the King, you discover that all your negative attitudes and weaknesses melt away and you find faith, hope, love, peace, and joy flowing effortlessly within you.

I have personally chosen this approach to overcoming self. I feel it is what the New Testament teaches, and it is what works most effectively in my own life. So, for example, when I want to overcome rational thinking, I never attack my thoughts and tell them to stop (which I found doesn't work), but instead I refocus from self to Jesus. I picture myself together with Jesus in a comfortable setting, and I write down a question I want to ask Him. I put a smile on my face, tune to spontaneity and write down the flow of thoughts that come while my eyes are fixed on Jesus.

The ultimate way to overcome self is to focus on God through Jesus Christ in prayer.

What Is Prayer, Anyway?

Prayer is two friends sharing love together. If you look back to the Garden of Eden and see how God walked and talked with Adam and Eve in the cool of the day, if you consider that God is described as manifesting incomprehensible love, you begin to realize that our sharing with Him is the communion of two lovers. You can find many examples of this in the Psalms. Therefore, when we pray, we are coming to Jesus, our Friend. Jesus said, *"No longer do I call you servants, I now call you friends"* (John 15:15). We are building a friendship.

The 4 Keys

Once again I want to remind you of the four words that summarize the four keys to hearing God's voice:

- Spontaneity

- Stillness

- Vision

- Journaling

So far, we have explored spontaneity and stillness. In the next chapter, we will delve into the exciting subject of vision—seeing with the eyes of our hearts.

Examples of Two-way Journaling

Michael—Christ Being Our Life

Lord, what do You want to speak to me concerning Your being my life? What does that mean practically?

My greatest desire is to see My children come into a place of complete rest in Me. This is mentioned in My Word over and over, and yet most of My children continue to strive and resolve within themselves to live and do better.

I desire to see each one of My children truly enter this place of rest, where there is a complete ceasing from their own strivings, efforts and self-determinations. This place is a place where self is no longer asserting itself, a place where it is no longer the determinations of the will, no longer the efforts of well-meaning intentions, but simply a place of utter abandonment to Me and to My life within. A place where there is such a trust and reliance on the divine flow and power of My resurrection life within that I said would flow like rivers out of your innermost parts.

The great cry for today is to do, to try harder, to live holier lives, to press in, and all those are worthy and good intentions. Yet, when they are not done solely out of My life and divine enabling, it produces greater bondage and greater condemnation in the hearts of My children.

I am your very life. I am everything that you need. I know you know these words, and you have quoted them many times, but the truth and the reality of these words are still not deeply ingrained in your spirit. It is coming. Rest assured. I know the way.

It means a daily, and constant choosing to draw on Me. At the very moment of temptation or weakness, you must cease your striving and effort to conquer and simply tune and turn in to My vast supply that I have for you. Resurrection power and life abide within you: the same resurrection and power that raised up the Lord Jesus out of the grave and the lower parts of the earth.

It's a refusal to turn to yourself, a determined choosing not to allow yourself to be drawn into the web of religious striving and effort that will certainly only produce failure and death. It is a realization that of yourself you can do nothing. Out of that you will truly be able to turn to Me and to draw upon the rich resources that I have. When it is My power and My Spirit, you will experience overcoming life and an abundant living that you have desired for so long.

You have seen this from afar off for many years and you have desired this and have yearned for it. This has been My doing and My wooing within you. I will see to it that you come fully to Me and to My rest and out of that you will do greater, much greater things than you have ever done, by far.

The life that you will then live will truly be that of the Son of God, it will not be your life through His, but His life through yours. The treasure coming through a surrendered and yielded vessel. You are simply a vessel. I am the life and the glory that will come forth.

This is the great groaning of all creation, to see My glory through a yielded people. To see the life of the Son of God manifested in a many-membered body, the Body of Christ. This is how I have chosen to show My glory. Not through strong and able men and women, but through weak and yielded people. There is no other way. This is the way I have chosen.

Continue to call upon Me and continue to ask Me to be ever reminding you of this glorious revealing and how simple it really is. Christ in you, Christ through you.

✳ ✳ ✳

Della—Jesus Provides Freedom and Hope

Dearest Jesus, I love You. Come closer. What do You want to say?

Your ministry is not over. I have much in store for you. There always is a breaking, letting go, and a releasing before new things can take place. Rest in Me. I know the storm rages. Stay close to Me and let your ear rest on My chest. I do know what's best. Be comfortable with not knowing. Let go. It is

OK not to know about tomorrow. Hippie Della is OK. She was very loved and taken care of by Me. She felt secure and had a child's heart. Embrace her. She is not gone. That is who you really are. Free like the spirit running with the wind. Draw close to Me. Open your soul's eyes. You will see Me waiting there for you. I have plans for your life. Rest in Me.

Thank You, Jesus.

✳✳✳

Karen—Death of a Vision

Father, what do You want to say to me today? What would You have me do?

Karen, look to Me. I know you are uncomfortable and wondering how this is all going to come out. Yes, you are in the death to the vision stage wherein you think life is falling apart on you, and you realize there is nothing you can do about it. You see doors closing on you and none opening at the moment. You feel boxed in with no place to go. This shall soon pass.

I am Your place and I want you to simply trust Me. The ministry I am calling you to is to be accomplished by My power so all will know it is from Me. When I am lifted up, I will draw all men unto ME. I will provide for you as I have promised. I know your needs. I know all about the bills. I know your desire to give more into My kingdom. You are important to Me, so important that I am taking special care to teach you these lessons. Relax, and enjoy Me and the life I have set before you. I am always with you and I am giving you time to come apart with Me in this wilderness. Rejoice in My love and that all is well even though to you it doesn't seem that way. I am refining you so you can be the clean, pure vessel of gold that you desire to be for Me and so I can work mightily through you. You have nothing to fear.

Thank You, Father. Take me. Work out Your precious will. By the power of the Holy Spirit, I take my hands off my life, my finances, my health, the ministry You are calling me to, work, everything.

Personal Application

Write the following questions in your journaling notebook or in a journaling file on your computer:

1. "Lord, what means have I used to effectively still myself?"

2. "What methods would You like me to cultivate?"

Now relax. Picture yourself with Jesus in a comfortable gospel setting—maybe walking along the Sea of Galilee or strolling through the fields of Judea. Turn to Him. See His love and compassion, and joy and excitement at being able to spend this time with you. Smile! Become a child and take His hand. Let the scene just happen as He wants it to. Ask Him the question on your heart. Tune to spontaneity and write down the answer He gives you. Do not test it while you are receiving it. Stay in simple childlike faith. You will have plenty of time to test it after the flow is finished. Then submit it to your spiritual counselors.

Free Online Resources to deepen these truths available at: www.cwgministries.org/FreeBooks

- **Checklist for Abiding in Stillness**

- **Come Away With Me—A prophetic meditation on the Song of Solomon**

CHAPTER 7

Key #3: Look for Vision as You Pray

We are now ready to review and then explore key number three for hearing God's voice:

- Key #1: Recognize God's voice as spontaneous thoughts that light upon your mind.

- Key #2: Quiet yourself so you can hear God's voice.

- **Key #3: Look for vision as you pray.**

- Key #4: Write down the flow of thoughts and pictures that come to you.

> *I will pour forth of My Spirit...and your young men shall* **see visions**, *and your old men shall* **dream dreams** (Acts 2:17).

Looking for vision as you pray is not a new concept. The following biblical examples bring home this key for you to accept as your own. Abraham's faith erupted when God gave him a vision.

> *And He took him outside and said, "Now look toward the heavens, and count the stars, if you are able to count them." And He said to him, "So shall your descendants be."*

Then he believed in the Lord; and He reckoned it to him as righteousness (Genesis 15:5-6).

Daniel **looked** toward Jerusalem as he prayed.

Now when Daniel knew that the document was signed, he entered his house (now in his roof chamber he had windows open toward Jerusalem); and he continued kneeling on his knees three times a day, praying and giving thanks before his God, as he had been doing previously (Daniel 6:10).

Habakkuk kept **watch** to see what God would speak.

I will stand on my guard post and station myself on the rampart; and I will keep watch to see what He will speak to me, and how I may reply when I am reproved. Then the LORD answered me and said, "Record the vision and inscribe it on tablets, that the one who reads it may run. For the vision is yet for the appointed time; it hastens toward the goal and it will not fail though it tarries, wait for it; for it will certainly come, it will not delay" (Habakkuk 2:1-3).

John looked inwardly for a **vision** and heard a voice say, "*Come up here, and I will show you what must take place after these things,*" and immediately *he saw a vision.*

After these things I looked, and behold, a door standing open in heaven, and the first voice which I had heard, like the sound of a trumpet speaking with me, said, "Come up here, and I will show you what must take place after these things." Immediately I was in the Spirit; and behold, a throne was standing in heaven, and One sitting on the throne (Revelation 4:1-2).

Jesus spoke the things He had **seen** in the presence of His Father.

I speak the things which I have seen with My Father; therefore you also do the things which you heard from your father (John 8:38).

Our ability to see in the spirit is a primary sense by which we perceive the spiritual dimension. Since Christianity is a heart-to-heart or Spirit-to-spirit relationship, we would expect this faculty to be central in our relationship with God. Unfortunately, it is not used as much as it should be because we have been trained to live out of our head rather than our heart. We tend to live more in the world of logical concepts and rational thinking than in the world of heart impressions, dreams and visions. If we are going to allow our hearts to be released, we must learn to live in the world of the dream and the vision (see John 5:19-20, 8:38).

God wants to communicate through the eyes of our heart, giving us dreams, visions, and godly imagination, but first we must recognize this sense within us and the importance it can have as we present it to be used by Him. For ten years as a Christian, it never occurred to me to use the eyes of my heart or look for vision. As a result, I never received any visions. Now that I've learned to look, I find vision readily appears to me.

Obviously, the "eyes of our hearts" (see Eph. 1:17-18) is a sense of our hearts. It is one of the ways our hearts communicate—possibly one of the primary ways. I have found that the key that unlocks the door to the inner world is the use of vision. Many spiritual leaders agree with this. Dr. David Cho, pastor of the world's largest church with over 750,000 members declares, "The language of the Holy Spirit is the dream and vision."[1] Watchman Nee, pastor and writer, states that, "The picture is the Holy Spirit memory."[2] These statements are astounding in the value they place on seeing in the Spirit.

I have come to the conclusion that the ability to think in terms of images is extremely important in the Christian's life (see Isa. 1:18). I believe that maturity involves knowing how to present both our logical faculties and our visionary faculties to the Holy Spirit to be used by Him. The results are Spirit-led reasoning and godly imagination, visions, and dreams.

If we look at Scripture, we see that dreams and visions have been prevalent throughout the history of God's dealings with people. The following is just a very small sampling of the hundreds of scriptural references to dreams and visions.

Genesis 15:1	1 Samuel 28:6	Acts 11:5-6
Genesis 40:5-7	1 Kings 3:5-6	Romans 11:8,10
Exodus 3:1-6	Ezekiel 12:22-27	Ephesians 1:18
Numbers 12:6	Daniel 8:15-18	Revelation 1:10,14
Deuteronomy 13:1-5	Matthew 2:12-13	Revelation 4:2-3
Joshua 5:13-15	Acts 9:10-12	Revelation 15:5

If you have any doubt about the validity of dreams and visions, or about the place of seeing with the eyes of your heart as an integral part of your Christian life, I strongly encourage you to look up each of these verses and find out exactly what the Bible has to say. Our opinions and beliefs are only as strong as the scriptural foundation upon which they are built. In fact, I recommend you do a concordance search of all verses on dream, vision, see, look, and eyes. Pray over the verses as you meditate on them. This way you will have hundreds of verses and a solid biblical perspective. Ask the Lord how He wants to use the eyes of your heart, and how He wants you to use them. This meditation was foundational to my understanding and conviction concerning the eyes of our heart. I encourage you to do the same! The Church needs firsthand revelation, not passed down theology.

Words Describing Dream and Vision

In the Greek New Testament, there are many different words and phrases used to describe encountering God through dream and vision, and experiencing revelation. They are as follows:

- *Onar*—a common word for "dream." Precisely, it is a vision seen in sleep, as opposed to waking. It is used in Matthew 1:20; 2:12-13,19,22 and 27:19.

- *Enupniom*—a vision seen in sleep. It stresses the given-ness, almost surprise quality, of what is received in sleep. It is used in Acts 2:17 and Jude 8.

- *Horama*—translated "vision." It can refer to visions of the night or sleeping experiences, as well as to waking visions. It is used in Matthew 17:9; Acts 7:31; 9:10,12; 10:3,17,19; 11:5; 12:9; 16:9-10; and 18:9.

- *Opasis*—can signify the eye as the organ of sight, an appearance of any kind, even a spectacle; but there are also two instances where it means a supernatural vision: Acts 2:17 and Revelation 9:17. The distinction between the perception of the physical and the nonphysical is lacking in the Greek. Both "seeings" are genuine perception.

- *Optasia*—translated "vision." It has the sense of self-disclosure, of "letting oneself be seen." It is used in the following four passages: Luke 1:22; 24:23; Acts 26:19 and 2 Corinthians 12:1.

- *Ekstasis*—the word from which the English word "ecstasy" is derived. It literally means standing aside from oneself, being displaced or over against oneself, and ordinarily there is a sense of amazement, confusion, and even of extreme terror. It may refer to either sleeping or waking experiences. Psychologically, both the dreams of sleep and the imagery that occurs on the border of wakefulness, hypnagogic or hypnopompic imagery, fit the condition that *ekstasis* describes. Although translated "trance," it is misleading to use the word "trance" as a direct translation. It is used in Mark 5:42; 16:8; Luke 5:26; Acts 3:10; 10:10; 11:5 and 22:17.

- *Ginomai en pneumati*—translated "to become in Spirit" (see Rev. 1:10). This signifies a state in which one could see visions and be informed or spoken to directly by the

Spirit. Related phrases are found in Matthew 4:1; Mark 1:12; Luke 1:41 and 4:1.

- *Ephistemi, paristemi*—simply referring to the fact that some reality stands by in the night or in the day. It is used in Luke 1:11; Acts 10:30; 16:9; 23:11 and 27:23.

- *Angelos or angel*—meaning an actual physical envoy, a messenger, or a divine being sent by God, and *daimon, daimonion, diabolos* or demon, devil and satan, referring to nonphysical entities or powers from satan. Both angels and demons can be encountered in dreams and visionary experiences as shown in the following references: Acts 10:3; Jude 8; and many instances in the Book of Revelation.

- *Blepo* and *eido*—meaning "to see," "to perceive." These words are used to mean "see" in the normal outer sense, yet are also used to refer to seeing in the spiritual sense as evidenced in the following passages: Revelation 1:2,11; Mark 9:9 and Luke 9:36. Obviously, because of the dual use of these words to describe both inner and outer sight, the early Church considered visionary experiences to be just as easy to perceive and observe, to be given as often, and to be equally valid as the perceptions one has of the outer physical world.

  Blepo simply means physical seeing but *eido* has the additional meaning of seeing all that is there, the essential nature of a thing, perception.

- *Apokalupsis*—translated "revelation," literally means disclosure, divine uncovering, or revelation. It is used in Romans 16:25; First Corinthians 14:6,26; Second Corinthians 12:1,7 and Galatians 2:2.

When considering the great variety of words New Testament Christians had to choose from to describe their visionary experiences, it is evident that they were able to very precisely define the exact type of visionary encounter they were having. Probably our poverty of vocabulary in finding one or two suitable words to clearly define our visionary experiences reflects the scarcity of direct spiritual encounter we experience in the Western culture. May we restore to our vocabulary a host of suitable words to clearly define the variety of inner spiritual experiences we are having!

Defining Kinds of Vision

The following summary may help us draw together all of the expressions and gain a clearer understanding of the kinds of experiences we can expect as believers.

1. Spontaneous Vision on the Screen Within Your Mind

We may receive a spontaneous inner picture in the same fashion as we receive spontaneous *rhema*. For example, God may give a vision of the face of a friend or relative, and we just know we are to pray for them. The picture is light and gentle, and is seen within. It may be sharp or hazy, precise or unclear. As I poll Christian groups, I find that almost everyone has had this type of vision.

2. Spontaneous Vision While in Prayer

These are identical to the previous level except that we receive them while seeking God in prayer. We have no part in setting them up. They just "appear," or pop into our minds. We may even find ourselves trying to change them in some way (although really we don't want to change them, because we want His visions, not ours). However, this, in turn, helps us to realize that it was His vision initially that lighted upon our minds (see Dan. 7:1,13-14). About 70 percent of the Christians I poll have experienced this type of vision.

3. Seeing a Vision Outside of Yourself

On this level, a person actually sees a vision outside himself, with his spiritual eyes. For example, Elisha prayed and said, *"'O Lord, I pray, open his eyes that he may see.' And the Lord opened the servant's eyes, and he saw; and behold, the mountain was full of horses and chariots of fire all around Elisha"* (2 Kings 6:17). Only about 15 percent of the Christians I poll have experienced this type of vision.

4. Vision While in a Trance

A vision can be seen while in a trance. Peter had this experience in Acts 10:10-23. Trancelike visions are not very common in Scripture or in the contemporary Church. About 3 percent of the Christian groups I poll have had trancelike visions.

Ekstasis, being taken outside of oneself, is reserved for those with strong preconceived notions that close them off from God's voice. Peter, who believed firmly that Gentiles could not be saved without first becoming Jews, had to be taken (with some sense of force) outside of his stubborn self and be shown the vision of the unclean animals and then be commanded to "rise, kill, and eat." Those whose spirit is open to God's voice seldom experience *ekstasis*, or trances. Trance is the common experience of New Age channellers such as Edgar Cayce, who are used by evil spirits.

5. The Visionary Encounter of Dreams

Paul received a vision in the night as he slept (see Acts 16:9-10). Dreams are common in Scripture (about 50), and they are also common today. About 85 percent of Christians have had a dream that they recognize as coming from God.

Visions on each of these five levels are equally valid and spiritual, and all are to be thoroughly tested, weighed, and considered.

Full-Color or Black and White Pictures?

The groups I poll are about evenly divided between those who see visions in full color and those who see in black and white. Some people seem to have much better internal antennas and clearer reception than others. My visions are nebulous, and black and white. Some people's are sharp, clear, and full color, like watching a movie in high definition.

I am more left-brain. My experience indicates that left-brain people (analytical, logical) generally do not see as clearly as those God has gifted with more right-brain leanings (intuitive and visionary).

That is fine. When I need to know more clearly, I simply team up with a seer, one who can see more clearly than I can. Jesus taught cooperation; He sent the disciples out in twos. The Book of Acts indicates that the teams were composed of a prophet and a teacher. It is likely that the teacher was more left-brain and the prophet more right-brain. We are not in competition with each other. We use our giftedness to serve one another. I think it is wise for you to minister with a person who is the opposite of yourself, and honor the different-ness of each other's gifting. Much more complete ministry is offered this way, and more people will be truly helped.

My First Steps to "See"

The Bible says we have not because we ask not. For years I never saw, because I never looked, nor did I ask to see. As I teach people to look, I witness their experience of becoming seers. This sounds simple and it is for many, particularly those who are intuitive, spontaneous, and visionary by nature, those who have not cut off their natural spontaneous openness to vision because of the pressure of a culture that idolizes logic.

However, for those like me who were born with the natural tendency toward the analytical and cognitive and who have had these leanings reinforced by the rationalism of their culture, becoming a "seer" may not be so easy. Often, the intuitive and visionary functions have literally atrophied or died through lack of use. Therefore, it is not as simple as just "looking" and "seeing." When a muscle has atrophied, it must first be exercised and strengthened before the body can call it into use again. In the same way, our weakened, dormant capacity for visualization must be exercised and strengthened before the Holy Spirit can fill it and call it into use.

The first step is to believe in the value of living in the world of dreams and visions. We must see it as the language of the heart, a primary means that God wants to use to communicate with us.

As pastors have often preached, our hearts are like a radio—we must tune them so we can hear God's voice. We must also tune them to see God's vision. Unfortunately, my heart's radio was not only out of tune, it was broken and in need of complete renovation by the Master. I began the process of restoration by repenting of having scorned my visionary capacity. I asked God's forgiveness for not honoring and using what He had created and bestowed upon me as a gift. I also repented of my participation in making an idol of logic and analytical thinking, a form of thinking that had bewitched me as well as my culture. I covenanted to seek and honor His ability to flow through vision as much as I sought and honored His ability to flow through analytical thought. If you need to pray the same prayer of repentance, do so now.

I next asked God to breathe upon my visionary capacity and restore it, to bring it back to life and teach me how to allow Him to flow through it. I laid my hands on my physical eyes and prayed for healing of the eyes of my heart in Jesus' name.

Then I was ready to take my first few wobbly steps. As I sat in my study seeking God's face, I was drawn to a scene from the fourth chapter of John in which Jesus sat by the well and talked with a Samaritan woman. Sensing that God wanted to sit and talk with me, I pictured the scene with a slight adaptation. Instead of the woman, I was the one sitting there next to Jesus. I prayed and asked the Holy Spirit to take over this godly imagination, and I tuned to flow. The scene came alive through the Holy Spirit. Jesus moved and gestured, as someone does when he is talking. With His movement, there came into my heart spontaneous or flowing thoughts, His words and directives for my life.

This was the first time I had ever sought for vision in this way, and I was thrilled to see that Scripture could so readily come alive and be moved upon by the power of the Holy Spirit. I had, in essence, poised myself for the divine flow by choosing a Gospel story, meditating upon it, and asking God to fill it. I found as I repeated this experiment in later days that God continued to move through these Gospel scenes, causing them to come alive with His own life and become supernatural visions direct from the throne of grace.

You, too, will find that the more you present this channel to the Lord, the more it will be used. It will grow and grow until you follow the example of our Lord and Savior Jesus Christ: for He did nothing Himself unless it was something He saw the Father doing (see John 5:19-20).

The Bible says as we come to God, we must come in faith. We must also come to the world of dream and vision in faith. *"Without faith, it is impossible to please God"* (Heb. 11:6). If we enter the world of dream and vision with doubt, we will find it taking us nowhere.

As we grow up, instead of rejecting the inner world as many of us were taught to do, we must learn to distinguish it from the outer world, yet live in it comfortably.

When we look at life, we see that we are more deeply affected by pictures than by simple cognitive communication. For example, we prefer television over radio, a speaker who tells vivid stories over a didactic lecturer, a testimonial over a book of theology. Analytical thought does not have the same power as thinking in images. Pictures give us a way of thinking that brings us closer to actual experiences of the spiritual world than any concept or merely verbal idea. We say, "a picture is worth a thousand words." God directed Dr. Cho to "always be 'pregnant' with dreams and visions," and he found that the ability to become creative came into his life only when he learned to "incubate" the visions and dreams God gave to him.

I desire earnestly to live as Jesus did, out of the Father's initiative, doing only what I see my Father doing (see John 5:19-20; 8:38). However, before I can live that way, I need to learn how to become a seer. In a rationalistic culture where "seeing" is generally looked upon with scorn, it takes a monumental effort to become at ease with seeing vision as Jesus did.

"Lookers" Become Seers

The spirit world is there, whether I am seeing it or not. By becoming a seer, I am simply beginning to see what is. I am learning to bring alive an atrophied sense (my visionary ability) and present it to God to be filled. Once my visionary sense has been restored to life and is presented before Almighty God, I have the opportunity to live as did Jesus of Nazareth, out of the continuous flow of divine vision.

My experience, as well as the experience of many others, has convinced me that once we have grown accustomed to looking expectantly into the spirit world for a vision from the Lord, it readily appears. The simple act of looking in faith opens us up to begin seeing what is there.

The expression "I was looking" is found about 13 times in Daniel alone (NASB).

> You...*were looking* [in the dream] *and behold...* (Dan. 2:31).

> *I saw a dream...and the visions* **in my mind**... (Dan. 4:5).

> *Now these were the visions* **in my mind** *as I lay on my bed: I* **was looking***, and behold...* (Dan. 4:10).

> **I was looking** *in the visions in my mind;* **I was looking** *as I lay on my bed, and behold an angelic watcher, a holy one, descended from heaven* (Dan. 4:13).

> *...Daniel saw a dream and visions* **in his mind** *as he lay on his bed; then he wrote the dream down and related the following summary of it. Daniel said, "***I was looking*** in my vision by night, and behold..."* (Dan. 7:1-2).

> **I kept looking** *until...After this* **I kept looking***, and behold...After this* **I kept looking** *in the night visions, and behold...* (Dan. 7:4,6-7).

> **I kept looking** *until thrones were set up, and the Ancient of Days took His seat...* (Dan. 7:9).

> *Then* **I kept looking** *because of the sound of the boastful words which the horn was speaking:* **I kept looking** *until...* (Dan. 7:11).

> **I kept looking** *in the night visions, and behold, with the clouds of heaven One like a Son of Man was coming...* (Dan. 7:13).

> **I kept looking***, and...* (Dan. 7:21).

*A vision appeared to me...and **I looked** in the vision, and it came about while **I was looking** that...and **I looked** in the vision...Then I lifted my gaze and **looked**, and behold... While I was observing...then I heard a holy one speaking... When I, Daniel, had seen the vision...* (Dan. 8:1-5,13,15).

And I heard the voice of a man between the banks of Ulai, and he called out and said, "Gabriel, give this man an understanding of the vision." So he came near to where I was standing, and when he came I was frightened and fell on my face; but he said to me... (Dan. 8:16-17).

The prophets of Israel could simply say, "*I looked*," and as they quieted themselves before God "*they saw*" (see Dan. 7:2,6,9,13).

When we first begin to look for vision, it may seem awkward and almost forced, anything but natural. For this reason, its very unfamiliarity makes some people suspicious of it. As we do it more and more, however, it becomes a natural posture that we do almost without conscious thought. Those who have walked in vision since early childhood find discussing it comparable to discussing the dynamics of breathing.

Since I have reclaimed the use of my visionary ability, I too can simply quiet myself in the Lord's presence, look, and see the visions of Almighty God. I am a "seer" simply because I have become a "looker."

Protestantism's Bitter Root Judgment And Inner Vow

I believe that when Protestantism protested and left the Roman Catholic Church, it reacted against Catholicism's use of imagery. I believe Protestants have held an ungodly belief that "All use of images constitutes a graven image." Their corresponding inner vow was that they would "Reject all uses of imagery in their Christian lives." The result is that most Protestant books on systematic theology do not even include a section on dream, vision, imagination, or any other application of the eyes of one's heart. This is startling, considering that the biblical stories and actions that came as a result of dreams and visions form a section of Scripture equal in size to the entire New

Testament! Their ungodly belief has given them the right to ignore one-third of the Bible.

✳ Another fruit is that Protestants do not lead in the arts. Protestants have great conservative political think tanks (a left-brain function), but few great Christian performing or visual arts (a right-brain function). We need to repent of this 500-year-old ungodly belief and inner vow for ourselves and our forefathers and receive all that the Bible says is ours.

Seeing in the Spirit, Not Worshiping an Image

Perhaps the verses that are most often interpreted as speaking against setting a scene are those that prohibit setting up a graven image.

God commanded the Israelites not to *"make a graven image or any likeness of what is in heaven above or on the earth beneath or in the water under the earth. You shall not worship them or serve them; for I, the Lord your God, am a jealous God"* (Exod. 20:4-5). Therefore, we must carefully distinguish between seeing in the spirit and idolatry.

There is obviously no problem in receiving a vision from God as one prays and waits before Him. This has occurred throughout the Bible, one example being in Revelation 4:2. Here John receives a heavenly vision of Christ, given by God, and as it unfolds, John becomes actively involved, dialoguing with heavenly and angelic beings and participating in the vision (see Rev. 10:8-11).

However, when I set the first scene and look for a vision of Christ, do I find myself in violation of Exodus 20:4, because I am making a likeness of a god that I am then bowing down to and worshiping? No, definitely not.

A graven image is "an object of worship, carved usually from wood or stone."[3] Obviously, the scene we set in our minds is not carved wood or stone, or worshiped, but simply serves as a stepping stone to the living flow of divine images.

God incarnated Himself in Jesus of Nazareth, *"the image of the invisible God"* (Col. 1:15). This God/Man then lived out a full life in our midst, showing us pictorially, over and over, the *"radiant glory of God"* (Heb. 1:3), revealing to us, image upon image, the kindness, gentleness, mercy, and power of God. God is not only invisible, He is also visible in Jesus of Nazareth—the greatest of all images given to humankind—through the Gospels as they record for us the powerful, life-changing stories of His life.

Now we have an image that is not a human-initiated representation of the likeness of God, but a God-given picture, perfectly portraying Himself to us in the multiplied stories He has recorded for us. We can turn to the Gospels, open to the story of His choice, and see the invisible God in visible action. Often, the story itself will give us the precise answer to our need.

For example, in asking the Lord one day how I should counsel in the situation of an illegitimate pregnancy, the Lord immediately reminded me of the story of Jesus saying to the woman caught in adultery, "Go and sin no more." He did not condemn, reject, or hate her; He received, protected, and loved her, sending her on with His instruction. Thus was brought before my heart the story, complete with sound and vision—the story I could enter into and feel—the story and image of God's choice.

I did not bow down and worship that image of Jesus forgiving the adulterous woman. Rather, that picture instantly helped me to focus on the eternal, invisible God who revealed His love and mercy.

Carrying this one final step, I have found that when I want to commune with God in general, share love together, or share our lives together, I can focus my inner being on the invisible, intangible God and tune to Him by focusing on His Son, Jesus Christ, in one of the casual, relaxed scenes from the Gospels. He becomes alive as His indwelling Holy Spirit quickens Him within me, and we commune together and experience any vision that He chooses to bring forth. We may walk together along the Sea of Galilee, sit on a mountainside, or experience any other scene He chooses to quicken to my heart. It is clearly commanded in Scripture that I *"fix [my] eyes on Jesus, the author and perfecter of faith"* (Heb. 12:2).

Differences Between Idolatry and Setting an Image in One's Mind		
	Idolatry	Image
Authorized By	Man (Exod. 32.1)	God (Exod. 25:8-22; Col. 1:15; Heb. 12:2)
The Goal	Worship the idol (Exod. 32:8)	Never worship the image; use image as a stepping stone into divine flow. (Rev. 4:1)
The Action	Idol remains dead (Isa. 44:19)	Divine flow is prompted (Rev. 4:2)
The Prayer	Pray to idol (Isa. 44:17)	Never pray to image; as divine flow is activated communication with God is established. (Rev. 4-22)
The Purpose	To worship "the thing" (Isa. 44:15)	To focus your heart before God (2 Cor. 3:18, 4:18)
The Attitude	Stiffnecked; proud of heart (Exod. 32:9)	Seeking God humbly (Prov. 2:1-5)
The Control Issue	Manipulating God; magic (1 Kings 22:20-23)	Watching God in action; Christianity (Rev. 4-22)

figure 7.1

I have looked at Jesus sitting on the edge of a well (see John 4) and asked Him to speak to me the things He desires; and He has, through a gentle flow of spontaneous thoughts. When I first began to use vision I would see Jesus from the shoulders down, and just sense His loving countenance. I did not see His face. After working with vision for a few weeks, I began to see Him more clearly. I saw His eyes full of laughter and a great big smile on His face. Others have told me that when they began to use vision, they, too, did not see Jesus' face. So be patient if that is your experience, also.

In no sense do I feel we are making a "graven image" or a "likeness." Rather, we are tuning in to God's image, Jesus Christ. Nor are we worshiping an image, because the image is readily alive with the moving of the Holy Spirit as He leads us into an encounter with and the worship of the ever-living Almighty God.

Summary So Far
Concerning Dreams and Visions

1. God does speak to us through dream and vision, as attested by hundreds of Scripture verses.

2. Since Jesus is our perfect Example, we are to learn to live the way He did, that is, constantly open to the divine flow of vision.

3. The Bible tells us that God provides a ready and free flow of dreams and visions since we have received the outpouring of the Holy Spirit. Therefore, the normal Christian life is to experience vision readily (see Acts 2:17).

4. Samuel established schools of the prophets to train seers (the original term for prophets). There is no indication that this process would not be continued.

5. It is also interesting that the prophets' constant statements were, "I looked." The Bible clearly tells us that we have not because we ask not. Therefore, if we want vision, we most certainly will begin looking and asking for it, something that many of us have never been taught to do. The best way to train a person to become a seer is to train him to become a "looker." Probably the major reason people are not seers today is because no one is instructing them to become lookers. We must once again learn to *look to see*.

6. We are plainly commanded to fix our eyes upon Jesus (see Heb. 12:1-2). The Greek for fixing our eyes is *aphorao* which literally

means "to view with undivided attention by looking away from every other object; to regard fixedly and earnestly, to see distinctly."[4] According to the above definition, part of fixing our eyes upon Jesus is "to see Him distinctly." This is precisely what I am encouraging the Church to do as they pray, worship, and walk through life.

Notice that *aphorao* is made up of *apo*, "away" and *horao*, "a visionary seeing." So, we are commanded to look away from other objects and to see Jesus in vision. Visions of Jesus, far from being unusual and infrequent, should be an essential part of our daily Christian experience.

7. May I suggest as an interpretation of Revelation 4:1-2 that John is preparing himself to visually receive the bubbling flow of the Holy Spirit's vision here? In chapter 4, verse 1, John said, *"I looked,"* and then he went through a door in the heavens. *Immediately following* his decision to answer the urging to go through this door, verse 2 records, *"At once I came under the [Holy] Spirit's power, and lo..."* (AMP).

It is interesting that the Greek behind this specifically states at the beginning of verse 2, *rather than the beginning of verse 1*, that John came under the Holy Spirit's power. May I suggest that since John felt a desire to meet God in the spirit realm, he visualized an open door in the heavens and, upon walking through it, *"came under the [Holy] Spirit's power,"* (AMP) finding an active flow of divine vision issuing forth.

Admittedly this is a somewhat personal interpretation and you should feel free to set it aside if you are not comfortable with it. The interested student may want to search for other places in Scripture where this process is indicated or taught. It is fascinating to me that John was priming the pump for this vision by picturing a scene in his mind which was the *last scene* of the *previous vision* he had received from the Lord (see Rev. 3:20). We can do the same thing. Try it!

8. God uses images extensively in His communion with us, as evidenced by the following:

   • God knows our needs. He knows that we are very aware of our own history and frequent failure. He has provided in the Bible a story, recording His dealings with humankind. As we prayerfully ponder these Bible stories, we discover them merging with "our story" as God speaks to us from them. Although parts of the Bible contain systematic theology, God has made the Bible mainly narrative.

   • When God designed the Holy of Holies, the place where man would stand directly before the presence of God, God used an image to represent Himself to Moses and the other high priests. If God were opposed to the use of images to symbolize Himself to man, He could have had Moses stand alone in an empty room and speak to Him face to face and mouth to mouth without the use of images. However, God chose to use a symbol—the Ark of the Covenant and the mercy seat with cherubim on top.

   • Individuals, laws, feasts, rituals, sacrifices and events were used throughout the Old Testament as types or pictures that help us grasp and appreciate the complexity and beauty of New Testament realities.

   • Rather than just telling us how glorious and splendid and full of love He is, God sent His Son Jesus Christ to be the *"radiance of His glory and the **exact representation** of His nature"* (Heb. 1:3). Colossians 1:15 tells us that Jesus is *"the image of the invisible God."* Jesus said to Philip, *"He who has seen Me has seen the Father"* (John 14:9). When God most clearly and powerfully revealed Himself to us, He did not do so with words and rational concepts but with the life of a person, His Son Jesus Christ, who was a living image of all God is. The truths of the invisible God have been revealed to us through Jesus' life story. When the theology is beyond our understanding, we can look at the life of Jesus and if we walk in Christ, we walk in God.

- Matthew 13:34 says, *"All these things Jesus **spoke** to the multitudes **in parables**, and He was **not** talking to them **without a parable**."* Jesus turned everything in life into a parable. He converted issues into symbols of heavenly values and realities. All of life was a meaningful story to Him. Jesus lived, thought and spoke in the world of the vision (or parable), and that is an important key to the release of God's power through Him. Jesus turned the matter of getting a drink of water into a discussion of living water (John 4). He saw in a field white for harvest the spiritual reality that the people of the earth need to be spiritually harvested into the storehouse of heaven. The commonplace pictures before Jesus were constantly used as stepping stones into images of spiritual realities.

9. I believe it is proper to enter into an image or picture to meet God in a direct spiritual encounter because the structure of the entire Bible is such as to lead us into this experience. As we have noted earlier, the Bible is primarily a book of powerful, life-changing stories, rather than a book of analytical theology. We are commanded to come unto the Lord as little children. When a child reads a story, he pictures the scene and action as he reads or listens. Most adults do so as well.

   According to Ephesians 1:17-18, God wants to open the eyes of our hearts, granting us a spirit of wisdom and of revelation as we read His Word. The process of Bible meditation, as God has designed it, involves us imagining a Bible story (i.e., to "imagine" is part of the biblical definition of the word "meditate"), allowing God to speak to us out of the midst of the scene (created by the Word) that is before our eyes, and living out that response.

10. When the vision within our hearts comes alive, we may encounter and interact with heavenly beings *in the vision*.

- In Daniel 4:13-14, King Nebuchadnezzar encountered an angel in a vision *in his mind*. *"I was looking in the visions in my mind as I lay on my bed, and behold, an angelic watcher, a holy one, descended from heaven. He shouted out and spoke as follows...."*

- Daniel encountered the Ancient of Days and one like a Son of Man in a vision he had in his mind. *"In the first year of Belshazzar king of Babylon Daniel saw a dream and visions in his mind as he lay on his bed; then he wrote the dream down and related the following summary of it.... I kept looking in the night visions, and behold, with the clouds of heaven one like a Son of Man was coming, and He came up to the Ancient of Days and was presented before Him.... As for me, Daniel, my spirit was distressed within me, and the visions in my mind kept alarming me"* (Dan. 7:1,13,15).

We see, therefore, that it is very biblical to encounter God, Christ, and angels *in the visions of our minds* as these visions come alive with the flow of the Holy Spirit within us.

11. Our ability to see in the spirit was designed to be presented to God and filled by God. We know *everything* God created was good, and that "everything" obviously has to include our visionary capacity. As all that God has created is presented before Him to fill, God's Kingdom is realized and His purposes established. When we present the eyes of our hearts to Him, His vision fills our spirits. Our responsibility is to present all our abilities quietly before Him, allowing Him to move upon and through them. That includes our minds, our hearts, our hands, our mouths and our visionary capacity, along with everything else that we are.

God will not force Himself on anyone who is not opening himself before Him. We generally will not speak in tongues until we offer Him our mouths. We probably will not receive words of wisdom and knowledge until we offer Him our minds. We normally will not receive visions until we offer Him the eyes of our hearts.

Therefore, in cultivating our visionary capacity, we are presenting the eyes of our hearts before God, asking Him to fill them.

Examples of Two-way Journaling

Remember that in cultivating our visionary capacity, we are presenting the eyes of our hearts before God and asking Him to fill them. Read the following examples.

Jennifer Anne Kramer

Lift up thine eyes, My little children! Lift up thine eyes to your Provider and Sustainer. Do you believe that I can save you? Do you believe that I give you food to eat and water to drink? What has the enemy stolen from you? Do you believe that it is I who has stolen from you? Oh, that you may know My heart for you! Oh that you would know that I have stolen nothing from your life, that it is I who has saved you from despair! I AM your God, I AM your Savior, I AM your only hope for the days ahead.

My children, hold one another up in prayer, be tightly knit together as the three-fold cord but look to Me to save you. Lift up thine eyes, lift up thine arms in worship and weep not for My thoughts for you are love! There is much human suffering and self-pity, but if you will just lift up thine eyes and worship your Creator and know that He will draw you out of your pit of despair, I will save you! Yes, I will save you and all your household! My heart grieves, My heart feels your pain and you must look to Me for your provision and security. Believe in Me, believe and have faith that I can do all that I say. Lift up thine eyes to meet Mine, let Me see that you are looking to Me and I will bring you out!

People fear rejection because they look upon others as their sources of approval, love, success, when actually people are only the channels.

Satan can block or dry up a channel but he cannot stop the flow or block the Source.

Knowing Me as your Source frees you from fear, worry, doubt, sickness, poverty and failure. It frees you to love and give to others, to meet their needs without expecting anything from them in return. You are free to give knowing your return comes from Me.

I have set you free; free to live for Me without fear; free to love and give unconditionally. You are free to love others without regard to their behavior or actions. You are free to be the person I want you to be.

✳ ✳ ✳

Gbemi—I Am the Patient Gardener

Lord, I am Your garden, have Your way. I am not my own, but I give You my all. I lay all my desires at Your throne.

I felt the Lord say: *I accept your garden of sacrifice, let Me work in it, let Me break up the fallow ground, remove the weeds and some deeply rooted misconceptions. I want to plant beautiful, life-giving and fragrant plants in your garden so that all can see My beauty and smell My fragrance.*

The process might hurt, but the end result is My beauty. I am the patient gardener; I will cause no harm to you. I need to treat the soil of your heart, so that whatever seeds I plant may grow and produce fruit or give fragrance. I will plant seeds that will give beauty, fragrance, healing and joy. I will tend the garden as long as you let Me in. I know you still have your requests, I am not ignoring them. Trust Me that I will answer in My time.

Lord, what about visions? I want to see more.

I felt the Lord say: *But you do, My child. I speak to you in your dreams. Practice seeing in your mind's eye; remember it must be done via faith. The more you do it, the better and clearer it becomes. Enjoy your day and remember I am with you.*

✳ ✳ ✳

A CLU Student Asks God to Redeem His Imagination

Lord, how do You view females? Will You redeem the sinful images that I have seen with my eyes?

I am the Great Artist. I am the Painter of the skies. I add color to all of nature. Indeed I formed and designed woman to be beautiful—she is indeed a work of art. Oh, can you picture Me sitting there, painting a picture of her? I do not look at her as a sinful man would look upon a prostitute. I do not look upon her nakedness, her sin. I look upon her as clothed with the radiance and beauty the Father has lavished upon her. I see the white robe of innocence that Jesus has given her, purchased for her by His own blood.

I see the gold that is placed upon her by the Father. Her head is crowned—indeed, it is crowned with glory and beauty. The angels themselves carry the train of her gown. She is altogether beautiful, altogether lovely. She is like a lovely rose—she is the Bride of the Great Bridegroom—covered with the same innocence, purity and virtue of Jesus. It is not that she possesses these qualities of herself—they are given her by the Bridegroom.

When compared to all the other works and wonders the Father has created in the heavens above, in the sea below, in the stars—the heavenly creatures themselves cannot compare to her beauty. She is to be revered, respected, the way the Great Princess of Creation should be.

How can eyes see the way the Great Bridegroom does? How can they see that she is a precious stone, she cannot be coveted nor can she be bought? No woman on earth is a gem to be sold. She is of great value, importance. The Father has called her His daughter, to be daughters of the King.

You have seen the female form with eyes of the flesh. Now I want you to see a woman with the eyes of your heart—eyes that look upon the body, soul, spirit to see the complete vision that the Father, the Son and the Holy Spirit see. See with new eyes.

Personal Application

In a separate journaling notebook or on your computer, write down the following three questions: Lord, how important is it to use the eyes of my heart? How have I been using them? How would You have me use them?

Picture yourself and Jesus in a comfortable Gospel story. See the scene around you. Then fix your eyes on Jesus. Smile! Enjoy His presence. Ask Him the questions written above. Tune to spontaneity and begin to write the flow of thoughts and pictures that come back to you. Do not test them while you are receiving them. Stay in faith. Know that you can test them later.

Prayer: *Thank You, Lord, for what You say to us. May the eyes of our hearts be constantly filled with Your vision.*

Free Online Resources to deepen these truths available at: www.cwgministries.org/FreeBooks

- **Dreams and Visions Throughout Church History**

- **Principles of Christian Dream Interpretation**

Endnotes

1. Dr. David Yonggi Cho, *The Fourth Dimension* (Alachua, FL: Bridge-Logos Publishers, 1979).

2. Watchman Nee, *Anointed Preaching.*

3. *The American Heritage® Dictionary of the English Language*, Fourth Edition (New York: Houghton Mifflin Company, 2009).

4. *The Analytical Greek Lexicon*, Zondervan.

CHAPTER 8

How to Restore Your Visionary Capacity

Ways to Strengthen the Eyes of Your Heart

Summarizing the lessons I learned, if you want to become a seer, here are five principles you can follow to open yourself up to a divine flow of dreams and visions:

1. Our goal is to be like Jesus who was a constant visionary (John 5:19-20; 8:38). *"The Son can do nothing of Himself, unless it is something He **sees the Father doing**...."*

   Make this confession aloud: I make it my goal to live as Jesus lives, out of a constant stream of divine pictures, and whatever needs to change within me for this to happen, I speak to it now to change, in Jesus' name!

2. We are looking for vision (Hab. 2:1-2). *"I will keep watch to see what He will speak to me...Then the Lord answered me and said, 'Record the vision.'"*
   "Watch and pray...." (Matt. 26:41).
   "Fixing our eyes on Jesus...." (Heb. 12:2).

   Pray this aloud: I will look for vision, all the time. If I forget to do this, Holy Spirit, please remind me and I will repent and look again for vision. Thank You.

3. We are looking ***in the vision*** until the vision has stopped flowing (Dan. 4:10,13; 7:2,9,13).

   "I was looking...."

   "I was looking in my vision by night...."

   "I kept looking until thrones were set up and the Ancient of Days took His seat."

   "I kept looking in the night visions...."

   Declare aloud: When a vision begins, I will continue looking (in a relaxed posture—without striving), and I will honor those pictures which alight upon my mind.

4. We must realize that we can have encounters with Jesus, God, and angels in vision *in our minds, and that these are actual spiritual encounters* (see 1 Kings 3:5-15; Dan. 4:4-5,10,13-14; 7:1, 13-16; Matt. 1:20; 2:12-13,19,22).

   Pray this aloud: I can live as Daniel lived. I can meet Jesus on the screen inside my mind (see Dan. 7:1,13-16), and this is an actual spiritual encounter. I choose to live as Daniel lived. I believe I can have the same experiences that people in the Bible had. Lord, meet me with Your grace. You have promised You will give me dreams and visions (see Acts 2:17), and I believe Your promise, and I honor the pictures that light upon my mind as I come to You in prayer.

5. A natural way to present the eyes of our hearts before God is to visually enter a Bible story in prayerful contemplation and allow God to move in it as He wills, or to fix our eyes upon Jesus, the Author and Perfecter of our faith, asking Him to meet us and shower us with His grace (see Heb. 12:1-2; Rev. 4:1-2).

   Confess this out loud: I will picture Gospel stories as I read them, and I will ask the Holy Spirit to bring me into a direct living encounter with my Lord and Savior Jesus Christ. I will believe that what I see is coming from the Holy Spirit. I will share my journaling and dreams and visions with my spiritual counselors for confirmation.

But—But—But!

Before we go any further, let's consider some common questions you might have.

First, "Don't I limit God by forcing Him to move in a Gospel story that I present before Him to fill?" The answer is, "Absolutely yes!" Of course, God has some flexibility as He speaks through the Bible story. He can move it in one direction or another (see Rev. 4:1,3). Moreover, if the Gospel story is totally removed from what God wants to show me, I may find that nothing happens. The vision does not come alive. It remains dead. God is not able to move in it. I have had this happen, and in response I have simply relaxed and said, "God, what would You like to say to me today?" With that, God implants the vision through which He can and does move.

The question follows, "Well then, why don't I just look for His vision in the beginning, rather than starting from a Bible story?" As I have said before, this works fine for the naturally intuitive and visionary person. However, the person with an atrophied visionary capacity will often need a learning tool to get him started. Once he is accustomed to vision, he may be able to discard the learning tool and simply "look" and "see."

Someone else may ask, "Am I saying that my 'godly imagination' is a divine vision?" Of course not! My image is my image. God's supernatural vision is His vision. We never mix up the two. We never say that my *priming of the pump* is God's vision. It is simply my *priming the pump*. John *"looked to see"* (see Rev. 4:1) what the Lord wanted to show him, the Holy Spirit took over, and a heavenly vision unfolded before him. We, too, can look to see what God wants to unfold.

When I invite the Holy Spirit to take over the scene in my mind. The inner flow is experienced and the vision moves with a life of its own, flowing from the throne of grace, it is obviously no longer my own. At this point it has become God's. My godly imagination is mine, and God's vision is God's. For example in Genesis 15:5, God gives Abram a vision of the stars of the heaven, and says Abram will have that many descendents. Following this vision, Abram is able to use his godly imagination and re-picture the scene, knowing that he will have that many descendents. So heart faith (see Gen. 15:6) can be inflamed again and again as Abram re-looks at this scene in his mind over and over and over again. I believe God wants us to receive visions from Him and hold them in our hearts through the use of godly imagination.

Another may question, "Where in the Bible does it teach that we are to set the scene ourselves in order for God to begin flowing in vision?" Part of my response is, "Where does it say in the Bible that we are *not* to set a scene and ask God to fill it?" Since there is no clear verse for either position, we resort to pulling together several verses, which we then interpret in light of our chosen position. An alternative to this approach is to allow our brothers and sisters the Christian liberty to work out their own understanding in this area, since there is no absolutely clear biblical teaching on the issue.

To most of the world, who have not been steeped in rationalism and analytical thinking, openness to the realm of the Spirit is a natural part of human awareness. Only to us in the Western world does it seem strange to the point of at first being scary. When we begin to do it, it soon becomes part of our normal awareness, and we become whole persons again! The bottom line for me is that we are to become like Jesus, and part of becoming like Jesus is we live in pictures. So let's all press with divine passion into that inner reality and heart experience of learning to see vision all the time.

On the Positive Side

On the positive side of this question of the capacity to think visually, I would like to make two points: (1) All of the children and two-thirds of the adults I have polled *usually* picture Bible scenes as they read them. As we are picturing these Bible stories and praying for a spirit of revelation (see Eph. 1:17), God causes the story to come alive and speaks to us out of it. This is essentially the same process we are describing, of setting scenes in our minds and asking God to grant us revelation, then tuning to the flow of the Holy Spirit and watching the scene come alive as God speaks to us. (2) One-fourth of the adults

I have polled normally picture the scenes of songs when they worship. As God inhabits our praises, the scenes come alive and move with a life generated from the throne of God. Both of these illustrate the very process I am describing.

Our ability to think visually is currently being used unknowingly by many Christians, particularly those who are intuitive and visionary by nature. In reality, visual thinking is not a new thing. We are just defining and clarifying what has been happening naturally for some. As a result of this clear definition and statement, all believers can now be taught to become more sensitive to the divine flow within us.

A Temporary Learning Tool

It must be remembered that setting a scene is a temporary learning tool needed only by some. The naturally intuitive person *may* not need this device. This person may simply look to see, and the vision will be there. The analytically oriented person may put aside this learning tool after learning to open up naturally and normally to vision. Nonetheless, I have used this tool successfully for more than 30 years and highly recommend it to all!

If we lived in a more biblical culture, perhaps we would not have so many obstacles to overcome before we could live easily and naturally in the divine flow of vision. If our dreams and their spiritual meaning were a typical part of our conversation at breakfast with our families, as they were for Joseph and other Hebrews, we would find a natural skill built into our lives concerning visionary things. However, who in the United States takes their dreams seriously, discussing them regularly in a family gathering? Practically no one. If we did, we would be considered crazy. Is it any wonder that skill and openness to visions are almost totally lacking in our culture?

As a Church, we need to repent for allowing the rationalism of our time to distort our own perspective of a balanced lifestyle. Some people fear that there may be seeds of Eastern thought in some of the teaching of the Church today. Did we ever stop to realize that Jesus was not a Westerner? God did not give us logic to idolize and put on a pedestal. He did not give us vision for us to squelch it with our scorn. No, it was others who encouraged these attitudes. If you need to repent, please do so now. Pray this prayer: *Lord, I repent for idolizing logic and scorning pictures. Forgive me, I pray, and wash me clean of my sin. From this day on, I choose to present both my reasoning capacity and my visionary capacity to You to fill and flow through. I will honor flowing thoughts and flowing pictures, as coming from the river within my heart. Thank You, Jesus, for Your love and grace toward me.*

Church, let us come back to the balance of Jesus of Nazareth, who did nothing on His own initiative, but only that which *He saw and heard* the Father doing (see John 5:19-20,30; 8:26,28,38). I have shared my struggles and experiences that have brought me closer to an ability to live this way. I challenge you to find the way that will *work for you.* The veil is torn, access is available, fellowship with the Holy Spirit is possible. Will you enter in? Will you seek the way? Will you go within the veil and experience God in direct encounter, or will you be satisfied to experience Him secondhand through the Book He has written?

Making Jesus Our Perfect Example

God is calling those who will make Jesus their perfect Example, who will aspire to live and walk as He did, who will do nothing on their own initiative, but will live out of a constant flow of *rhema* and vision within them. Will you search until you find the way to that lifestyle and experience? Will you continue on until you discover Him?

> *You search the Scriptures, because you think that in them you have eternal life; and it is these that bear witness of Me; and you are unwilling to come to Me, that you may have life* (John 5:39-40).

Prayer: *Lord, we come to You in repentance for allowing our culture to dictate to us, telling us that we are to scorn a part of our inner capacity that You have created and placed within us. We seek Your forgiveness and ask that You restore to our hearts a proper use of dream and vision. Restore our ability to hear and to see. Draw each of us into all that You have for us.*

Allow God to Restore Your Visionary Capacity

Some people find that seeing vision is almost impossible. They are not even able to call a picture of their loved ones onto the screen of their minds. There may be several reasons for this. It is best to seek the Lord for revelation concerning what the block or hindrance is, and then ask for His revelation of the steps to take to heal the problem. The following are some common problems that I have run into, along with some solutions that have proven helpful.

Problem #1—Disdaining the Visual and Idolizing the Rational

Some people have unwittingly been swept into the Westerner's idolization of logic and disdain (or disregard) of the visionary. Westerners generally do not believe in the value and power of the visionary capacity within them. They do not hold it in esteem and honor, as one of the gifts that God has placed within us. This was my problem.

To heal this problem, you must: (1) Repent for not fully honoring and using a gift and ability that God has placed within; (2) Repent for idolizing logic and cognition; (3) State your commitment to present both your visionary and analytical capacities to the Holy Spirit to fill and to use; (4) Ask God to breathe upon and restore your visual capacity; and (5) Begin practicing and exercising it by learning to live in pictures as readily as you live in thoughts. Then you are ready to begin presenting the eyes of your heart to God to fill, *by looking* for His vision as you walk through life.

Problem #2—Fear of Entering into Cultism

Some are unable to use their visual capacities effectively because they have been taught that it is cultish.

To heal this problem, you must: (1) Realize that the ability to think and see using pictures was given to you by God, not by satan; (2) Realize that even though satan seeks to fill your visual abilities, so does God, (3) Realize that satan can attack the thought processes as easily as he can attack the visionary processes; therefore, both must be presented continuously before the Lord for Him to fill and to flow through; (4) Acknowledge that God does not want you to turn away from use of the visual capacity, but rather He wants you to present it continuously to Him to fill; (5) Renounce fear of receiving a satanic counterfeit, while confessing faith in God's ability to fill the visual capacity; (6) Confess fear as sin and receive God's gift of faith.

Problem #3—Cutting Off the Visual Capacity to Avoid the Sin of Lust

Some people have chosen to deal with the problem of lust by simply making a decision to cut off all use of the visual capacity. These people probably cannot visualize anything, including their living room couch.

To heal this problem, you must: (1) Realize that there are effective means of dealing with lust, other than cutting off one of the capacities that God has placed within. It is infinitely more effective to fix our eyes upon Jesus with our visionary capacity when we are tempted by lustful images than it is to refuse to use our visionary capacity at all. Moreover, when we constantly fill our vision with Jesus, we will find that destructive images simply cannot and do not intrude. It is the idle and empty mind that falls prey to sin; (2) Learn to appropriate some of these other alternatives to effectively deal with the sin of lust; (3) Repent for cutting off the visual capacity; (4) Ask God to restore it and recreate it; (5) Begin using it again; and (6) Ask God to fill it with His divine vision.

Problem #4—Shutting Down the Visual Capacity to Avoid an Unpleasant Memory

Some people have shut off their sensitivity to the visual capacity because they are trying to avoid seeing a scene of pain in their lives. This may be an experience of molestation or a recurring nightmare or some other terrifying scene. They have decided that the most effective way of handling these frightening scenes is to cut off their visual capacities. These people probably cannot visualize anything, not even their family pet.

To heal this problem, you must: (1) Recognize and discover the precipitating reason for cutting off your visual sense; (2) Offer the scene to God, asking Him to walk into it and heal it with His loving, all-powerful presence. Seek the help of someone skilled in the ministry of inner healing if necessary to help you receive the complete healing God has for you; (3) Ask God to restore the use of your visual capacity; (4) Begin again to use pictures and visions as you walk through life; and (5) Present the eyes of your heart to God for Him to fill and flow through.

Suggestions for Seeing in the Spirit

Part of the solution for each of the preceding problems was presenting the eyes of your heart to the Lord and beginning to use pictures in your daily life. Here are some suggestions that may help you begin to be open to God, allowing Him to fill the eyes of your heart with His dream and vision. When you want to strengthen your arm muscles, you do push-ups. These are "eye-ups" that will help you strengthen the eyes of your heart.

1. You must "be still" outwardly and inwardly so the Holy Spirit can issue forth with a flow of living images. Review Chapter 6 on stillness. You will sense a bubbling flow within you as the vision comes alive with a "life of its own" (the Holy Spirit's life).

2. Enter a biblical story by picturing the scene. This is probably the most common method Christians use. Simply allow yourself to see what you are reading. And you can do more than just imagine the scenes yourself. Ask God what He wants to show you from what you are seeing, and then tune to flow. A flow of inner images can take over that is directed by God.

3. Open the eyes of your heart during your quiet times, allowing God to show you things. I have found that *focusing intently* on Jesus while asking the Holy Spirit to take over the vision will cause the scene to come alive.

4. In intercession for others, see the person for whom you are praying, and then see Christ meeting that person. Relax

and ask the Holy Spirit to show you what Jesus wants to do in the situation. Allow the vision to move under the direction of the Holy Spirit. Watch what He does, then pray that into existence.

5. Listen to your dreams, which are a natural expression of the inner world. Ask God to speak to you during the night (see Ps. 127:2). When you awaken, *immediately* record your dreams and then ask God for an interpretation. He will give it. We have a book and teaching series available entitled *Hear God Through Your Dreams* that instructs you how to receive God's counsel during your dreams at night.

6. Praying in the Spirit opens up communication with the Holy Spirit and allows Him to flow, especially if you are presenting the eyes of your heart to God to fill.

7. Quiet prayer, simply affirming your love for Jesus and His toward you, opens you up to reflections and insights that are a form of vision in action.

8. When you come before the Lord in praise and worship, open the eyes of your heart to see what you are singing and allow the Holy Spirit to carry the vision where He wants.

One Inner Screen

In the verses from Daniel quoted previously, you may have noticed where the vision was that he was looking at: "in [his] mind." That is where you will normally see visions also—in your mind. The kind of vision that you see "outside of yourself" is very unusual, both in Scripture and in today's experience.

The following diagram may help you see and understand that the eyes of your heart can be filled by self or satan or God. But it will almost always be the same "screen" that each uses.

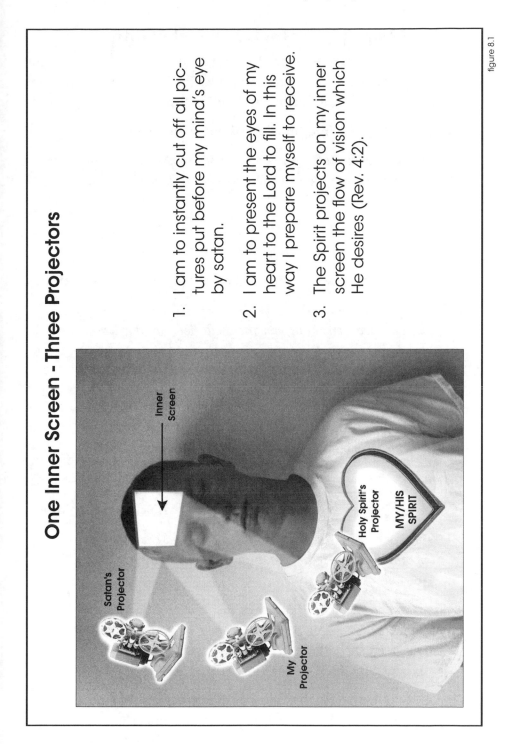

One Inner Screen - Three Projectors

1. I am to instantly cut off all pictures put before my mind's eye by satan.

2. I am to present the eyes of my heart to the Lord to fill. In this way I prepare myself to receive.

3. The Spirit projects on my inner screen the flow of vision which He desires (Rev. 4:2).

figure 8.1

Improper Uses of Our Visual Ability

When I use my own projector to create a slide show or movies out of my own heart and mind, I get in trouble. The Bible warns of several misuses to which I might put the eyes of my heart.

We can follow the imagination of our own heart.

> *But have walked after the imagination of their own heart, and after Baalim, which their fathers taught them* (Jeremiah 9:14).

In this case, man is using his capacities and God-given giftedness himself, rather than yielding it to God to use and fill.

We can use our imaginations the same way we use every ability we have–for evil.

> *But they hearkened not, nor inclined their ear, but walked in the counsels and in the imagination of their evil heart, and went backward, and not forward* (Jeremiah 7:24).

We can imagine evil against one another.

> *How long will ye imagine mischief against a man? Ye shall be slain all of you...* (Psalm 62:3 KJV).

Anyone can imagine evil, mischievous, and vain things.

Carving a graven image and worshiping it is strictly forbidden.

> *The workman melteth a graven image, and the goldsmith spreadeth it over with gold, and casteth silver chains* (Isaiah 40:19 KJV).

> *Thou shalt not make unto thee any graven image, or any likeness of any thing that is in heaven above, or that is in the earth beneath, or that is in the water under the earth* (Exodus 20:4 KJV).

> *And the residue thereof he maketh a god, even his graven image: he falleth down unto it, and worshippeth it, and*

prayeth unto it, and saith, "Deliver me; for thou art my god" (Isaiah 44:17 KJV).

"Graven" image in the Hebrew literally means "to carve, whether wood or stone."

Fashioning an image of our own choosing and then bowing down and worshiping it is strictly forbidden.

Using our visual capacity in lust is strictly forbidden.

I say to you, that every one who looks on a woman to lust for her has committed adultery with her already in his heart (Matthew 5:28).

Look at What We Gain By Using the Eyes of Our Hearts!

1. God has commanded us to imagine His Word ("meditate"— see Josh. 1:8; 1 Chron. 29:18). I will approach the Bible as God has commanded me to. I will imagine it and pray over it and ponder it and meditate upon it! I will not let my Bible times descend into Western rationalism!

2. Divine creativity comes through image (see Exod. 25:9-22; 35:35). I will not give over my birthright to be creative to anyone or any group. I will release God's divine creativity!

3. When God reasons, He uses imagery. I will never reason on my own. I will only reason together with God. That means I will reason using imagery, as exemplified in Isaiah 1:18.

4. When Jesus taught, He used imagery (see Matt. 13:34). I will be a powerful speaker. I will communicate using pictures.

5. As Jesus lived, He ministered out of vision (see John 5:19-20). I, too, will minister out of pictures and visions that the Lord gives to me (words of wisdom, words of knowledge, discerning of spirits, prophecy).

6. God has declared that one of the primary ways He communicates with us is through dream and vision (see Num. 12:6; Acts 2:17). I thank God for this primary method of communication He has created and I will use it!

7. God counsels us through our dreams at night (see Ps. 16:7). If I don't interpret the symbolism of my dreams, I miss God's nightly counsel to me!

8. Spiritual sight is better than spiritual blindness (Jesus healed the blind—see Mark 10:46-52). Yes, I can get through life being spiritually blind, but I don't have to!

9. The Lord's Supper utilizes imagery ("This is My blood, this is My body, do this in remembrance of Me"—see John 6:53-54; 1 Cor. 11:23-25). I could not appreciate the fullness of the power of the Lord's Supper if I could not appreciate imagery.

10. Personal transformation occurs while we look into the spiritual realm (see 2 Cor. 3:18; 4:18). I see how Jesus is responding to the situation I am facing and I respond the same way. I take on Christ's response.

11. Pictures are powerful and produce heart faith (see Gen. 15:1,5-6). I need visions from God so my heart can be inflamed with divine faith.

12. The Bible is full of pictures, dreams, visions, metaphors, similes, parables, and images (Genesis through Revelation). If I cut all pictures out of my Bible, it will be really skinny!

13. Our prayers are to be full of imagery (see Ps. 23). Pictures enliven prayer!

14. Our worship is to be full of imagery (see Ps. 36:5-6). Pictures energize worship!

I am not willing to lay aside all the benefits I receive from using the eyes of my heart. Even though some are fearful, I will not strip my

Christian experience of these things. Fear must and will be overcome in my life, and full Christian experience will be mine!

Journaling About Using Vision

The speaking of your spirit is to be the speaking of My Spirit, and it will be if you are centered and focused on Me. As you look clearly and only to Me, the intuitive impressions you receive are from Me.

Lord, when you say "look to Me," do you mean inner vision?

It is not absolutely necessary, although it is extremely helpful. Remember the pattern of My Son. He saw and heard. The looking with inner vision facilitates an easy, pure flow. However, the flow can come through inner dependence—simply "relying on." When looking to Me, you will find that intuition progresses beyond your subconscious knowledge to things that I reveal.

Vision and Inner Healing

I define *inner healing* as "allowing God to replace pictures in the art gallery of our minds, substituting pictures which do not have Him in them with pictures that do have Him." If we look back at a painful scene and Jesus is not there, it is obviously a lying image, since Jesus is always present. We need to replace the picture that contains the lie (Jesus wasn't there) by seeing the truth, that Jesus was there moving, loving and healing. Then our hearts will be healed.

An example of the use of vision in inner healing in the New Testament is the twenty-first chapter of John where Jesus heals the deep hurt in Peter's heart caused by his threefold denial of his Lord (see Matt. 26:69-75). In order to minister profound, lasting healing, Jesus used imagery to deepen the reality of the forgiveness and love He was offering Peter.

Both the hurt and the healing happened: (1) at dawn, (2) around a charcoal fire, and (3) involving a threefold confession. The Lord brought about an encounter that served to remind Peter of his denial. Here the Lord showed something of what "drama" in His hands can do by way of healing memory and equipping for service. Simultaneously, *what had been and what was going to be* were present in Peter's mind and heart—a moment of intense, deep imagining and cleansing, as Jesus three times recommissioned Peter to go back into the ministry and feed His sheep (even though he had just committed a colossal blunder and failure). Jesus revealed His love and His acceptance of Peter's weakness, and said, "Continue on." It may well be compared with the Lord's use of "drama" in the parables; for all who are responsive, "my story is being told there." The Lord is *at work* in this activity. It is central to His ministry. If the Church wants to heal the heart of man, we must be comfortable telling and entering into stories.

Examples of Two-way Journaling

Robert—God Heals Heart Wounds

My son, you have received much by way of healing and your progress has been good. Although you have ministered in these realms and have received ministry yourself at certain times in your life, you have still been a little cynical over certain areas of inner healing. It is because of this cynical side of you that I have not been able to touch certain areas of your life, therefore you have only received a measure of freedom on some things.

The situation that you mentioned at twelve years old is clear in My mind too, because I was there and saw it all. The only thing was, in those days, you didn't know Me and you were not aware of My presence, or that I even cared for you. But I do care for you, I always have. At that time, you were very introverted, unconfident and filled with much anxiety. This was because of inherited traits, and from family circumstances outside of your control.

This situation would not have normally hurt you at all and had you been whole at that time you would have shrugged it off, but you didn't. You thought you had, but you didn't. That is why you can remember it in vivid detail. It had a profound effect on you, so much so, that you went from being an A and B student to a C average. You gradually lost interest in school and couldn't wait to leave. Do you remember this, My son?

Yes, Lord, I do.

I want you to visit that classroom again in prayer, but this time we are going together. What do you see?

I see You, Lord, standing by my side as he made fun of me.

What did I do with you?

Lord, You are bending down, putting Your arm around me and saying, *"It's okay, it's only a joke, he doesn't mean anything by it, don't take it to heart. I love you just the way you are, you are not inferior to them. So hold your head up high, you are Mine, and you don't know it yet, but I have great plans for you in the future."* I feel warm and secure with Your arm around my shoulder. I feel protected and at peace.

Now I want you to forgive Mr. Green and your class friends.

Lord, I forgive them for their careless remarks. I ask You to cleanse my thoughts in the conscious, unconscious, and subconscious parts of my mind and fill them with Your thoughts. Thank You, Lord, for showing me and healing me!

Now, My son, go in My love and know that I am with you always. Know also, that this is why you have been given to comparing yourself to others and feeling inadequate and discouraged at times. But this day I have made you free.

✳ ✳ ✳

Darin from Korea—Inner Healing

Here are three testimonies of how [this message] has helped me have "life to the full":

I was going to seminary in Kansas City and driving a school bus to support the family. One day I subbed in on a high school route. The regular driver had been letting the kids off at their houses instead of at the designated stops on the route. When I started to drop the kids off at the designated stops instead of at their houses, they started verbally assaulting me. I've never ever been called such bad names in all of my life. When I got to the end of the route I was ready to park the bus, leave the keys, and just quit! I was so emotionally hurt.

Several years later, still feeling the pain, in prayer I asked God, "Where were You?" As I closed my eyes and reflected back on the situation, I could see Christ standing behind me as I sat and drove the bus. I could see that the pain of the verbal darts of the kids was being taken upon the back of Jesus Christ. He had been with me all the time, simply standing behind me as I was driving and being my shield. Since then, when I think back on the situation, all I can see is Christ Jesus standing behind me and shielding me. I can't even "work-up" any pain. What release! Thank You, Christ Jesus!!

✳✳✳

When I was growing up, I got into trouble quite a bit, like most kids. As a young boy, when my mom would punish me (as is right for mothers to do) she would send me to my room. I was then supposed to stay in my room until I could come out without crying. The problem was, as I was in my room crying, I always wanted my mom to come in and love me. It wasn't the physical pain that hurt me, but the emotional pain of thinking that I was being abandoned or rejected by my mom. (Please know that I have great parents and I'm sure they had no idea how I was feeling.)

As an adult, and still feeling this emotional pain of rejection, in prayer, I asked God, "Where were You?" As I closed my eyes and reflected back, I could see Christ sitting behind me, putting His arms around me and holding me as I sat in my room. He was there all the time and loving me. It brings such great comfort even as I write about it now. Since then, when I think back on the situation, all I can see is Christ Jesus holding a small little boy, me. It's hard to even "work-up" any pain over this situation. Thank You, Christ Jesus, for holding me.

✳✳✳

As a young 4-year-old boy, I remember being picked on by a local bully named Kenny. I remember being in his old, dirty, brick house and being verbally "pushed around." I was very hurt. Even as an adult in my late 30s, that memory still caused me a great deal of pain and brought feelings of revenge.

One day, in prayer, I asked God, "Where were You?" As I closed my eyes and reflected on the situation, I could see Christ Jesus simply standing beside me, with His right hand on my right shoulder. He was the size of an adult. Just His presence beside me relieved my emotional pain.

I was also curious as to why this seemingly small incident had been such a sore spot for 30+ years. I could sense God saying, *Things that happen to small children have a great impact on their lives.* My only feeling now about Kenny is sympathy. I hurt for him. How terrible to be so lonely that you have to bully people around to get a sense of relief. Thank You, Lord Jesus, for Your presence and Your healing."

✳ ✳ ✳

Jean from England—Brokenness

Lord, please speak to me about this Discipleship Training School as I walk through these delightful grounds. Lord, I feel Your presence, Your closeness in the beauty of this place.

What do you see lying on the ground?

Lord, I see many fallen chestnuts. Some are completely exposed, their hard, prickly shells have long since broken open and they are bright and shiny.

What else do you see?

Lord, some have only a crack in their shells, others are partly exposed and some are still unripe and are on the trees.

My child, this is a picture of the different stages of My children within this school. Some have allowed Me to break open their hard shells that they had placed around themselves for protection. They are open and exposed, and My Holy Spirit will continue to do a deep work in their lives. Others are partly open and, as the power of My Holy Spirit is released, their bondages will break asunder. Others are in different stages of openness, and some are not ready at this present time. Remember the chrysalis? It is not My purpose to wrench away hard shells before the maturing process is completed. If you help the butterfly to break the shell it will be damaged and it will die. My timing is always perfect. So allow Me to initiate and My people to respond at their own pace.

Personal Application

In your journaling notebook or on your computer, write the following: "Lord, what do You want to say to me concerning the ideas presented in this chapter?" Now quiet yourself down into a comfortable scene with Him. Tune to flow and write what He says back to you. Share it with your spiritual advisors for confirmation.

Free Online Resources to deepen these truths available at: www.cwgministries.org/FreeBooks

- **Poised Before Almighty God**

- **Questions to Help Others See Vision**

CHAPTER 9

Key #4: Two-way Journaling

We have come to our fourth essential key to hearing God's voice:

- Key #1: Recognize God's voice as spontaneous thoughts that light upon your mind.

- Key #2: Quiet yourself so you can hear God's voice.

- Key #3: Look for vision as you pray.

- **Key #4: Write down the flow of thoughts and pictures that come to you (Two-way Journaling)**

Two-way Journaling: A Means of Discerning God's Voice

As you know by now from previous discussion as well as the numerous examples you've read, two-way journaling is a biblical method that can help you grow in the discernment of the voice of God in your heart. It has been a most helpful tool for me, probably the key tool that has taught me to discern the Lord's voice. Two-way journaling, or simply journaling, as I use the term, is basically recording your prayers and what you sense to be God's answers. The Psalms are an example of this process, as well as the books of the prophets and Revelation. Clearly, this is a common biblical experience.

To be precise, I try to say *two-way journaling* to ensure that people know I am talking about a dialogue with God where both you and God are talking and you are recording it all. If I just say journaling, I still mean two-way journaling. In two-way journaling, I want God to do most of the talking, since His words are life (see John 6:63), not mine. The Bible clearly tells us to limit our words when we are before His throne and to let Him do most of the talking. Make sure you do this!

> *Guard your steps as you go to the house of God and draw near to listen rather than to offer the sacrifice of fools; for they do not know they are doing evil. Do not be hasty in word or impulsive in thought to bring up a matter in the presence of God. For God is in heaven and you are on the earth; therefore let your words be few* (Ecclesiastes 5:1-2).

Some people have asked me if it is not true that the journaling commands and examples we find in Scripture are different from the journaling we are doing, since in the Bible all the journaling became the inerrant Word of God. Not so! In First Chronicles 28:12-19, we have an example of journaling that did not become Scripture, exemplifying the exact procedure we are recommending. In First Chronicles 28:19, David says, *"The Lord made me understand in writing by His hand upon me, all the details of this pattern."* What he received was the blueprint for the temple, which is not recorded in Scripture in its entirety.

God is speaking to His children much of the time. However, we often do not differentiate His voice from our own thoughts, and therefore, we are timid about stepping out in faith. If we can learn to clearly discern His voice speaking within us, we will be much more confident in our walk in the Spirit. Journaling is a way of sorting out God's thoughts.

One of the greatest benefits of using a journal during your communion with the Lord is that it allows you to receive freely the spontaneous flow of ideas that comes to your mind, *in faith* believing that they are from Jesus, without short-circuiting them by subjecting them to rational and sensory doubt while you are receiving them. Journaling allows you to write in faith believing the flow of thoughts and pictures is from the Lord, knowing that you will be able to test them later.

I found that before I began keeping a journal, I would ask God a question, and as soon as an answer came into my mind, I would immediately question whether the idea was from God or from self. In doing so, I short-circuited the intuitive flow of the Holy Spirit by subjecting it to rational skepticism. The flow of God is arrested by doubt. He that comes to God must come in faith (see Heb. 11:6). I would receive one idea from God and doubt that it was from Him, and therefore receive no more. Now, by writing it down, I can receive whole pages in faith, knowing I will have ample time to test it later. Keeping a journal greatly facilitates the flow of *rhema* into your heart.

Also, maintaining a journal keeps your mind occupied and on track as you are receiving God's words. My mind wants to do something while I am receiving revelation from God. If I tell it to be quiet and do nothing, it has a fit and starts critiquing every word I write. So I tell my mind to help me by spelling the words correctly. Even though I am not a great speller, my mind is happy to be helping. Journaling puts my mind on my side as a facilitator of divine encounter, rather than a critic of it.

Another advantage of writing revelation down is given in Habakkuk 2:2-3. Habakkuk was told that he should write what he received, because there would be a period of time before it came about. Therefore, your journal becomes an accurate reminder of revelation God has given you that has not yet come to pass.

After keeping a journal for more than 30 years, I cannot fully express how it has deepened my relationship with Christ. It has been one of the most helpful tools I have discovered for growth in the Spirit.

The Difference Between Journaling and Automatic Writing

Obviously, automatic writing is satan's counterpart to journaling. Those who have experienced automatic writing before becoming a Christian tell me that in automatic writing, a spirit comes and controls the person's *hand*, whereas in journaling there is a spontaneous flow of ideas birthed by God in their *hearts* and then recorded in their journals by a hand freely under the person's own control. Therefore, in journaling, the entire being is involved, the heart, the mind and the mind's guiding of the hand in writing, whereas in automatic writing only a limp hand is involved. The rest of the individual is bypassed by the evil spirit that controls the hand.

The Difference Between Journaling and Adding to Scripture

One objection to journaling is that it seems to come perilously close to writing new Scripture and, thus, adding to the Word of God. Some take this objection and use it against hearing from God in any fashion apart from reading the Scriptures. This is an honest objection and we must not dismiss the matter lightly.

The Bible is complete in that it contains the revelation God desires to give us in order to grant us salvation and to restore us to a life of fellowship with Him. Nothing needs to be added to it! It is inerrant and inspired by the Holy Spirit and has been the best-selling Book in all of history, even after 2,000 years!

This does not mean that God has stopped speaking to His children. On the contrary, the Bible says God does continue to speak to us even as He did from Genesis to Revelation (see John 10:27). We still get to take walks with God in the garden in the cool of the day and dialogue with Him. This does not mean that all our personal dialogue now needs to become Scripture. No, it is just two friends sharing love together. Our journaling does not become Scripture.

Practical Suggestions for Journaling

Here are some things I have learned that can help you continue to enjoy dialoguing with God through two-way journaling for the rest of your life:

1. Since you are coming to meet with your Creator and Sustainer and commune with Him, your time of journaling should be when you are in your prime condition and not overcome by fatigue or the cares of the world. I find early morning best for me. Some find the middle of the night best for them. Find your best time and give it to God.

2. A simple spiral-bound notebook is sufficient. If typing comes easily for you, you may want to type rather than write. Some people use a recording device and commune with God while driving in their cars. They simply speak the words they feel are coming from God. I have found journaling on my computer is the easiest for me. I can type much faster than I can write, and I can put it through spell checker when I am done. Then I can e-mail any journal entries I would like to my spiritual advisors for their input, and generally have an answer back within 24 hours.

3. Correct grammar and spelling are not critical when journaling. (Hallelujah!)

4. Keep your journal secluded and use codes when necessary, such as when praying about sensitive situations or other people. As you bare your soul to God and He counsels you, some of your material will be of a private nature and should be kept confidential (i.e., coded). You may even want to destroy extremely sensitive entries after you have completed the journaling.

5. Date all entries.

6. Include in your journal your communion with God, your dreams and their interpretations, visions, and images the Lord gives you, and personal feelings and events that matter to you (angers, fears, hurts, anxieties, disappointments, joys, thanksgivings).

7. When you begin journaling, you will find that the Holy Spirit gives you healing, love, and affirmation as He speaks edification, exhortation, and comfort to your heart (see 1 Cor. 14:3). He will lead you into a fuller love relationship with Jesus and provide the encouragement and self-acceptance the Divine Lover wants to give to you. Then, as time goes on, you may allow your journaling to expand into a flow of the gifts of the Holy Spirit (prophecy, word

of wisdom, word of knowledge, discerning of spirits, etc.). If you try to use your journal to cultivate the gifts of the Holy Spirit before you have sharpened your journaling ability through use, you may find that your mistakes will set you back so severely that it will be hard to press on with use of a journal. After you are firmly established in journaling, you will find the gifts of the Holy Spirit beginning to flow naturally through it. Allow them to come *in their time*.

8. Have a good knowledge of the Bible so that God can draw on that knowledge as you journal. Not only is **rhema tested against the *Logos*, but it is also built upon the *Logos***. God told Joshua to meditate, confess, and act on the Law of God day and night so that God could give him success (see Josh. 1:8). If I fill my heart and mind and life with God's principles, and then pause in dependence on Him in a given situation, my spirit will bring forth, through a flow of spontaneous thoughts, a perfect construction of exactly the right biblical principles. Thus I am able to speak a more pure, life-giving word from God. *Rhema* is built on the *Logos*, in that God, by His Spirit, is selecting, through illumination, the specific principles that apply and then is constructing them in precise order. My mind cannot pick out and construct with nearly the precision that His Spirit can. Thus, *rhema* is grounded in *Logos* and is illumined by *Logos*.

9. If you want to add more structure to your journal, you may use the first few pages to list people and items God is burdening you to pray for regularly. You would want to be sure to stay tuned to flow as you prayed through these lists.

10. When you sit down to journal, *write* the question you have, rather than just thinking it. This simple act will assist greatly in facilitating the Lord's response. At a

minimum I write, "Good morning, Lord. What would You like to say to me?"

11. As you are learning the art of journaling, you may want to journal *daily* until it is established in your life. Then you should be free to be spontaneous about your journaling. I generally journal several times a week.

12. Skip a line in your journal when you move from God speaking to you speaking, and vice versa. This will help you keep the transitions clearer when you reread it.

13. Reread your last journal entry before you begin your next day's entry. It helps you check whether or not you have been obedient to the previously spoken *rhema* word.

14. It is good to review your entire journal when the notebook is full and write a brief summary of the key themes God has spoken about to you. Put this summary in the front of your next journal.

15. I have found that every time I have asked the Lord for a date, the dates have always been wrong. Therefore I have stopped asking. When God speaks, He simply says "soon," which means anytime in the next 1,000 years! He said, "Behold, I come quickly" (see Rev. 22:12) and that was 2,000 years ago! He says, *"Trust Me."* I recommend that you don't ask for specific dates in your journal, either.

16. God gives us revelation for the areas in which He has given us responsibility and authority. A homemaker will receive revelation for within the home and family. A husband will receive revelation for caring for his family and functioning in his job. A pastor will receive revelation for the church for which God has made him responsible. An entrepreneur will receive revelation concerning business decisions. Along with a God-given ministry comes God-given revelation to wisely fulfill the ministry. Therefore,

look for revelation in the areas in which God has given you accountability.

Stay away from the ego trip in which you begin seeking revelation for areas where God has not placed you. When Peter asked Jesus for information about John, Jesus essentially told him it was none of his business and he should worry about being obedient to what the Lord had spoken to him. As a result of Peter's curiosity about something outside his area of responsibility, confusion and false information spread through the Church (see John 21:18-23). You do not want to be the cause of such error!

Safeguards for Journaling

The following recommendations will allow you to experience more fully the benefits of journaling.

1. Cultivate a humble, teachable spirit. Never allow the attitude, "God told me, and that's all there is to it." All revelation is to be tested. In learning any new skill, mistakes are inevitable. Accept them as part of the learning process and go on.

2. Have a good knowledge of the Bible so that you can test your *rhema* against the *Logos*.

3. Be fully committed to sharing with two or three spiritual advisors on an ongoing basis. Walk together with others who are seeking spiritual intimacy with Almighty God. Realize that until your journaling is confirmed, it should be regarded as "what you *think* God is saying." Time is also a confirming factor, as *"wisdom is vindicated by her fruit"* (see James 3:13-17; Luke 7:35).

4. Occasionally, I might write something down and the flow stops or seems to become impure or unusual. In this case, I assume that I have gotten my eyes off the Lord. I simply refocus and ask God to speak again because I feel I've

gotten off-track. The Lord is always gracious to repeat Himself and I can usually see where I missed Him.

5. Check to be sure your journaling experiences are leading to greater wholeness and ability to love and share God. If your experiences become destructive to you, you are contacting the wrong spirits and you should seek out your spiritual counselors immediately.

Limit Your Journaling to the Categories Given in the New Testament for Prophecy

After many years of personally journaling and teaching others, I have arrived at the conclusion that journaling essentially amounts to personal prophecy, where the Lord is speaking directly to you. It is therefore wisest to limit your journaling to the three categories given in First Corinthians 14:3—edification, exhortation, and comfort.

Edification means to "build up," so your journaling will be building you up. It empowers your faith and makes you stronger in your walk with God.

Exhortation means to encourage toward a specific way of living, such as Jesus' exhortation to the woman caught in adultery: "Go and sin no more." Other examples are, "Love your spouse," or "Forgive this person," or "Display mercy rather than judgment." All these are exhortations to a certain way of living.

Comfort means to counsel, to bind up, to pour on healing oil. When God is simply loving you and healing you, that is comfort.

You see, journaling is primarily for building a love relationship between you and God. In our journals, God will call us to rest, believe, have faith, and trust, regardless of what the outcome will be. And because we believe, trust, and have faith, we maximize the opportunity for God's supernatural grace to work in our lives and the lives of others. Life is worth living because we are not full of negatives. So God must call us to faith, and He will over and over.

Ask the Right Questions!

As we continue in our relationship with the Lord, we want to discuss issues of importance with Him: "Lord, should I take this job that has been offered to me? Should I ask this person to marry me? Should I continue to attend this church? What should I say to this person who is angry? Is this the house we should buy? What should I do to improve my health and receive my healing?"

Jesus declared that the Father knows the number of hairs on your head (which changes every time you run a brush through it!), and that He sees even the little bird when it falls. He cares about every aspect of your life, and He wants you to know His will. He wants you to make wise decisions, and He offers His grace to give you strength to grow in holiness every day. He is pleased when you ask for His wisdom and He will generously give it to you (see James 1:5). Just remember to keep your heart pure, allowing no idols (your own will) to distort the pure *rhema* of God to you.

However, it is very easy for this kind of directive question ("*Should I* ask this person to marry me?") to subtly alter and become a predictive question about the future: "Lord, who will I marry? *Will I* marry this person? Will I get this job? Will our offer on this house be accepted? When will I receive that raise? Will this person be healed?" These are the questions that will get us into trouble! Throughout the Bible there are repeated prohibitions against seeking out or listening to soothsayers or diviners—those who claim to predict the future. Tomorrow belongs to the Lord, and He wants us to face it armed only with our faith in Him.

In addition, questions about future outcomes nearly always involve the will of other people. That makes it **always in a state of flux** (see Ezek. 33:13-16; Jer. 18:7-10). God may tell you His will in the Scriptures or in your journal, but unfortunately, sinful man does not always act in accordance with God's will. God is not willing that any should perish but that all should come to repentance. Yet, sadly there are those who do not repent and who do perish. As long as people have *free will,* the future is *fluid.*

When Jonah predicted the future and told Nineveh they would be destroyed in 40 days (see Jon. 3:4), that did not come to pass because Nineveh repented, and therefore God did not do what He said He would do. When God told Israel He had given them the Promised Land (see Exod. 12:25), they ended up dying in the wilderness and not receiving God's blessing, because they would not trust Him. My understanding is that when God says He is going to do something, that thing is jurisdictionally available to you if you want to go after it and war legally for it. And if He says a calamity is coming, it can be avoided by repenting. Thus, I believe the future is changeable to a great extent.

By His own initiative, God may choose to tell us something of our future, particularly in the areas of His promises to us and His plans for us. However, He will usually answer our nosy questions for more detail than He has given with the exhortation, *"Trust Me."* If we keep pressing and asking questions He has already refused to answer, we will generally get an answer from a lying spirit or according to our own desires. Demanding to know more than God wants to share with us opens us to deception.

The Lord said this to our friend and mentor Maurice Fuller in his journal: *"My will is not for hire. It is not for sale. It is not for you to inquire, as from an oracle. My will is plain to those who will do My will."*

Maurice also gave us the following insights concerning this question:

> Like you say, journaling is not some kind of Ouija Board. We cannot use journaling as a way to get around God's reluctance to reveal certain things to us. Journaling—as well as hearing God more naturally in our spirit—enables us to hear what God wants to tell us. It is not a method to persuade God to tell us things He doesn't wish to reveal to us.
>
> Witchcraft, as you rightly discern, seeks knowledge of the future for our own personal (and maybe selfish or even evil) benefit. In fact, some witchcraft

practitioners have developed the ability to trick the demons into divulging information they did not at first want to reveal. Deuteronomy 18 strictly forbids practicing witchcraft but, more than that, that passage and others forbid us to approach God and try to use Him as the witchcraft practitioners use their familiar spirits.

Not taking the name of the LORD your God in vain is actually a prohibition against Israel (and us) using the name of God as a talisman or to attempt to approach God as in witchcraft, trying to conjure information from Him. God will not allow Himself to be conjured up or to be conned into providing information as though He were no more than an Ouija Board.

My sense of receiving information from God is that, unlike witchcraft, God ties His revelation to us to what He is doing in our lives at the moment. It may not be beneficial or helpful to us to know certain facts at certain times in our life. He may wisely and lovingly withhold the future from us for our greater good. We do not decide what we want God to tell us and then try to persuade Him to conform to our imperfect agenda.

God tells us what He wants us to know and when He wants us to know it. God may tell us a little at a time, rather than everything at once because He does not do all His work in us in one fell swoop. Our approach should always be, in my view, not "God, tell me this or that," but, "What do You want to tell me about this or that?"

God may certainly tell us about some things far in the future in great detail, but it is at His initiation, not ours. My sense is that this is relatively rare, simply because we usually cannot easily handle too much information too far in the future. But it does happen and it is a very interesting experience watching how it comes to pass.

I hope you can see the difference between the questions, "Should I ask this person to marry me?" and "Will I marry this person?" The first is seeking personal guidance and direction about what I should do. The second seeks to know the future, and involves the free will of another individual. Be careful that you ask the right questions in your journal.

And you should be aware that even if the Lord says, "Ask her," that is not a guarantee that her answer will be "yes." Your responsibility is only to be totally obedient to what you believe the Lord is saying to you. You may not understand why things turn out as they do, even when you have obeyed. The working of God may not become clear to you until eternity. Yet, you must be obedient and faithful.

A subcategory of the predictive questions we are to avoid is the ever-popular, "Will this person be healed?" Sadly, many, many people have lost their faith in hearing God's voice, and even in God Himself, because they believed with all their heart that they had God's assurance that someone they loved would recover, yet they died. I have to tell you that I do not understand healing—why some people live and some die. But I will share with you the conclusion God has brought me to, and that I encourage you to consider for yourself.

I am absolutely, 100 percent convinced that it is God's will to heal everyone who comes to Him. Everything I read in the Bible and everything I have learned about my Father through our personal relationship demands that this be so. Jesus healed all who asked, and He said that He was doing exactly what He saw the Father doing. I believe that complete healing is always the will of God. I believe that if I ask the Lord if it is His will to heal someone, the answer will always be "yes."

However, I also know that not everyone is healed. As I reminded you earlier, God's perfect will is not always accomplished on this earth. There are factors in healing that I simply have not comprehended so far in my life, search and meditate and pray and experiment and ask as I might.

So what do I do when someone I love is diagnosed with cancer? I believe that God will heal him. I believe that it is absolutely God's will that this child of His walk in health and serve Him his allotted threescore and ten years (at least). I pray with total confidence for the healing touch of God. I journal about what other steps we should take to promote his healing, and I share them with conviction and passion. I constantly stay tuned to the spontaneous impressions the Spirit may send to me so that nothing in me hinders the power of God from flowing. I understand that healing is a conditional covenant (see Exod. 25:26), and so I encourage him to ask God if there are any conditions He wants him to meet in order for His healing to be released into his life. We listen to what He says, and we obey His instructions. We nourish and care for his spirit, soul, and body so that divine health can be manifest.

And if he is not healed? I still believe it is absolutely God's will that His children walk in health. I still believe it is always God's will to heal. I do not understand why His will was hampered in this life, and I grieve the loss of the one I loved. But I do not allow any circumstance, no matter how tragic, to undermine my faith in my God. My understanding of the Lord and His will is not based on physical conditions but on the unchanging Word and character of God.

More Ways to Test Our Journaling

Let's return again to the question of how I can know for sure that my journaling came from God. How do I test it, and hold fast to what is true, setting aside the rest (see 1 Thess. 5:21)?

In previous chapters we have discussed some powerful methods for discerning if our journaling is from God: (1) When my spiritual advisors check their spirits, do their hearts tell them it is God or not? (2) Did I come to the Lord with the right heart attitude? (3) Does the *Logos* confirm the *rhema*? (4) Were my spiritual eyes fixed on Jesus, or was I holding an idol in my heart? If all of these confirm that what you received is from the Lord, your confidence level should be very high.

Now I want to build on what we have already learned, and add a methodology that I have used for many years and found to be extremely helpful in discerning truth in a variety of arenas.

✗ The Names and Character of God

Anything that God says to us is going to be in harmony with His essential nature. Journaling will help you get to *know* God personally, but knowing what the Bible says *about* Him will help you discern what words are from Him and when the accuser may be trying to deceive you. Make sure the tenor of your journaling lines up with the character of God as described in the names of the Father, Son, and Holy Spirit.

Through journaling, these names will become revelation knowledge to you. You will no longer simply know that a name of God is *Jehovah-Shalom*; you will know God as *the Source of your peace!* Wonderful Counselor will no longer be just a title of the Son; it will be an apt description of your Friend. The comfort of the Holy Spirit will not be merely a theological statement of faith but the living truth that you have experienced.

So these names are given both as a standard against which to test the content and spirit of your journaling, and as an inspiration of the ways in which you can expect the triune God to make Himself known to you as you spend time with Him.

Names of the Father

Jehovah-Jireh (The Lord will provide)—Genesis 22:14

Jehovah-Raphe (The Lord my Healer)—Exodus 15:26

Jehovah-Nissi (The Lord my Banner)—Exodus 17:15

Jehovah-Shalom (The Lord my Peace)—Judges 6:24

Jehovah-Raah (The Lord my Shepherd)—Psalm 23:1

Jehovah-Tsidkenu (The Lord my Righteousness)—Jeremiah 23:6; 33:16

Jehovah-Shammah (The Lord is there)—Ezekiel 48:35

Almighty—Genesis 17:1

Judge—Genesis 18:25

Fortress—2 Samuel 22:2

Lord of lords—Deuteronomy 10:17

Heavenly Father—Matthew 6:26

Holy One of Israel—Psalm 71:22

Most High—Deuteronomy 32:8

I AM—Exodus 3:14

Names of the Son

Advocate—1 John 2:1

Almighty—Revelation 1:8

Author and Finisher of our faith—Hebrews 12:2

Bread of Life—John 6:35

Captain of Salvation—Hebrews 2:10

Chief Shepherd—1 Peter 5:4

Consolation of Israel—Luke 2:25

Cornerstone—Psalm 118:22

Counselor—Isaiah 9:6

Creator—John 1:3

Dayspring/Sunrise—Luke 1:78

Deliverer—Romans 11:26

Desire of all Nations—Haggai 2:7

Door—John 10:7

Good Shepherd—John 10:11

Governor—Matthew 2:6

Immanuel—Isaiah 7:14

Just One—Acts 7:52

King of kings—1 Timothy 6:15

Lamb of God—John 1:29

Lawgiver—Isaiah 33:22

Life—John 14:6

Light of the World—John 8:12

True Light—John 1:9

True Vine—John 15:1

Truth—John 14:6

Names of the Holy Spirit

Comforter—John 14:16

Free Spirit—Psalm 51:12

Holy Spirit—Psalm 51:11; Ephesians 1:13; 4:30

Power of the Highest—Luke 1:35

Spirit of Adoption—Romans 8:15

Spirit of Grace—Zechariah 12:10

Spirit of Holiness—Romans 1:4

Spirit of Knowledge—Isaiah 11:2

Spirit of Life—Romans 8:2

Spirit of Might—Isaiah 11:2

Spirit of Prophecy—Revelation 19:10

Spirit of Understanding—Isaiah 11:2

Spirit of Wisdom—Isaiah 11:2

Testing the Spirit, Content, and Fruit

The Bible tells us that we can test the spirit, the content, and the fruit of a revelation to determine whether it is of God. The following chart may help differentiate the three sources. Take some time to become familiar with it now, and if you receive any journaling that is questionable, use it to help clarify your discernment.

Testing Whether an Image Is from Self, Satan, or God		
Self	Satan	God
Find Its Orgin (Test the Spirit - 1 John 4:1)		
Born in mind. A painting of a picture.	A flashing image. Was mind empty, idle? Does image seem obstructive?	A living flow of pictures coming from the innermost being. Was your inner being quietly focused on Jesus?
Examine Its Contents (Test the Ideas - 1 John 4:5)		
A painting of things I have learned.	Negative, destructive, pushy, fearful, accusative, violates nature of God, violates Word of God. Image afraid to be tested. Ego appeal.	Instructive, upbuilding, comforting. Vision accepts testing.
See Its Fruit (Test the Fruit - Matthew 7:15-20)		
Variable	Fear, compulsion, bondage, anxiety, confusion, inflated ego.	Quickened faith, power, peace, good fruit, enlightenment, knowledge, humility.

figure 9.1

The fruit of inner spiritual experiences should be an increase in love, reconciliation, healing, and wholeness. If, instead, you find the opposite happening, you should immediately discontinue your journaling until you receive help from your spiritual counselor.

A Spirit-Anointed Paradigm for Discovering Truth

A Spirit-anointed paradigm (system) can also be used to confirm that your journaling is correct. I have used many systems for determining truth in my past. Following are some of them:

- If dad said it is true, then it is true.
- If my teacher said it is true, then it is true.
- If my pastor said it is true, then it is true.
- If my professor said it is true, then it is true.
- If an apostle said it is true, then it is true.
- If my reasoned theology said it is true, then it is true.
- If a double-blind scientific study said it is true, then it is true.

Finally, after years of doing all of this, it dawned on me that perhaps I should search through the Bible and discover *what God says is the appropriate method for discovering **truth**!*

It is amazing to me that I was nearly 40 years old before it occurred to me that I ought to research Scripture looking for God's methodology for determining truth!

My research involved meditating on more than 5,500 verses, and all that I learned is presented in a book titled *How Do You Know?* On the following pages I have summarized in two charts what I believe is God's design for discovering truth. I have called it "The Leader's Paradigm," and it is a methodology that utilizes God's speaking to us through six different means, which I have pictured as pillars. I believe that, to be a successful leader, you will need to use this system or a system very close to it.

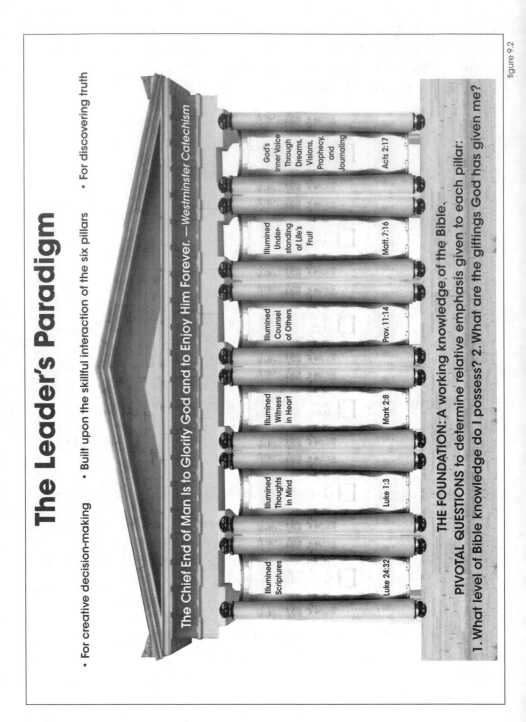

The Leader's Paradigm

- For creative decision-making
- Built upon the skillful interaction of the six pillars
- For discovering truth

The Chief End of Man Is to Glorify God and to Enjoy Him Forever. —*Westminster Catechism*

Illumined Scriptures	Illumined Thoughts in Mind	Illumined Witness in Heart	Illumined Counsel of Others	Illumined Understanding of Life's Fruit	God's Inner Voice Through Dreams, Visions, Prophecy, and Journaling
Luke 24:32	Luke 1:3	Mark 2:8	Prov. 11:14	Matt. 7:16	Acts 2:17

THE FOUNDATION: A working knowledge of the Bible,
PIVOTAL QUESTIONS to determine relative emphasis given to each pillar:
1. What level of Bible knowledge do I possess? 2. What are the giftings God has given me?

figure 9.2

Pillar #	Key Verse	How Experienced	How Compared
Pillar One Illumined Scriptures	And they said to one another, "Did not our hearts burn within us, while He talked with us by the way, and while He opened to us the Scriptures?" (Luke 24:32)	This pillar is experienced as the Holy Spirit illumines Scriptures to you—you sense them leaping off the page or just coming to your attention spontaneously.	This pillar could be viewed as enhanced Biblicism; however, we go beyond studying the Bible with our intellects only, asking for the Holy Spirit to illumine Scriptures to our hearts and minds.
Pillar Two Illumined Thoughts in One's Mind	It seemed fitting for me as well, having investigated everything carefully from the beginning, to write it out for you in consecutive order, most excellent Theophilus. (Luke 1:4 NASB)	This pillar is experienced as the Holy Spirit guiding your reasoning process through spontaneous impressions. It is obvious that Luke's Gospel was more than simply investigative research of his own mind, as what he wrote has stood as the Word of God for 2,000 years.	This pillar could be viewed as enhanced rationalism; however, we go beyond simple rationalism to allowing the Holy Spirit to guide our thinking process (through combining intuition and reason) rather than guiding it ourselves.
Pillar Three Illumined Witness in One's Heart	And immediately when Jesus perceived in His spirit that they so reasoned within themselves, He said unto them, "Why reason ye these things in your hearts?" (Mark 2:8)	This pillar is experienced as an impression perceived in your spirit. Deep inner peace or unrest is often part of this experience.	This pillar could be viewed as enhanced hedonism in that we are doing what "feels" good; however, in our case, we are going with the "feel" within our hearts, rather than the "feelings" of the flesh.
Pillar Four Illumined Counsel of Others	Where no counsel is, the people fall: but in the multitude of counselors there is safety. (Proverbs 11:14)	This pillar is experienced as you ask your spiritual advisors to seek God for confirmation, additions, or adjustments in the guidance you sense God has given you.	This pillar could be viewed as enhanced humanism, as we are receiving counsel through others; however, we go beyond people's wisdom and ask them to impart the wisdom of God to us.
Pillar Five Illumined Understanding of Life's Experiences	Ye shall know them by their fruits. Do men gather grapes of thorns, or figs of thistles? (Matthew 7:16)	This pillar is experienced as you ask God to give you insight and understanding concerning the fruit life is demonstrating. God gives you revelation as to what has caused the fruit.	This pillar could be viewed as enhanced empiricism, in that we are examining life carefully; however, we go beyond our own limited understanding of life and ask God to give us His understanding of what we are seeing.
Pillar Six Illumined Revelation from God Through Dreams, Visions, Prophecy, and Journaling	"And it shall come to pass in the last days," saith God, "I will pour out of My Spirit upon all flesh: and your sons and your daughters shall prophesy, and your young men shall see visions, and your old men shall dream dreams." (Acts 2:17)	This pillar is experienced as you receive direct revelation from God through dreams, visions, and journaling. Journaling is the writing out of your prayers and God's answers	This pillar could be viewed as enhanced mysticism; however, we go beyond just "any" spirit-encounter as we pursue Holy Spirit encounter.

The Objective: To have all six pillars in agreement before making a major decision.

figure 9.3

As you review these charts, you will see that I present a biblical basis for each of the six pillars. I have also compared these pillars to six key philosophies that have been promoted over the centuries. I have shown that all six philosophies do hold a fragment of truth, and that when you combine the Holy Spirit to each one, and then merge all six together, you have a wonderfully broad-based paradigm for discerning and clarifying truth. I have used this paradigm very successfully for the last 20 years of my life, and encourage you to prayerfully reflect on it and then try it.

Major Decisions

I expect that the leading of God will be consistent through all six pillars of the Leader's Paradigm before I make a major decision. Because I wait for all six to line up, I am spared making many major mistakes. I cannot tell you how valuable this paradigm has been for me.

Just because I have a broad-based methodology for discovering truth is no guarantee I will receive full truth. The Bible says that "we see through a glass darkly," so we still may not know the total truth in an area. However, it is as accurate as we can be in the circumstances we are in. That is why we walk humbly. That is why we remain teachable. "Blessed are the poor in spirit...."

Balance the Six Pillars Based on *Your* Gifts

I think the more right-brain intuitive person will place more weight on the intuitive aspects of these six pillars. This is probably right because their gifts in the area of intuition and vision make them more precise and wise when they lean upon these gifts.

By contrast, the more analytical left-brain person will likely lean a bit more heavily on the analytical aspects of these pillars, because their strengths in the area of Spirit-led reasoning and examining the fruits make them more precise and wise as they lean upon these gifts. This, too, is right.

However, both left- and right-brain people should stretch themselves somewhat so that they integrate both left- and right-brain faculties into their decision-making process.

If you are an accomplished Bible scholar, you will probably weigh more heavily on the pillar of illumined Scriptures. If you are very new to the Bible, you may not put as much weight on that pillar because of your lack of knowledge of the principles of the Word. It is not that the Bible is not reliable for the young Christian. It is that they are more ignorant of its contents.

Determine Your Journaling Skill Level

May I suggest that when we begin to journal, we are babes, and we grow through several stages. As we go through these phases, our skill level (our spiritual dexterity) increases, and we find we can receive more precise data and information from the spiritual realm.

Each of us has different skill levels. I am under the distinct impression that right-brainers can reach further and with more dexterity into the spirit realm than left-brainers can. I also believe that with practice, anyone can go further than they could before. This is a natural law God has built into His universe.

Journaling's Beginner Stage—Operating in the Spirit of Prophecy (Rev. 19:10)

One working definition for this stage is, "Not being able to personally capture the prophetic flow unless you have been led into it by another." When I guide a group in journaling, I consider this an example of leading the group into experiencing the spirit of prophecy in the room.

When operating on this level, you should definitely keep your journaling restricted to the areas of edification, exhortation, and comfort. Most people will begin here.

Journaling's Intermediate Stage—Operating in the Gift of Prophecy (1 Cor. 12:10)

A working definition for this stage is, "Personally able to flow in the prophetic even when it is not manifest in the meeting at large." These people are able to be prophetic, sensing the Spirit within their hearts even when the circumstances without do not lend themselves to being prophetic. They have cultivated the ability to stand still before God while walking among men.

When operating on this level, you will journal in the areas of edification, exhortation, and comfort. In addition, you will find wisdom from the Lord, especially when functioning in the area of *your call and responsibility and ministry*. For example, you could journal about your family. If you are a teacher, you might journal about your teaching, or if an evangelist, you could journal about what God is speaking to you concerning evangelism, and so on.

After you have acquired skill in journaling by doing it regularly for six months to a year, you may find the gifts of the Holy Spirit beginning to flow through your heart and pen. One of these gifts is prophecy. I have found that I can ask the Lord for a prophetic word for our Sunday service, and He will give it to me before the service begins—possibly even several days before. I write it down and share with the pastor in charge of the service that I have a word from the Lord. He then calls on me to share it at an appropriate time. One such prophecy follows.

My children, fear not your weaknesses. Be not discouraged by them. Are they mightier than I? Are they greater than the living God? NO! They are not! No! They are simply to be consumed by MY Power. Even as you are consumed in MY Presence, so are your weaknesses consumed by MY Power. MY Power and MY Presence are one. Therefore when you are consumed in your weakness, you are not consumed in MY Presence. Conversely, when you are consumed in MY Presence, MY Power has consumed you, and your weaknesses are no more. So come, My children, unto Me, and you shall be healed.

Growing into the operation of the gift of prophecy is available for all who seek it. Second Timothy 1:6 indicates it is also imparted through the laying on of hands.

Journaling's Advanced Stage—Operating in the Office of a Prophet (Eph. 4:11)

A working definition for this stage is, "Personally developed until you are recognized by other leaders in the Body of Christ as having a mature prophetic ministry." This is not a call everyone has, as is evidenced by Ephesians 4:11: *"He gave some prophets...."* So we will not all reach this level. Those who have the call to do so can; the rest of us will become what God is asking us to become. For me, it is to be a teacher in the Body of Christ, not a prophet. Perhaps I can be a prophetic teacher, but not a prophet. In my estimation, people who grow into the office of a prophet are often a bit more right-brain than I am.

When operating in the office of a prophet, you not only can receive edification, exhortation, and comfort, but you may also have a matured skill and precision in speaking truth to the Church and possibly, occasionally, even predictive prophecies. You also display the fruit of the Holy Spirit in your life and have the character qualities of an elder in the Body of Christ. Do not press for this office unless that is what God has called and gifted you for. There are other offices and functions that are also vital to the Body where you may be needed.

Mistakes in Your Journaling: Celebrating the Learning Curve!

There will be times, especially when you are just beginning, that you will find errors in your journaling. How do you handle this? I didn't deal with it very well at first. Usually I would become angry, fearful, discouraged—tempted to throw my journal down and quit. I did that at least a half-dozen times during my first year. I was of the opinion that since it was supposed to be God's words, it had to be right; and if it wasn't right, then it wasn't God, and the whole exercise in journaling was a farce.

As I reflect on my initial responses, I realize how immature they were. Who does anything perfectly the first time? Who ever began riding a bike without falling more than once? Who ever learned to play tennis without missing the ball? The fact is, there is always a practice time before we perfect any skill. And even when we have become skillful, we still make mistakes from time to time. We must carry this same attitude and realization into our spiritual growth as well. If we do, the pressure of having to be perfect in our journaling is removed. We will allow ourselves the freedom to fail at times, without giving up the whole enterprise. We simply laugh and say, "Whoops, that was a mistake!" and go on. I encourage each of you to adopt this attitude.

Common Reasons for Journaling Mistakes— and Solutions

1. **Improper focus.** Sometimes you may discover yourself inadvertently praying with an idol in your heart. That is, you are focusing more intently on the "thing" you are praying for than you are on Jesus Christ. Thus the answer comes back through the "thing" rather than purely from Jesus' heart.

   The solution: Fix the eyes of your heart on Jesus as you pray. Watch Him address the thing you are praying about.

2. **Improper interpretation.** Sometimes I think God has said a certain thing. I go out and act on it, but it doesn't come to pass as He said it would. I have often found that when I go back and read the actual words that are in my journal, they are different from what I had thought them to be. I had immediately jumped to a conclusion, interpreting the words in a certain way. However, when I looked again at the precise words, I found that these actual words were fulfilled. It was my interpretation that was wrong.

   The solution: Be careful not to interpret what God says. Ask Him to interpret it. He will!

3. **Not acting as God instructs.** I have found that if I do not act on the words of God in the way and according to the timing that He gives me, the release of God's perfect will into the situation can be hindered.

   The solution: Do what God says, when He says it, the way He says to do it. Our actions become acts of faith, prophetic actions and acts of obedience, and as such they open the door for God's miracle-working power to be released.

4. **Not being a large enough conduit to release God's power.** God chooses to have His power flow through channels, allowing His will to be released. These channels most often are individual Christians. If God has spoken that His will is to do a supernatural feat through me, and my channel is clogged through improper spiritual care and exercise, my constricted channel can thwart God's miracle, and my journaling may appear to be wrong. However, my journal probably did reveal God's perfect will, but it was not accomplished because of the channel being too small to allow a sufficient amount of the Holy Spirit's energy to touch the point of need.

   The solution: Take good care of your spirit through continually praying, spending time with Jesus, meditating on the Word, picturing what God has promised as already fulfilled, confessing all sin and obeying the voice of God in your heart. You may also be interested in our book *How to Release God's Healing Power Through Prayer.*

5. **Not having the right word in my vocabulary to fit the feeling within my spirit.** As God grants impressions within our hearts, our spirits search for an adequate vocabulary to attach to these impressions so they become understandable. If I do not pause to get exactly the right word, or if I do not have the right word in my vocabulary, I can hastily assign a wrong word to the inner sensation and find I have messed up my journaling.

   The solution: Wait for the "right" word to be formed within your heart, the word that fully and completely conveys the feeling of your spirit.

6. **Blocking the divine flow by having my sights fixed on a limited number of options.** Sometimes when I ask a question I am looking for a "yes" or a "no" and have thus

closed my heart to other creative possibilities. Often God has ingenious approaches to situations that I never hear because I am locked into a narrow framework. In this case I may find myself journaling the answer I most want to hear, since I have blocked the divine flow.

The solution: Be careful to be open to limitless possibilities.

7. **My advisors may answer quickly without hearing from God.** Sometimes when you share your journaling with your spiritual friend, he may disagree with what you have written. In this case, make sure that he has not just answered "off the cuff," or just given you "his best opinion" concerning the issue. You are not asking for his best judgment; you are asking him to seek God's voice in his heart concerning the issue.

The solution: Ask him to pray about it and tell you what God says to him.

8. **Some of God's commands in my journal are never meant to be fulfilled.** They are simply positioning moves. *"Now it came about after these things, that God tested Abraham, and said to him, 'Abraham!' And he said, 'Here I am.' And He said, 'Take now your son, your only son, whom you love, Isaac, and go to the land of Moriah; and offer him there as a burnt offering on one of the mountains of which I will tell you"* (Gen. 22:1-2). Later the angel of the Lord countered this command, saying to Abraham, *"Do not stretch out your hand against the lad, and do nothing to him; for now I know that you fear God..."* (Gen. 22:12).

I wonder if God was concerned with Abraham making an idol out of Isaac, so He had to show Abraham that nothing, not even a miraculous offspring, could be allowed to come between Abraham and God. God "tested" Abraham (see Gen. 22:1) and when He saw that Abraham was willing to offer Isaac as a sacrifice, He said, *"...now I know that you fear God."* Fearing God means coming completely out of all idolatry and worshiping God only.

I believe this happens numerous times in our lives. God speaks a certain thing, moving us in a certain direction for a period of time, and then after getting us to a specific point or action, He totally reverses His command. I believe this is done in order to position our attitudes in holiness before Him, and to more effectively place us and others for future purposes that He has planned.

The solution: We must be open to this eventuality and hold on to all words loosely. It is Christ Himself, and Christ only, to whom we hold tightly. All words, visions, and journaling are held loosely.

9. **God will not violate our free will.** God desires that all come unto repentance; however, some do not. Therefore, God's perfect will is not always realized in each person's life.

   The solution: When we are journaling, and a word is given that involves another person, we need to realize that that person can choose a direction contrary to God's perfect will and that our journaling, even though it may be reflecting God's perfect will, may not be fulfilled.

10. **Reject any journaling that speaks of the death of someone from whom you would like to be freed.** If you believe you are being told that your spouse is going to die and you are going to marry another, this should be dismissed. Every close relationship contains a certain amount of stress. There may be a conscious or unconscious desire to be freed from the relationship. This unconscious desire can emerge in your journal and appear to be the voice of God.

   The solution: Do not incubate such a vision or speak it or act upon it. Instead, focus your journaling on ways of enhancing your relationship with that person and give increased attention to cultivating your relationship with the Lord.

Destructive journaling is almost always from the deceiver. This is one of the ways satan comes to us as an angel of light. He will use Scripture to prove his point; however his message betrays him. He is speaking of death. It should be actively resisted and rebuked in the name of Jesus. My spiritual advisor's wife had a feeling soon after their oldest daughter was born that she was not going to live very long. He sensed immediately that it was from satan and together they rebuked his lie in Jesus' name.

11. **Beware of your own strong desires as you journal.** If you feel strongly about a certain thing, it is very easy for your own desires to come through your journaling. Prominent examples would include: romance, sexuality, power, greed, lust, fame. These things can flow so easily and effortlessly into your journal that you are most certain it is Christ, yet it is only a reflection of your own desires.

    The solution: Crucify your own desires daily, and walk near the cross of self-sacrificing love. Make sure your journaling comes only from that vantage point. Share any questionable journaling in these areas with your spiritual advisors for their input.

12. **Asking questions outside of your scope of knowledge and giftings.** If you need insight on obtaining financial freedom and you know nothing about how to go about doing it, you may find your journal a fruitless place to look for a direct answer, other than God telling you to go and do some studying or instructing you to enter into a relationship with an entrepreneur so you can become

discipled. Journaling breaks down when you have not deposited anything in the "hard drive."

I see our minds like the hard drive of a computer, and our hearts and the intuitive flow as the software. As we fill our minds with both the Word of God and the testimonies and principles of successful people, we prepare our hard drives by loading them up with information to draw upon. Once the hard drive is loaded, then the software can, upon command and under the direction of the Holy Spirit, select information that is the right application for the problem set before us.

The solution: I recommend not journaling about a problem or an area in which you have no knowledge, because in most cases I believe you will receive little or nothing of value. You may experiment for yourself and decide if I am right or not. I suggest you keep detailed records and analyze your findings. I would love to receive a copy of your conclusions. I have found that I must fill my hard drive before I activate my software if I want meaningful results.

These cover some of the most common reasons for errors in our journaling. Accept your errors with grace and laughter and go on, knowing that *practice makes perfect* (see Heb. 5:14).

Sharing Your Journal With Others

Often we become emotionally attached to the revelation in our journals and demand others receive it. Sometimes, we share it with strong conviction, not mindful of the fact that our interpretation or application may be off base. Occasionally, the revelation itself might be just plain wrong.

Personally, I always try to share revelation in a way that allows the other person the most room in responding to the word. For example, I will often share it as an appeal or as counsel. That way, the other person is free to come to his own conclusion and take whatever action he feels is appropriate, or no action at all. If I really feel strongly about the issue, I might share it as an "impression."

Seldom do I add the emphasis of "thus saith the Lord." After all, if it is a word from the Lord, it will accomplish all that God intended for it to do (which, by the way, may be very different from what I expect), without any need of my stating God's endorsement.

The Body of Christ could save itself much grief by allowing revelation to move under its own authority rather than trying to bring others under our authority by claiming that they need to submit to what we believe we have received from God. All true authority rests in the *rhema* word directly from God. We only have authority to the extent that we speak true *rhema*. And true authority does not need to be demanded or coerced. True authority is recognized and responded to without force or manipulation.

The Word of the Lord Breaks

As Psalm 29:5 states, *"The voice of the Lord breaks the cedars,"* so often the voice of the Lord spoken in our quiet communion with Him will break us and humble us. Remember the Israelites at the mountain of the Lord. They refused to listen and have fellowship directly with Him because His voice was accompanied by His fire. The purifying fire of God always accompanies His voice. Yet the essence of that fire, the power that fuels it, is always Love. It is Love that draws us to Him, and by His Love, we become holy as He is holy.

Another reason the Lord speaks to us and reveals things to us is to build our faith. Jesus said in John 14:29, *"And now I have told you before it comes to pass that when it comes to pass, you might believe."* Our faith is of supreme importance to God. It is only what is done in faith that pleases Him. The growth of our faith is a high priority to the Lord, and you will recognize it as a major goal in all that He says to you through your journal.

Knowing Him

Let's remember that hearing God's voice is not about knowing "stuff," but about *knowing Him.* God's goal is the building of character rather than the revealing of futuristic insights. We must have faith in God, not in our revelation. We must be skeptical of our interpretation of the revelations God gives us, and realize that most things will not be fulfilled in the way we expected them to be fulfilled.

I pray these considerations will help your journaling be a life-giving experience. I pray for your victory and success.

Examples of Two-way Journaling

Several of our students have allowed me the privilege of passing their journal entries along to you so you may be blessed by hearing the kinds of things that the Lord is speaking into their lives. Celebrate the goodness and greatness of God as you read.

Renay—God's Voice Strengthens Marriage Relationship

Lord, how do You want me to approach my husband?

Oh dear little one, I am your Maker, your Creator. I placed this special man in your life because I alone know what you need. Man needs to feel loved and attended to. You are small and precious to him as you are small and precious to Me, yet he has greater expectations of you.

Just love him, little one. For he must know your love. He must see it and feel it. He does not know your heart as I do. You must show him, you must make your love known. You must show him your respect, little one. For you are righteous and beautiful through Me and it is I Who give you strength. It is I Who will help you overcome and win your husband back. He longs for you as you long for him. He is lonely and empty without you, for you fill him as I intended it to be.

***

Della—A Pastor's First Three Journal Entries

You still have many things you fret about. Fix your eyes on Me, not just for journaling. I do care for you and I meet your needs one day at a time. You feel that you are unprotected and need to take action for the future, but you have always been under My wings, daughter. I have always been there protecting you. These are just facades and they are coming down for you. Let them fall down.

Go to the edge of the cliff and just jump. I will catch you. You will learn to enjoy life as you asked and you will see Me. Keep your eyes fixed. You are making progress. Let go, and let Me. I do have somewhere that I am taking you and it is a journey. Let the heaviness and pressures go. It is OK to be lighthearted and carefree, especially because I care for you and about you. You have many that love you. Keep your eyes on Me.

✱✱✱

Lord, what would You like to say to me today?

Come and sit in My lap today. This weekend I have been doing many things in your life and in the lives around you. Remember to take quiet time and rest in Me. Mondays are really your Shabbat. You need to find your peace and center in Me. You are learning that I can do more than you possibly could think about. I have surprised you this weekend to show you I am working in these relationships.

Lay your head on My chest. Let Me hold you tight. It is OK to let go of everything and relax in Me. When I massage your temples, your stress will leave because that is where it is held. Quit thinking so much and sense your spirit. Stay focused in vision and expecting vision. I will come to you in vision and you will see Me clearly. You will see clearly. Letting go is a process. This is the day to let go and download.

Thanks, Jesus.

✱✱✱

Dear Jesus, why do I want to eat all the time?

There have been great disappointments inside of you. With the disappointments come great emptiness and that is what you have been trying to fill. It is true that food isn't that filling. It's just a habit that is associated with pleasure. You have been making great strides in bringing your disappointments to Me and acknowledging them. It will get better in this area. You are pressing into Me and finding out about My nature. I am not troubled or concerned with circumstances as you are. I have a much larger plan and a larger view.

As you continue to trust in Me and envision Me, you are seeing Me in a new light. I don't want you cloaked in heaviness, nor with the cares of this world. It is true that you have come such a long way this past year. This year will be lighter and freer for you. You will experience more joy and deeper intimacy with Me. It will be worth all your prayers and perseverance. The river is coming and your heart is being healed. My daughter, I have gifts for you. Get ready to open them. Receive them, believe in them and use them. They will help others get set free. Rest your chest on My heart today. Lean into Me.

Thanks, Jesus.

✳✳✳

Benji, 10-year-old Boy—Interpersonal Relationships

Why does Dad always get so mad all the time?

Benji, I'm bringing you through many tests right now. And I'm teaching you and him many things. You are now going into spiritual adulthood, and you must learn many things. Your dad and mom will get stricter on you for a short time, and during this time I will teach you many things. Some of your friends will dislike you because you are getting wiser and more spiritual. I love you and your parents love you, and I will be interceding for you at the right hand of the Father during this time.

Lord, will You help me have a better attitude towards my elders and my schoolwork?

Yes! All you have to do is ask for My help!!

Please help me have a better attitude.

OK. But first I want you to yield yourself to Me and allow Me to take control.

OK. I want You to take all control over me and I yield myself to You.

Benji, you will have a better attitude all the time. You are very very special to Me. Thank you for yielding to Me!

I love You very much!

I love you, too, Benji.

✳✳✳

Mark Virkler—"God, Why Aren't You More Specific in Our Journals?"

Situation: I was frustrated because I see in other people's journaling what I saw in mine—the constant encouragement of God to trust Him and to believe and to have hope, but not (in my perception) all the specifics they need for breakthrough in their lives. When I would provide the specifics they need by way of counseling, a breakthrough would come.

Lord, why don't You provide these specifics to me and to others directly through our journaling? I do understand that faith, hope, and love are central, but the specifics that provide the release are also extremely valuable.

Mark, I have shown you in your spirit the answer. It is because I have ordained apostles, prophets, evangelists, pastors and teachers in the Body of Christ, to whom you are to relate for instruction and help and counsel. If you could get it all from Me directly, then you would not need each other. Thus, you would fragment. Therefore I do not give you all you need through your journaling. I give you faith, hope and love and some other extras, but I purposely hold back some of the information you need and I give it to others to give to you. This way, each one must walk in relationship with others in the Body of Christ in order to become all that I have called and destined them to be.

Journaling is a wonderful key, but it is not all that a person needs. He also needs My revelation through the other ways I speak. This includes instruction coming through others in the Body of Christ.

I shared this journaling with the following two spiritual advisors for their input:

Maurice Fuller's comments: I agree with God. Journaling, to me, is a way to learn to hear from God until we can hear Him clearly in our spirit. So whether or not we continue to journal, it seems to be in the same category as hearing from God in our spirit. And that is only one way God speaks to us. Other ways are, as your journaling says, through others (which should confirm what God has already been speaking to us), through divinely ordained circumstances, through prophecy (word of knowledge, word of wisdom, etc.), and through visions, dreams and so on. I do not put a lot of weight on one particular method.

God often speaks to me when I am not specifically waiting for it. I submit a question to Him and He answers me in His time in the way He chooses. It is not a long wait but I have never been successful at pressing Him for a total answer right now. I have never found that I hurry the process up significantly by journaling. I always hear something through journaling but seldom does a complete solution come that way. Sometimes I don't hear anything in so many words but a conviction or a particular sense of direction begins to grow and grow until it crowds out all doubt and indecision.

Gary Greig's comments: This makes entire sense to me and resonates with my spirit. It's also the point of First Corinthians 12 and Hebrews 10:25.

✳ ✳ ✳

Remember, Journaling Is Only a Tool

We do not worship the tool or get stuck on the formula, as fantastic as journaling is. No, we come to the Creator and Sustainer of our souls, the Lord God Almighty. Can He speak outside of our journals? Obviously, yes! I have discovered that after journaling for awhile, I am much more aware of the inner sensation of the flow of the Spirit of Almighty God. Now even without my journal at my side, I find myself hearing that intuitive voice within speaking to me. Do I continue to journal? Yes, because it is such a powerful tool. But I also hear from God in other ways, including the counsel of friends, the Bible, circumstances of life, and dreams. When all these line up, I feel most confident that I am truly flowing in God. I do not live out of any one of these alone, but rather out of all of them.

Do I sometimes miss God? I imagine so. It's so hard to tell. There are really so few mentors in this area to show us the way. I accept the fact that we are children just beginning to learn to walk in the realm of the Holy Spirit. I expect that in such a stage of growth there would be numerous mistakes. However, I just keep on pressing on. *Lord, keep me from faltering.*

Personal Application

Write down the following questions in your journal or on your computer: "Lord, what do You want to say to me about the use of journaling as a tool to help me in hearing Your voice? How important is it? What do You want to speak into my life at this time?"

Now pick a comfortable scene of you and Jesus together, either in Galilee or perhaps in your home with you. Make sure you are in a comfortable setting with Him so you can be relaxed!

Fix your spiritual eyes on Jesus, put a big smile on your face, relax and ask Him the questions above. Then tune to flowing thoughts and pictures and record what He tells you.

When your journaling is complete, reread it and share it with your spiritual advisors to ensure it is from God and to build your faith so you continue on in journaling.

Free Online Resources to deepen these truths available at: www.cwgministries.org/FreeBooks

- **Examples of Journaling**

- **Journaling from Mark Virkler on Galatians 2:20**

- **Passionate Intimacy with God Through Dialog**

- **Robe, Crown, Nails, Cross—Journaling about the powerful symbolism of Easter**

CHAPTER 10

A Tuning Dial—The Tabernacle Experience

How Do I Tune My Heart to Hear God's Voice?

Our minds and physical senses cannot receive the fullness of God's revelation to us. It must come to our hearts intuitively through the operation of the Holy Spirit, living within us.

> But just as it is written, things which eye has not seen and ear has not heard, and which have not entered the heart of man, all that God has prepared for those who love Him. For to us God revealed them through the Spirit; for the Spirit searches all things, even the depths of God (1 Corinthians 2:9-10).

I have heard it used in sermon illustrations that our hearts are like a radio, which we need to tune to hear the signals that are coming from God. I would agree with that. However, no one could ever show me the tuning knob that would help me to adjust my heart more perfectly to the voice of God. Therefore the illustration always left me frustrated.

In this chapter we are going to give you a tuning dial. We are going to look at ways God has said we can tune ourselves to hear His voice. Most of the aspects of tuning deal with preparing the condition of our hearts, since it is into the heart that God speaks. We will look at three biblical patterns of approaching God to hear Him speak: the tabernacle experience; the prophet Habakkuk; and the instructions given in Hebrews 10:22.

Approach God Through the Tabernacle Experience

On Mount Sinai, God gave Moses the design for the tabernacle where the Israelites were to worship God, offer sacrifices, and hear directly from Him. Hebrews 8:5 tells us that this tabernacle and the services offered there were a copy, a shadow and example of the heavenly realities. It not only established the way for the Israelites to approach God and hear His voice, but it also demonstrates the way for us to approach God. (See following diagram on page 259.)

The tabernacle represents the spirit, soul, and body of man. The Outer Court corresponds to man's body, where we receive knowledge mainly through our five senses. To illustrate this, the Outer Court didn't have a covering but was illuminated by natural light, showing that we receive light (knowledge and revelation) through natural means.

The Holy Place corresponds to man's soul. It had a roof over it, but inside it was illuminated by oil burning in a lampstand, representing the Holy Spirit revealing truth to our minds. (Oil often symbolizes the Holy Spirit in the Bible.)

The Holy of Holies was a totally dark, enclosed tent with no natural or artificial source of light. The only illumination that ever shone in the Holy of Holies was the light of the *shekinah* glory of God. When God was present, there was light. If God departed, all was dark. This represents man's spirit, where the glory of God lights our innermost being, giving us direct revelation within our hearts.

Each of the *six pieces of furniture* in the tabernacle *represents an experience* in our approach to God.

First I enter the tabernacle through the gate of salvation. The tribe of Judah was before this gate. The name Judah means *praise,* so I enter His gates with thanksgiving in my heart and I enter His courts with praise as I prepare myself to hear God's voice.

The Tabernacle Experience — God's Design for Approaching Him

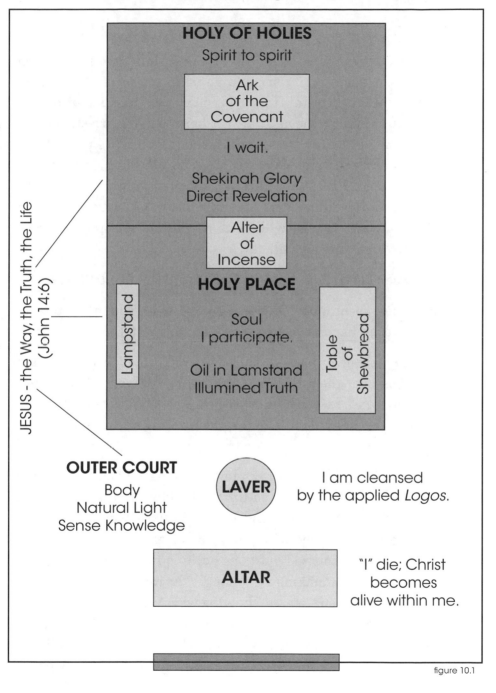

figure 10.1

There were two items in the Outer Court: the brazen altar and the brazen laver.

The Brazen Altar, Symbolizing the Cross (see Exod. 27:1-8)

The brazen (or bronze) altar was the first thing you faced when you entered the tabernacle. You could **not skip any piece** of furniture as you went into the Holy of Holies. If you wanted to meet with God, you first had to stop at the altar. It was here that the priests offered the animal sacrifices. The brazen altar, then, represents my need to make Jesus the Lord of my life and present myself as a living sacrifice to Him (see Rom. 12:1-2). This is an absolute prerequisite to approaching God. If I already know what I want to hear as I approach God in journaling, my strong will, will contaminate the spontaneous flow from within. I must lay my will down.

The Brazen Laver, Representing God's Word (see Exod. 30:17-21)

The brazen (or bronze) laver was a large basin where the priests would clean their hands and feet before moving into the Holy Place.

The New Testament says in Ephesians 5:26 that Jesus cleanses and sanctifies us by the washing of water with the Word. So the laver signifies that I wash myself by applying the *Logos* (Word of God, Scripture) to my life. The applied *Logos* has a cleansing effect on my heart and mind.

It is interesting that the brazen laver was made from the mirrors that the Hebrew women donated for the building of the tabernacle. In James 1:22-25, those who read the Word but do not obey it are compared to someone who looks in a mirror and sees that his face is dirty and his hair mussed but does nothing to fix himself up, just walking away without making any changes. As we read the Bible, God holds up a mirror to our hearts, showing what we really look like. As we approach God, He wants us to be changed, sanctified, and made holy by applying the cleansing power of His Word to our lives daily. So here I ask, "Am I meditating upon and applying the Bible to my life?"

After stopping by the brazen laver to be washed, the priest would then move to the *Holy Place*. This was a large room with a roof of animal skins. Inside the Holy Place were three pieces of furniture.

The Table of Shewbread, Symbolizing Our Will (see Exod. 25:23-30)

The table of shewbread was a table on which the priests placed 12 special loaves of bread. Just as flour is ground fine for the making of the bread, so our will is ground fine as we totally commit our way unto the Lord. God wants our wills to be set only to obey Him when we enter His presence to hear from Him. The priests would come together to eat this bread week by week. God uses our fellowship with other believers as a means of grinding our wills and shaping us into His image. As I stop at the table of shewbread, I ask, "Am I living in fellowship with the body of Christ? Is my will ground fine?"

The Golden Lampstand, Representing Our Illumined Mind (see Exod. 25:31-39)

Also in the Holy Place was a seven-branched golden lampstand lit by oil. This is what gave light to the Holy Place. The oil represents the Holy Spirit. So I ask myself, "Am I allowing God to illumine my mind as I meditate upon His Word?"

The Altar of Incense, Representing Our Emotions (see Exod. 30:1-10)

Right in front of the doorway to the Holy of Holies was a golden table where the priest burned an offering of incense morning and evening. This table was perfectly square or balanced. The incense represents the worship of God's people. The way into the Holy of Holies, the manifest presence of God, is through worship. As we offer up a continuous sacrifice of worship, our emotions are brought under the control of the Holy Spirit and come into balance. Here is where I ask, "Am I standing quietly in God's presence and am I worshiping Him, or have I become a grumbler?"

The Ark, Symbolizing Direct Revelation of the Spirit into Our Hearts (see Exod. 25:10-22)

Inside the Holy Place was a smaller, separate room called the Holy of Holies. Inside this "tent of meeting" was just one item: the Ark.

The Ark of the Covenant was a chest overlaid with gold that held symbols of God's covenant with Israel. The flat top of the Ark was called the Mercy Seat. On it, two golden angels stood facing each other with their wings stretched out toward the center as a covering over the Mercy Seat. It was from the Mercy Seat that God promised to meet with and speak to Moses and the priests. Here I ask this question: "Am I still and quiet in God's presence, fixing the eyes of my heart upon Jesus?" **Using the imagery of the tabernacle can be a powerful means of preparing our hearts to meet with our Lord.**

Habakkuk 2:1-3 Provides a *Tuning Dial* for Hearing God's Voice

We have already looked closely at Habakkuk who gave us our four keys for hearing God's voice.

Using all four of these keys is pivotal to your success at clearly discerning the Lord's voice in your heart. I quiet myself by fixing my eyes on Jesus, tuning to spontaneity, and writing down the flow of thoughts and pictures that come to me.

Hebrews 10:19-22 Presents a *Fine-Tuning Dial* for Hearing God's Voice

...we have confidence to enter the holy place by the blood of Jesus, by a new and living way which He inaugurated for us through the veil, that is, His flesh, and since we have a great priest over the house of God, let us draw near with a sincere heart in full assurance of faith, having our hearts sprinkled clean from an evil conscience and our bodies washed with pure water (Hebrews 10:19-22).

The passage says that we come before God by entering the "Holy Place." The literal word, which is translated "holy place," is *hagios* and refers to that inner room of the tabernacle, the Holy of Holies where I stand or kneel quietly in God's presence. Once there, we hear His voice in our hearts. The writer says that we come into God's presence with the following four attitudes:

1. *A sincere heart.* My heart must be true, with no hypocrisy, no deception, and no lying. I am wholehearted in my love, praise, and trust of God. I return to Him with my whole heart; I search for Him with my whole heart; and I cry out to Him with my whole heart.

2. *In full assurance of faith.* *"...he who comes to God must believe that He is and that He is a rewarder of those who seek Him"* (Heb. 11:6). I have come to a decision to believe all that God says about me is true! I have an unshakable conviction that God lives in my heart and that His river flows out from within me. When I come before God and tune to His inner river, *the resulting flow is **God!*** My God is Immanuel, God with me! All doubt and unbelief is vanquished! I am a believer!

3. *A heart sprinkled clean from an evil conscience.* I absolutely believe that as I confess my sins before God, they are totally washed away by the blood of Jesus. I stand clean and holy before God, not because of my righteousness, but because of Christ's cleansing blood. I am not trying to be good any more than Jesus would accept the title "Good Master." I am cleansed. That is what makes me righteous before God. It is not of me; it is through Christ.

4. *A body washed with pure water.* *"Christ also loved the church and gave Himself up for her; that He might sanctify her, having cleansed her by the washing of water with the word* [rhema]*"* (Eph. 5:25-26). Jesus speaks into my heart through my journaling and as I act on what He says, it cleanses my life. I am obeying the previous *rhema* God has spoken to me.

Keeping My Heart Tuned

I am to keep my heart tuned to God's channel all day long, receiving revelation continuously as I walk through life. That is the way Jesus lived (see John 5:19-20,30). That is how I am to live. I don't fall in and out of His presence. I *stay* in His presence by maintaining the biblical posture described above. The Bible calls it "abiding in Christ" or "praying without ceasing." So in my morning devotions, I simply say, "Good morning, Lord, what do You want to say to me?" And I fix my eyes on Jesus, tune to flow and write. However, if nothing comes, then that means I must be out of tune, so I go back and walk through the tuning lists above to see where the block is and to remove it.

Not Hearing God's Voice?

The following list of reasons why you may not hear God's voice helps you identify the problem, and the remedies offered empower you to overcome the road blocks.

1. You have a lack of faith.

    The Solution: Engage in "faith-builders" (tongue-speaking, worship in the spirit, praise, reading Bible promises, rereading your journal, using imagery, simply abandoning yourself to the God who is faithful, see Heb. 11:6); submit your journaling to your spiritual advisors for confirmation.

2. Your mind wanders.

    The Solution: Use a journal and use vision. Write down, pray through, and confess things that are on your mind. Make sure your heart is not condemning you. If it is, purify it through repentance.

3. You feel God is not speaking.

    The Solution: Pour out your heart *fully and completely.* Begin writing down anything you receive, even if there are only one or two words. Remember, the Spirit's impressions are slight and easily overcome by bringing up your thoughts. As you begin to write, more words will flow.

4. God is not speaking.

The Solution: It may be you are asking questions God does not want to answer. Perhaps you need to fast to release His answer. Check for problems on the fine-tuning dial. Maybe you have wrong motives (see James 4:3).

Even though Christ has opened the way before us into the Holy of Holies by rending the veil and sprinkling us with blood, many Christians do not enter frequently. The way is not burdensome or unduly complicated. Christ does the work, Christ sprinkles us with His blood, Christ grants us faith, Christ gives us a clean heart. We simply need to be willing vessels to receive His finished work. Our love and attention must be set toward Him.

Yet, how often our focus and devotion are diverted to things other than Christ. We do not always earnestly seek His overcoming power because we enjoy a desire of the flesh. We are not always willing to lose our life in order to find His life.

Also, it takes *effort* to learn to walk in a new realm. I watched with amazement as my two children learned to walk. They tried so hard, stumbled and fell so many times. They hit their heads and hurt themselves so much for a period of *many months*, yet they would not give up. Walking just beats crawling, and the Holy of Holies just beats the Holy Place. I believe that for us to learn to walk in the Holy of Holies, it will take the same kind of attention and effort, involve the same kinds of falls and bruises, and take a *number of months or years* before we become skillful. Please demonstrate at least as much persistence as a small child learning to walk.

May we take up the challenge to come confidently before God and receive His life and love. May we put forth the attention and effort that is needed. May we be willing to fully lose our life in order to find it.

My Personal Experience

I find God speaks to me from the Outer Court, the Holy Place, and the Holy of Holies. He has often directed me through the simple reading and application of the Bible (brazen laver in the Outer Court). He has often illumined a passage of Scripture to my heart, lifting it right off the page, letting me know it was His *rhema* for me at that moment (lampstand in the Holy Place). And He has often spoken with spontaneous thoughts, feelings, and images directly into my heart as I have waited quietly before Him (Ark of the Covenant in the Holy of Holies). Jesus has become my Way (Outer Court), my Truth (Holy Place), and my Life (Holy of Holies).

If I have ever found the Holy of Holies cut off to me, it was because I did not adjust my fine-tuning dial. I have gone with a lack of faith or a condemning heart, and therefore, have not had the confidence to approach God.

Luke wrote his Gospel as a Holy Place experience—through Spirit-led reasoning (see Luke 1:1-3). John wrote the Book of Revelation as a Holy of Holies experience—through direct revelation, bypassing his reasoning process (see Rev. 1:10-11). Both are equally valid. Both were 100 percent accurate in what they said.

Personal Application

Using vision, present yourself before each piece of tabernacle furniture. Focus on Jesus and ask Him what He wants to speak to you about the placement of this experience in your life. Tune to spontaneity and record what He says. You may want to also ask Him about the fine-tuning dial of Hebrews 10:22.

How to Possess Your Promised Land

...You may enter the land which the Lord your God gives you, a land flowing with milk and honey, as the Lord, the God of your fathers, promised you (Deuteronomy 27:3).

God says astounding things in our journals. He plans on using us in greater ways than we ever imagined. He plans on doing greater things through us than we dreamed of doing ourselves. He plans on blessing us more than we expected to be blessed. God told Abraham, *"...in you all the families of the earth will be blessed"* (Gen. 12:3). *"And He took him outside and said, 'Now look toward the heavens, and count the stars, if you are able to count them.' And He said to him, 'So shall your descendants be'"* (Gen. 15:5). These promises were spoken to Abraham by God when Abraham was 75 years of age and *had no children!*

Often in the Bible, when God told people what He was going to do through them, they turned around and explained to God that He could not do such a great thing through them, and why.

Moses said, "I can't lead millions of people because I can't talk" (see Exod. 4:10-11). That point didn't bother God, because God knew He could speak through Moses and make him better than he was. However, Moses refused to be convinced. God became angry with Moses and said, "Fine, I will give you Aaron as your mouthpiece, but I could have spoken through you if you would have believed Me" (see Exod. 4:12-15). The point is, don't look at your weaknesses and explain to God why He can't do something! Look at Jesus and the gifts of His Spirit, and say, "Yes, Lord, You can do it in me through Your wonderful anointing!" Focus on Jesus, and not yourself!

God plans on fulfilling these great promises He makes to us in our journals through His anointing working in and through us, and not through our own strength. If we will only **believe and obey**, God can and will do the supernatural through us!

God said to the Israelites, *"I have given you the promised land"* (Deut. 27:3). God will say similar things to each of us in our personal journals. He said to me, *"Mark, you are going to saturate the earth with the message of communion with God"* (teaching people how to hear God's voice). How are we to respond when God tells us such great things?

I used to respond by saying, "Hallelujah!" and sitting back to watch God accomplish what He had promised. Often nothing happened and I became frustrated. I had not yet learned that when God is speaking a prophecy like this through my journal, He is revealing my potential. If I walk hand in hand with God, this potential will be realized. If I don't, the potential will be wasted.

When God makes a promise to us, it is usually conditional on a number of things. Even if He doesn't say the promise has conditions, it still generally does. For example, God told Jonah to tell the inhabitants of Nineveh that He would destroy them in forty days (see Jon. 3:1-4). There was no "if clause" at all. That was the end of the sentence. However, when the Ninevites decided to repent, God, too, repented of the destruction that He had prepared to bring them and did not destroy them as He had planned (see Jon. 3:5-10).

God states this principle of conditionality:

> *At what instant I shall speak concerning a nation, and concerning a kingdom, to pluck up, and to pull down, and to destroy it; If that nation, against whom I have pronounced, turn from their evil, I will repent of the evil that I thought to do unto them. And at what instant I shall speak concerning a nation, and concerning a kingdom, to build and to plant it; If it do evil in my sight, that it obey not my voice, then I will repent of the good, wherewith I said I would benefit them* (Jeremiah 18:7-10 KJV).

Another classic example is when God told the Israelites that He had given them the Promised Land. Did that mean they could sit back and the Promised Land would drop into their laps? No, they had to seek God for direction and then go in and battle and conquer city after city.

So, too, when God says to me, *"I have healed you,"* my next question needs to be, "God, are there any specific actions You want me to take to precipitate Your healing flow?" Often there will be, because His covenant of healing is based on four prerequisites found in Exodus 15:26.

One of the prerequisites is to "keep *all* His statutes." So there are any number of His health laws that I may be breaking that are prohibiting me from obtaining the promise He has given to me both in His Word (Bible) and in my journal. Here is where the counsel of my advisors (who in this case know about health) comes in. I ask them to pray concerning any things God would tell them that I should be aware of or doing or changing in my lifestyle in order to release the healing flow of God's power.

I never used to do this. I would just sit back and wait. And nothing would happen. Now, I ask God and my spiritual advisors what I am to do and I receive their counsel. I remain active rather than passive. I am getting much better results this way. I believe it is a key answer to many people's dilemmas.

If God says He is going to heal your marriage, you then ask God what He wants you to do to be a catalyst for that healing. He will probably give you several things to do, attitudes to change, and actions to take.

You need to know that when another person's will is involved (as it is in this scenario), God will not overrule their will, but He and you will be doing everything possible to make the other party willing (in this case—to restore the marriage). However, in the final analysis, God will not overrule the other person's will, and so there is a possibility that a spouse may walk out, and God's declared will for the marriage would not be fulfilled.

This does not mean your journaling was wrong. This means God does not overrule people's wills to force His will to be done. By instructing you to believe and act in faith, God has positioned your heart to release the maximum force possible, intensifying the probability that a miracle of restoration will occur in your marriage.

The following is a short summary list of what Joshua and the Israelites had to do before they **possessed** the Promised Land that God said He had *already given* to them.

Steps the Israelites Took
To *Possess* Their Promised Land

1. They sent out spies into the land they were going to possess (see Josh. 2:1).

2. The people consecrated themselves for battle (see Josh. 3:5).

3. Their spiritual leaders led in battle (see Josh. 3:6).

4. They kept listening to the Lord every step of the way so that they knew God was with them in the actions they were taking (see Josh. 3:7).

5. They acknowledged a leader who was appointed by God, who in turn commanded the spiritual and the military leaders (see Josh. 3:8-9).

6. This leader could command a miracle to happen, and it did (see Josh. 3:10-17).

7. The Lord continued to give direction to this spiritual leader (see Josh. 4:1).

8. They took time out to follow God's instructions to create memorials to remind their descendents of the miracle-working power of God in their midst (see Josh. 4).

9. God's miracles made the enemies' hearts melt before them (see Josh. 5:1).

10. Complete obedience to God was required (see Josh. 5:2-10).

11. Joshua encountered and obeyed an angelic commander (see Josh. 5:13-15).

12. God gave detailed instructions about how to conduct the battle. These were followed to the letter and Jericho was taken (see Josh. 6).

13. Disobedience to God's voice within the camp brought defeat (see Josh. 7:1-5).

14. Seeking the Lord brought God's voice and revelation of why there was defeat and how to remove the sin that caused it. The sin was removed (see Josh. 7:6-26).

15. God gave detailed instructions of how to defeat the enemy. These were followed and the enemy defeated (see Josh. 8:1-35).

16. They were tricked by the Gibeonites because they did not seek the counsel of the Lord (see Josh. 9:14).

17. God's voice led Joshua into victory against five kings (see Josh. 10:8).

18. Obedience to God's voice brought victory (see Josh. 11:6).

19. Complete obedience and complete victory were finally obtained (see Josh. 11:15,23).

Obviously, hearing God's voice, believing it, and obeying it must rank at the top of anyone's list who wants to possess their Promised Land.

Journal, asking the Lord to speak to you from the list about the key requirements you need to know if you are going to possess the land the Lord has told you is yours.

What Keeps People From Entering Their Promised Land?

God told Moses to speak to the rock and water would come out, but instead, in his anger he hit the rock (see Num. 20:8,11).

> *But the Lord said to Moses and Aaron, "Because you have not believed Me, to treat Me as holy in the sight of the sons of Israel, therefore you shall not bring this assembly into the land which I have given them" (Numbers 20:12).*

Not honoring and absolutely obeying the voice of God kept Moses and Aaron out of the Promised Land.

How does God determine if we are prepared to walk into the promises He has for us?

> *You shall remember all the way which the Lord your God has led you in the wilderness these forty years, that He might humble you, testing you, to know what was in your heart, whether you would keep His commandments or not* (Deuteronomy 8:2).

God tests us to see if there is faith in our hearts—to see if, when under pressure, we say, "I trust in God as my Provider and Deliverer." Failing God's tests keeps us from receiving our inheritance here on this earth!

> *Surely all the men who have seen My glory and My signs which I performed in Egypt and in the wilderness, yet have put Me to the test these ten times and have not listened to My voice, shall by no means see the land which I swore to their fathers, nor shall any of those who spurned Me see it* (Numbers 14:22-23).

The Israelites failed ten of these tests while in the wilderness. Below are two of them. Rather than trusting in God, they began to whine and complain.

> *Then they set out from Mount Hor by the way of the Red Sea, to go around the land of Edom; and the people became impatient because of the journey. The people spoke against God and Moses, "Why have you brought us up out of Egypt to die in the wilderness? For there is no food and no water, and we loathe this miserable food"* (Numbers 21:4-5).

> *So they gave out to the sons of Israel a bad report of the land which they had spied out, saying, "The land through which we have gone, in spying it out, is a land that devours its inhabitants; and all the people whom we saw in it are men of great size. There also we saw the Nephilim (the sons of Anak are part of the Nephilim); and we became*

like grasshoppers in our own sight, and so we were in their sight." Then all the congregation lifted up their voices and cried, and the people wept that night. All the sons of Israel grumbled against Moses and Aaron; and the whole congregation said to them, "Would that we had died in the land of Egypt! Or would that we had died in this wilderness!" (Numbers 13:32–14:2)

God's response to the people's whining is: *"How long shall I bear with this evil congregation who are grumbling against Me? I have heard the complaints of the sons of Israel, which they are making against Me. Say to them, 'As I live,' says the Lord, 'just as you have spoken in My hearing, so I will surely do to you; your corpses will fall in this wilderness, even all your numbered men, according to your complete number from twenty years old and upward, who have grumbled against Me. Surely you shall not come into the land in which I swore to settle you, except Caleb the son of Jephunneh and Joshua the son of Nun'"* (Num. 14:27-30).

For the sons of Israel walked forty years in the wilderness, until all the nation, that is, the men of war who came out of Egypt, perished because they did not listen to the voice of the Lord, to whom the Lord had sworn that He would not let them see the land which the Lord had sworn to their fathers to give us, a land flowing with milk and honey (Joshua 5:6).

So they received what they expected and declared. They did not believe God was their Shepherd. They grumbled and complained saying they would die since God didn't care for them, and God said, "Fine, if that is what you want to believe for and confess, then that is what you will get." They all died in the wilderness.

It took me years in my own life to understand that God gives me exams on an ongoing basis. These tests come in the form of God allowing some pressure into my life, so He can see by my confession what I believe in my heart. Once I learned this, I became painfully aware that I had failed many tests over the course of my life and that this was hindering me from entering into the Promised Land God had in store for me.

I have repented of my whining and unbelief and my confession now is, "God is my Lover, my Provider, my Defender, and my Sustainer. I worship my God." This confession in times of pressure has allowed me to pass several tests, and helped me to press on into what God has promised me.

Entering God's Land of Promised Abundance

But My servant Caleb, because he has had a different spirit and has followed Me fully, I will bring into the land which he entered, and his descendants shall take possession of it (Numbers 14:24).

What kind of a spirit is God looking for in those who would enter into their promised lands?

Take care, brethren, that there not be in any one of you an evil, unbelieving heart that falls away from the living God. But encourage one another day after day, as long as it is still called "Today," so that none of you will be hardened by the deceitfulness of sin. For we have become partakers of Christ, if we hold fast the beginning of our assurance firm until the end, while it is said, "Today if you hear His voice, Do not harden your hearts, as when they provoked Me." For who provoked Him when they had heard? Indeed, did not all those who came out of Egypt led by Moses? And with whom was He angry for forty years? Was it not with those who sinned, whose bodies fell in the wilderness? And to whom did He swear that they would not enter His rest, but to those who were disobedient? So we see that they were not able to enter because of unbelief (Hebrews 3:12-19).

God's Plan for Our Lives

"For I know the plans I have for you," declares the LORD, "plans to prosper you and not to harm you, plans to give you hope and a future" (Jeremiah 29:11 NIV).

I believe God has a Promised Land experience for each of us. It touches our marriages, our health, our finances, our ministries, and our children. We can ask God to give us a detailed picture of what our Promised Land looks like in each of these areas.

What attitude must a leader have who is going to lead people into their promised lands?

> *Be strong and courageous, for you shall give this people possession of the land that I swore to their fathers to give them. Only be strong and very courageous; be careful to do according to all the law which Moses My servant commanded you; do not turn from it to the right or to the left, so that you may have success wherever you go. This book of the law shall not depart from your mouth, but you shall meditate on it day and night, so that you may be careful to do according to all that is written in it; for then you will make your way prosperous, and then you will have success. Have I not commanded you? Be strong and courageous! Do not tremble or be dismayed, for the Lord your God is with you wherever you go* (Joshua 1:6-9).

Unwavering faith in the power of Almighty God flowing in and through you is a must! Total obedience to the voice of God at all times is a must! Meditating on, speaking forth and obeying the Bible at all times is a must, because then you make your way prosperous and then you have success.

Death and Destiny

One issue that was a block to my walk of faith, and that I personally had to resolve, was my concern that if I openly confessed the promise of God to me, and the fulfillment of that promise was not yet manifested at the time of my death, I would look like a fool to all those standing around at my funeral. I suppose I shouldn't have been so concerned since at that point I would be out of here anyway, but I hate appearing foolish so I was always reticent to confess the amazing promises the Lord gave me in my journal.

Finally one day I talked to the Lord about this concern, and He answered me this way: *"Mark, if you die in faith confessing what I have told you to confess, you will not be a fool. I will consider you as a Hebrews 11 hero of faith."* Wow! That revelation had never dawned on me. They, too, died in faith believing that what God had said would come to pass even though they did not see it in their lifetimes (see Heb. 11:13).

In the same way, God may want me to die in faith, and not die complaining! I get it! I shall die in faith! I will give up whining! (Actually, God has taken a strong stand against complaining. He killed 14,700 people in one day for grumbling [see Num. 16:41-50]. It really is not healthy to whine.)

So God healed one more negative and unbiblical picture in my mind that was taking me backward and not forward. Now rather than picturing myself as a fool, I picture myself as a hero in faith! As you journal, God will heal your negative pictures also!

I remember very vividly a day I was being pessimistic about the world and life, and Roger Miller, one of my spiritual advisors, made this comment to me: *"Leadership is automatically transferred to those who remain optimistic."* Wow! That *rhema* of God burned in my heart like a searing fire. I wanted so much to be a leader in the world and make a difference for Christ, and yet my heart was in instant agreement with the *rhema* word Roger had spoken to me. Not many would want to follow me if I was a down-in-the-mouth pessimist!

That was the day I made a decision that I would be positive for the rest of my life. The quote from Roger stands in a frame on my desk for me to look at each and every day. Satan is *not* more powerful than God. Evil is *not* more powerful than Good. Darkness is *not* more powerful than Light.

My confession is:

- Light is more powerful than darkness!

- Truth is more powerful than error!

- Righteousness is more powerful than wickedness!

- God is more powerful than satan!

- Wherever I stand, darkness must flee!

- The Church *will* fulfill Christ's great commission to disciple all nations, and we *will* make His enemies His footstool! (See Acts 2:34-36.)

One of the riveting things Jesus spoke into my journaling one day was this: *"Mark, whatever you focus on grows within you and whatever grows within you, you become."* This *rhema* word galvanized my approach to spiritual growth. I will fix my eyes upon Jesus (not my self, my sin, my weakness, or my strength), and Jesus will grow within me.

Make sure that you are a child of faith so that people can follow you, and that you are a leader in discipling this world for our Lord and Savior, Jesus Christ. If you journal regularly, God will turn you into a child of faith as He did me. *Journal regularly! Become a child of faith* (see Heb. 11:6; 1 John 5:4)!

David Barrett, author of the *World Christian Encyclopedia* discusses the growth of the Church. In A.D. 100 there was one Christian for every 360 non-Christians. By A.D. 2000 there was one professing Christian for every three non-Christians. *So statistics confirm that over the last 2,000 years there has been no end to the increase of God's government* (see Isa. 9:7)! This, of course, means that there has been no end to the *decrease* of satan's government!

Let the Church rejoice and celebrate the ever-expanding Kingdom of God! Let each one of us be an integral part of this expansion, even as Joshua was! Let each one of us take dominion over the area God has assigned to us.

May you be one of the *"followers of them who through faith and patience inherit the promises"* (see Heb. 6:12). May *you* disciple the area God has allotted to you, bringing it under the rule and reign of Christ.

I pray that you learn to live in obedience to the voice of God and that His Spirit-anointed victories become the pattern for your life, even as they were for Joshua! To the King be glory forever and ever. Amen!

God says:

> *Of the increase of His government and peace there shall be no end*, upon the throne of David, and upon His kingdom, to order it, and to establish it with judgment and with justice from henceforth even for ever. *The zeal of the LORD of hosts will perform this* (Isaiah 9:7 KJV).

AMEN!

Examples of Two-way Journaling

Read how others have used the four keys to tune their hearts to hear God's voice and possess their Promised Lands.

Pastor Terry—Don't Dig Up the Seed

Father, here I am again, needing confirmation as to Your call on my life. Why do I seem to vacillate so much? Have I not settled the issue inside? What do I need to do that I may proceed in whatever way You desire with confidence? I can't seem to press forward when I'm not sure why.

And when I don't see the things we do bearing fruit, I begin to question the call, and then satan tries to put the old identity back on me...and tell me I'll never get out of this place...and will end up like Pastor Bob, and that will be my plight in life...always thinking some-day it's going to change...but it never does...and then you become disillusioned and weary, and lose hope...I don't like what I sense and feel at that time...Help me to know for sure what to do.

Terry, you keep digging up the seed to see if it's growing. Please, leave it in the ground. You know that I've called you here...and you know this is where I want you to be. If that were not true, I would have called you elsewhere. I would have opened up other doors and moved you. But I have planted you here. Can you remain here? Can you not believe Me for success?

How many times have I warned, yes warned, you to be patient. To hold on. Didn't My prophets tell you it would be a hard work? But Terry, hard, doesn't mean empty and futile. You haven't yet accepted the work I've given you to do. You are still looking out there...waiting for the fruit... waiting for the visible manifestation to decide whether this is true or not. I ask you, are you in a better place today than you've ever been?

Yes, Lord.

Are you flowing in more of Me than you've ever done?

Yes, Lord.

Are you waging war in the realms I've told you to?

I'm not sure what that means at this time, Lord.

I have given you the messages about fighting the giants...was that for your people only...or for you also?

I guess it was for me, too, Lord.

Then fight, Terry. Fight the good fight. Fight with Me. I have your back. I have your front. I will protect...and I will win the battle. But you must, you must, stay beside Me. You cannot get off on your own and expect that I will protect you. Stay in My covering. Stay with My plan. Stay with My agenda. And allow Me to lead and guide you in everything. Walk with Me, Terry...

Where are we going, Lord?

I'll show you...You see that? It is the ruined fruit from those who have dug up their seed and allowed it to die because they couldn't wait for the growth and development of the fruit...and they had to see it to believe it.

Where I am taking you is to a place where the fruit is not seen for some time, and then, by My Spirit, I will make it suddenly visible and all will

*see. Trust Me, Terry. Trust Me when it's hard to see, and hard to believe…
Trust Me with the church…Trust Me with your future…*

*Get close to Me, and I will direct you, and you will know My will and
purpose. And you will have confidence that no matter what happens you are
in the middle of My will and plan for you. See those fields…they are yours.*

But, Lord, there is nothing there…

*Terry, there is nothing there if all you can see is what is visible to your
natural eye. But underneath is a wealth of seed, waiting its time…germi-
nating, growing…ready to spring to life…But you must believe it's there,
and leave it there. Don't dig it up. Don't spoil what we've done…Let it be…
and simply trust Me….*

*Love those whom I've given you…and take the time to build what I told
you to do so far…put together your plan for discipleship…lay it out…design
as I have told you. It will be the path that I chose to work…and it is My
desire in you…to accomplish these things.*

*Take this time, before the growth happens, to organize and develop
this plan. Lay more seed, Terry…throw out more seed. Plant more seed.
And then wait…and water it with your prayer and tears and fasting…and
then watch…it will grow, and it will feed thousands upon thousands…*

*Give it time…it is germinating and growing, and I'm not done with
what I'm putting together into this "stew." It will be good, and others
will enjoy it…and you can be satisfied with what happens…Trust Me…I
will accomplish this if you will stay put, and let Me do what I've said I
would do….*

✳ ✳ ✳

Bill—Journaling Releases God's Creativity Into the Marketplace

I have been journaling since 1992 using your material. I have often
journaled about business issues and problems, and God has given me

wisdom to solve business problems as well as give direction in relationships, sales campaigns, and solution approaches.

There were two examples I felt that you might be interested in. The first occurred in a marketing meeting where we were trying to develop a new marketing tag line that captured the value of a new solution we were bringing to market. The team was stumped, so I journaled and the Lord gave me a marketing tag line. I told the team; they were amazed and said that was great, and it opened an entirely new approach for the team to work on.

On another occasion I was really stumped trying to write a marketing brochure for a seminar my wife and I are doing, I tried to write it but I was really stuck. I journaled and the Lord gave me the entire copy. I simply wrote it down.

In addition to my day job, Sue and I are also itinerant ministers. I used to take five hours to write sermons; now using journaling they are done in about 30 minutes.

The approach to hearing God that I learned from you has completely transformed my Christian life and business. Thanks for teaching me this very practical method for hearing God's voice. I have taught it to others all over the world in my Christian seminars, and Sue and I have written a children's Sunday school program called Kids in Renewal that teaches kids to hear God's voice using your method. This program has been taught in over 800 churches worldwide to date.

Taking God's Voice Into Your World

So far we have written 60 books demonstrating how to take God's voice into area after area of life. We have also developed over 100 college courses for Christian Leadership University that puts the voice of God in the center of your learning experience. These classes can all be taken from your home. For more information, please see our ministry page at the back of this book.

✳✳✳

Lynda—God's Voice Even as We Jog!

I was going out to jog (after about a three-month break) and was trying to determine how much to run. Against my feeling of compulsion, I listened to what was coming from within. I was able to run this amount, realizing that if I had followed my compulsion, I would have failed to succeed in the goal. As I thought on this (nearing the end of my jog) I felt God saying to me *Lynda, I want you to succeed.* This was a revelation to me.

The next day in my journal I said to God, "Lord, I have so many questions, what is real faith? What is success? Why is it so hard for me to believe You really have my best in mind? Speak to me, Father."

Yes, My child, I do want you to succeed. It has always been My plan that you would have success. But as your mind is telling you right now, the success I have for you, and for all My children, is not the success as the world knows, or measures. Your success is measured by your oneness with Me. That is how I made you to be. You become truly you, truly human, when your oneness with Me is complete.

The Father and the Son are one. Jesus did nothing out of His own initiative. He only did what He had already seen the Father do. That is why I want you to come to Me to rest in Me, to spend time with Me, so you will truly know Me and thus be able to follow in My ways.

As you have been gathering faith in My love for you, your ability to express that genuinely for others has increased. As you have shed tears over My mercy and grace and the price I paid for you, you have shed tears for others, and with compassion reached out in My name.

My Son did not have success in the ways of this world. He largely spent His time with 12 men and of those, primarily three. He had contact with a lot of people, healed many (but could have healed more) but He poured His life into that motley crew...fishermen, ordinary people. The more of an agenda these men had, the harder it was to truly see Me and be one with Me.

It's not that I don't want you to have visions and dreams and aspirations, but I want them to be seated in your oneness with Me...for I want you to succeed, to accomplish what I made you for...not because that is where or how you earn your value and love. Your value is a given. It just is. You are My daughter, My precious child. My love for you is complete. You have nothing to prove or accomplish or do to make My love any greater for you. Neither will you ever lose or be separated from My love.

You are beginning to discern some of your own deception of your strengths and weaknesses and even wisdom. Your deception comes from a yet unhealed heart. You are only beginning to grasp My view of you...it will take you time to put to death your view of you, and own how I see you. This is part of the renewal of your mind.

When you place faith and confidence in your old structures and behaviors and ways of thinking...you will fail. The old way is built on law, on striving, on succeeding by will power. The new way, My way, is based on rest, on humility, on becoming childlike, on dependency. These ways continue to be foreign to you but you are walking in them more and more. It is My desire to see you succeed, to see you one with Me, to let the river of life flow freely from you.

Don't look at this as somehow losing yourself. In fact, it is really becoming more of who you really are. What you are putting to death is the mask, the facade, the fortress that holds you in, imprisoning who you really are. Work with Me. Like Joshua, listen to Me. Sometimes you will think My instructions foolish, or of making no sense...but the walls come down. Be strong and courageous...in following My ways. For I will be with you. Do not be afraid or discouraged, for I will be with you. I AM WITH YOU NOW. Be still, rest and know that I AM GOD.

We hope and pray that learning about these four keys to hearing God's voice has moved you into a deeper relationship with your heavenly Father. May your confidence and motivation be increased as you too pursue an intimate daily conversation with the One who loves you and wants to reveal His everyday destiny for you—His beloved.

Personal Application

On six different days, journal out God's answer to the following questions concerning what His Promised Land blessings look like in your life:

- God, what is Your vision of my finances, and what conditions do You want me to meet to see these blessings released in my life?

- God, what is Your vision of my health, and what conditions do You want me to meet to see these blessings released in my life?

- God, what is Your vision of my marriage, and what conditions do You want me to meet to see these blessings released in my life?

- God, what is Your vision of my family, and what conditions do You want me to meet to see these blessings released in my life?

- God, what is Your vision of my ministry to the world, and what conditions do You want me to meet to see these blessings released in my life?

- Lord, what is Your vision of our nation and this world, and what conditions do You want me to meet to see this vision realized?

Maintain a journal that records the continuing instructions of God to you in each area and the steps you have taken and are taking to attain the Promised Land that God has given to you in each and every area.

Free Online Resources to deepen these truths available at: www.cwgministries.org/FreeBooks

- **Dialoging with God Through the Tabernacle Experience (by Ben C. Lunis, a Certified CWG Facilitator)**

- **How to Survive and Thrive in the Purging Before the Promised Land**

- **How to Release God's Healing Power Through Prayer**

- **Thy Kingdom Come on Earth as it is in Heaven— Dialogues with God (by Ben C. Lunis, a Certified CWG Facilitator)**

- **"The Lamad New Testament" which encourages Revelation Based Learning—A New Testament with Journaling Questions Throughout! (Developed by Andrew R. Hardy)**

- **Read our archive of newsletters, which contains many examples of journaling about real life issues** www.cwgministries.org/newsletters

Recommended Reading

Applying Vision to Your Encounter with God

The Bible teaches us that God gives dreams (see Acts 2:17) and that He counsels us at night through our dreams (see Ps. 16:7). This is a wonderful and fascinating area that we cover in our book *Hear God Through Your Dreams*.

There is a complete manual, *How to Release God's Healing Power Through Prayer*, on using vision and flow in healing prayer.

Key principles for interpreting your dreams and the full *How to Realease God's Healing Power Through Prayer* manual are available for download at www.cwgministries.org/freebooks.

For a description of the practical way Dr. Cho lives, pregnant with dream and vision, read his book *The Fourth Dimension*.

For a good book describing the use of vision in the ministry of inner healing, read *You Can Be Emotionally Free* by Rita Bennett.

Journaling Collections

Our Father Speaks Through Hebrews by Rev. Peter Lord

Peter Lord is the former pastor of a 6,000-member Baptist church in Titusville, Florida. He starts each entry with a verse from Hebrews and follows it with the journaling the Lord gave him concerning that verse. Very powerful. The first book I know of that consists of a man's journaling. A landmark book. Available from http://peterlord.net/.

Hearing God by Rev. Peter Lord

An excellent complement to *4 Keys to Hearing God's Voice*. Peter Lord is on our board of advisors and shares similar insights from his life's experience of over 30 years in the ministry. Available from http://peterlord.net/.

You will find more two-way journaling at:

www.cwgministries.org/freebooks

www.KoinoniaNetwork.org

APPENDIX A

The Origin of Thoughts, Biblically Speaking

The thoughts are in my head, so didn't they originate with me? The biblical answer is, "Not necessarily." The Bible is very clear to say that our thoughts may come from any of three sources: self, the Holy Spirit, or demons. This understanding is critical for the person seeking to live his life out of the voice of God since God's voice will often come as a spontaneous thought that is sensed as being in our minds. Some thoughts come from God, and yes, some come from satan.

God did not create man as a self-contained unit. God calls us vessels (see 2 Cor. 4:7). A vessel, of course, is designed to be filled with something. We are designed to be filled with God (see 2 Cor. 4:7). However, in the Garden of Eden, satan tempted man to live out of self, and man fell to the temptation. Since that point in time, man can have self's thoughts, and self is the filling station for satan. So now we find that we can also be filled with satan and his demons. Thus our thoughts can come from God, self, or satan.

Humans are composed of a spirit, soul, and body (see 1 Thess. 5:23). Our spirits are designed to be united or joined to another Spirit. Before we invited Jesus Christ into our hearts to be our Lord and Savior, the Bible tells us that we had evil spirits working within us *"[You were obedient to and under the control of] the [demon] spirit that still constantly works in the sons of disobedience"* (Eph. 2:2 AMP). Once we are saved, the Holy Spirit is joined to our spirits (see 1 Cor. 6:17) and His work within us quickly grows and expands.

Both demons and the Holy Spirit can give us thoughts (see Luke 22:3; Acts 5:3; 1 Cor. 2:10). In both cases, they are registered in our minds as spontaneous thoughts. Spontaneous or flowing thoughts come from the spirit world. John 7:37-39 teaches that the flow we sense within is coming from the Spirit. Conversely, analytical thoughts come from our use of our rational minds.

When we are attempting to discern the voice of God from our own or satan's impulses, we need to begin by determining if the thoughts were spontaneous or analytical. If they are spontaneous, they have come from the spirit world. Now we need to determine if they came from the Holy Spirit or from evil spirits.

If the tenor of the thoughts lines up with the names and character of satan, they are coming from satan; if the tone of the thoughts lines up with the names or character of the Holy Spirit, then they are probably coming from God. (Occasionally, satan will manifest himself as an angel of light and give us thoughts that appear to be God's thoughts.)

Spirit-led reasoning can be defined as allowing flowing pictures and words from the Holy Spirit to guide our reasoning process. We can ask for this and seek it out by properly posturing our hearts before the Holy Spirit (see John 7:37-39; Ps. 73—David reasoned in the sanctuary of God).

Demon-led reasoning is when we allow flowing pictures and words from demons to guide our reasoning process. An idle or undisciplined mind will quickly fall into this trap. The result will be thoughts that reflect the purposes of satan: condemnation, fear, lust, anger, lies, and every form of wickedness.

This is why the Bible instructs us to *"take every thought captive"* (see 2 Cor. 10:3-5). We must ensure that we only allow the Holy Spirit to use our minds, not self or satan, if we are to grow strong in faith and in the holiness of the Lord.

"Western study," which can be defined as "man using his reasoning capacity," gives us reasoned knowledge. "Biblical meditation," which is "the Holy Spirit utilizing all faculties in both hemispheres of man's brain," gives us revelation knowledge. Study is man in action. Meditation is God in action.

Study gives me what Paul called "knowledge," which comes through the strength of the flesh—me using my mind myself (see Phil. 3:4-8). Meditation gives me what Paul called "true knowledge" (see Col. 2:2), or revelation knowledge (see Eph. 1:17-18; Luke 24:32), knowledge birthed by the Spirit of God. Paul repudiated the reasoned knowledge he obtained in his Bible school learning (see Phil. 3:1-11), in favor of the revelation knowledge he received while alone with God in the Arabian desert (see Gal. 1:12,17,18).

God's plan from the beginning, from the Garden of Eden, was that we would be in daily communication with Him and He would grant revelation knowledge into our hearts (see Gen. 3:8-9). Living this way would result in the work we do being birthed by and anointed with the Holy Spirit's power. Jesus lived that way Himself, doing nothing of His own initiative but living totally from divine impulse, or we could say out of *rhema* and vision (see John 5:19-20,30).

Satan's plan was to tempt man to live out of himself, to figure things out on his own, without divine revelation. God had commanded him not to eat from the tree of the knowledge of good and evil for it would surely bring about spiritual death or loss of divine communication between them if they did (see Gen. 2:17).

Satan convinced Eve that if she ate from it (tried using her own mind herself), it would not result in loss of spiritual communion or death, but instead would make her smart like God and able to know things on her own, without having to get the knowledge from God through spiritual union. He said to Eve, *"For God knows that in the day you eat from it your eyes will be opened, and you will be like God, knowing good and evil"* (Gen. 3:5). This one step caused mankind to descend into a philosophy called rational humanism, which we will discuss in a moment.

A more complete discussion of the role of the mind can be found in chapter five of **Wading Deeper Into the River of God** by Mark and Patti Virkler.

Rational humanism is, of course, what satan was offering to Eve in the Garden of Eden. If you remember, the devil's temptation in the Garden was that man live out of himself, acquire his own wisdom and knowledge, and move with his own power. He said, *"You will be like God, knowing good and evil."* In accepting this temptation, mankind moved from being a vessel that contained God to being a vessel that manifested satan and his demons (as self is the filling station for satan).

The two key words in satan's temptation were "you" and "know." From these two words we now have built two philosophies, **humanism** and **rationalism.** Humanism reveres the efforts of humans as the center of life, and rationalism centralizes man's reasoning process. Both philosophies are satan's alternatives to God's original plan. Both are wrong, and both are idolatry. And God has made it extremely clear in the Ten Commandments that He hates idolatry and has forbidden it (see Exod. 20:3).

Jesus lived out of divine flow, and by becoming the Second Adam He reversed what the first Adam had done. Jesus insisted that He did nothing out of His own initiative but only said what He heard the Father saying and did what He saw the Father doing (see John 5:17,19-20,30; 8:26,28). Thus Jesus stepped away from both humanism and rationalism, and back to revelation knowledge and divine anointing, which are at the heart of Christianity.

When Paul declared that we have died and Christ is our life (see Gal. 2:20), and that we must die daily (see 1 Cor. 15:31), he was insisting that we must return to the lifestyle of Adam in the Garden of Eden and Jesus, as He walked in Nazareth. We die to our own self-initiative, except to choose to connect to the indwelling Christ and to release Him. We choose to labor to do only one thing—to come to rest, to cease our own laboring, and to touch and release the Spirit of Christ out through our beings (see Heb. 4:11).

I live out of the "Christ I" by continuously doing the following:

1. I look to the indwelling Christ, not my own wisdom or strength.

2. I tune to my heart—that is, to flowing thoughts, pictures, feelings, and anointing (see John 7:37-39).

3. I call forth His life (see Heb. 3-4).

4. I glorify God for all that flows out through me.

The "Christ I" releases the following through me:

1. **Anointed reason in place of man's reason**—Instead of looking to, trusting, and applying the analytical abilities of my own mind, I yield my mind to flowing pictures and flowing thoughts, and I journal these out (see Isa. 1:18).

2. **Divine vision in place of vain imagination**—Instead of evil or vain imaginations (see Gen. 6:5; Rom. 1:21), I use the eyes of my heart for "godly imagination" (see 1 Chron. 29:18 KJV) and to receive divine dreams and visions by asking the Holy Spirit to give me a flow of pictures, which I tune to within (see Acts 2:17).

3. **Anointing in place of my strength**—Instead of setting my will to accomplish or to overcome, I set my will to connect with the indwelling Christ and to release His power and His anointing through me (see 1 John 2:20).

4. **Divine emotions in place of my emotions**—Instead of living out of my feelings, I ask God to give me His feelings about the situation (see Gal. 5:22-23).

Christ's life and anointing make you better than you are! Let Christ live through you by the indwelling Holy Spirit! Apply the law of the Spirit of life in Christ Jesus (see Rom. 8:2). Choose to tune inward and draw on the river of power, anointing, wisdom, and revelation that is in the indwelling Holy Spirit.

May each of us ascend back to a biblical worldview and a Spirit-anointed lifestyle, following the example of our Lord and Savior Jesus Christ, as well as the original design that God laid out in the Garden of Eden.

Additional Journaling Questions

General

- Good morning, Lord. I love You and I give You this day. What would You like to speak to me?

- How do You see me?

- What do You want to say to me?

- Do You love me?

- What blocks keep me from moving forward in my relationship with You? How can these best be dealt with?

- What wrong beliefs would You like me to repent of, and what godly beliefs would You like to replace them with?

- Lord, are there any people whom I need to forgive and release to a greater extent than I have?

Marriage

- What do You want to say to me about my marriage?

- How do You see my marriage?

- How do You want me to see my marriage?

- What would You have me do to enhance my marriage?

- How can I show greater love to my spouse?

- Are there things You would have me do to show greater love, honor, and respect toward my spouse?

Children

- How do You see each of my children?

- Can You give me any special instructions about how we should raise these children? (see Judg. 13:12)

- What are the gifts and strengths You have given them that You want me to focus on and help them develop?

- What are their weaknesses, and how do You want me to come alongside to strengthen them?

- What are their special needs that You would have me meet?

- How would You have me enhance my relationship with each of my children?

- Is there anything You would have me do to enrich my children's walk with You?

- Are there things You would have me do to show greater love, honor, and respect toward my children?

Work

- Lord, what do You want to say about my work?

- How do You see it?

- How do You want me to see it?

- Are there any attitudes I have about my work or my work companions that You would like to speak to me about?

Ministry

- Lord, what is the primary ministry You would have me doing at this time?

- What would You have me do to continue preparing myself for effectiveness in this ministry?

Working Definitions Concerning Spiritual Realities

Precise workable definitions help us accomplish purposes swiftly, easily, and continuously. Because scientists have defined "gravity," they can also define "air pressure" and "lift." They can do this so precisely that airplanes can take off and land *effortlessly and with great regularity. I want the same clarity and consistency for my spiritual life.* I want "Spirit-anointed lift" on a daily, ongoing basis.

These definitions help me achieve this by teaching me to stay away from rationalism, humanism, man's reason, and dead works. I enjoy instead God's voice, His vision, and the anointing that comes through the Holy Spirit.

When I began my walk in the Spirit many years ago, and I asked others who had gone before me for working definitions, I received little help. When I asked what God's voice sounded like, they responded, "You know that you know that you know." Obviously, this is totally worthless if you don't know, and I didn't.

When I wanted to walk in the Spirit and I wanted to know what my spirit felt like, they said it was the innermost part of me. Of course that is not what it feels like, that is where it is located. Then they told me that it was the part of me that contacted God. That is not what it feels like, that is what it does. So no one could even give me a definition of what my spirit feels like. How could I possibly "walk in the

Spirit"? I didn't even have a clear understanding of what the experience was.

Well, it is pretty hard to live a life in the Spirit with no solid working definitions to build upon. The assortment of definitions below will get you started in this pursuit. Some come from this book and some from other books we have written. Below we simply state the definition without all the supporting Scripture that is in our various books. May this understanding assist you as you build your life in the Holy Spirit!

Working Definitions—Arranged Topically

God's voice—sounds like spontaneous thoughts that light upon your mind.

Man's spirit—is sensed as underlying attitudes, underlying motivations, and underlying character traits. For example, we could tune to God with an **attitude** of reverence, awe and respect, a **motivation** of seeking Him diligently, and a **character trait** of humility and dependence upon Him.

Man's spirit or heart—largely interchangeable words.

The function of the human spirit:

- To be joined to the Holy Spirit (see 1 Cor. 6:17).

- To receive and transmit the life of the Holy Spirit to man through the fruits and gifts.

Five faculties of man's spirit/heart:

- **Ears of my heart** (see John 5:30)—where I hear spontaneous thoughts from the spirit world.

- **Eyes of my heart** (see Rev. 4:1)—where I see spontaneous pictures from the spirit world.

- **Mind of my heart** (see Luke 2:19)—where I ponder, meditate, and muse.

- **Will of my heart** (see Acts 19:21)—where I establish convictions that I live out of.

- **Emotions of my heart** (see 1 Kings 21:2-5)—deep underlying emotions that affect my behavior; we can pick up God's emotions or demons' emotions.

Language of the mind—Man's analytical reason, which is rebuked by Jesus four times in the Gospels, and never encouraged in the Scriptures. Left-brainers must be instructed to turn away from this or they will naturally do it when they seek to come into the Lord's presence. Sometimes right-brainers, after hearing from God, will add to that word with left-brain thinking and will believe they are still in the right brain and still hearing from God. Both left-brainers and right-brainers must learn to distinguish what is from the Spirit and what is from their own minds.

Language of the heart—is flowing thoughts (see John 7:38), flowing pictures (see Acts 2:17), flowing emotions (see Gal. 5:22-23), pondering and meditation (see Ps. 77:6). Sensing God's movement in our hearts can be called illumination, revelation, revelation knowledge, perception, discernment, word of wisdom, word of knowledge, or prophecy.

Western study—man using his reasoning capacity.

Biblical meditation—the Holy Spirit using all faculties in man's heart and mind.

Proper fuel for our hearts—Faith, hope, and love (see 1 Cor. 13:13). If you journal, God will automatically fill you up on this fuel so you will run well for the day.

Four keys to hearing God's voice:

- Key # 1: Recognize God's voice as spontaneous thoughts which light upon your mind.

- Key # 2: Quiet yourself so you can hear God's voice.

- Key # 3: Look for vision as you pray.

- Key # 4: Write down the flow of thoughts and pictures that come to you.

Four words that summarize the four keys to hearing God's voice:

Stillness—Vision—Spontaneity—Journaling

Hearing God's voice is as simple as quieting yourself down, fixing your eyes on Jesus, tuning to spontaneity and writing. (MEMORIZE AND SHARE THIS!)

As exemplified in Habakkuk 2:1-2	Key Succinctly Stated
I will stand on my guard post	Quiet yourself down by...
And I will keep watch to see	Fixing your eyes on Jesus.
What He will speak to me	Tune to spontaneity.
Then the Lord answered me and said, "Record the vision."	Write down the flow of thoughts and pictures.

The heart posture that ensures the flow within will be the Holy Spirit!

Biblical Statement (John 7:37-39)	Key Confession
If anyone is thirsty	Lord, I am **thirsty** for Your voice
Let him come to Me	Lord, I **fix my heart upon You**
And drink	I **tune to flow,** drinking in Your words
He who believes in Me	I **believe** the flow within me is You!

The Leader's Paradigm—a broad-based system for discovering truth based on six ways God communicates with us: illumined thoughts in our minds; peace versus unrest in our hearts; illumined Scriptures; illumined counsel of others; illumined understanding of life's fruit; and direct revelation through dreams, visions, journaling, and prophecy. A consensus of all six is sought, especially when making major decisions.

Spiritual advisors—people who are alongside you or ahead of you in an area and whom you seek out for spiritual advice; who are willing to seek God with you and share with you, for your prayerful consideration, what they sense in their hearts.

Submission—openness to the Spirit-led counsel and correction of several others, while keeping a sense of personal responsibility for our own discernment of God's voice within.

Sorting out three categories of thoughts:

1. *Spontaneous positive thoughts* we will assume come from the Holy Spirit. They line up with the names/character of the Holy Spirit, including Edifier, Comforter, Teacher, Creator, Healer, and Giver of Life.

2. *Spontaneous negative thoughts* we assume come from demons, and thus will line up with the names/character of satan, which include accuser, adversary, liar, destroyer, condemner, thief and murderer.

3. *Analytical thoughts* come from self, from our own reasoning process, and are sensed as cognitive, connected thoughts.

A dead work—Man doing things through his abilities (see Heb. 6:1—to be repented of).

A live work—An activity birthed in the Holy Spirit (see John 5:19-20,30).

Law of the Spirit of Life in Christ Jesus—the energizing we experience as we fix ourselves upon God and call for His life to flow out through our spirits (see Rom. 8:2).

Know where the eyes of your heart are fixed at all times because:

- The intuitive/spontaneous flow comes from the vision being held before your eyes.

- Whatever you focus on grows within you and whatever grows within you, you become.

- We are transformed by what we look upon. We are to fix our eyes upon Jesus and be transformed into His likeness (see 2 Cor. 3:18; 4:18; Heb. 12:2). It is called "coming to the light."

- Looking at our sin and weakness and seeking to battle them really doesn't provide victory (called "stripping away"). Seeing and radiating Jesus is the only true approach to spiritual growth.

Philosophies:

- *Humanism*—puts *human effort* as the center of life.

- *Rationalism*—puts *man's reasoning* process at the center of life.

- *Christian Mysticism*—Puts *releasing the Holy Spirit* at the center of life (see 1 Cor. 2:9-10).

- *Satan's temptation* in the Garden of Eden was to step from direct spiritual encounter with God on a daily basis (mysticism), to rational humanism (*YOU* can be like God, *KNOWING*... see Gen. 3:5).

Man's reasoning—man controlling his reasoning process—self in action.

Spirit-led reasoning—allowing flowing pictures and words from the Holy Spirit to guide the reasoning process.

Demon-led reasoning—allowing flowing pictures and words from demons to guide our reasoning process.

Vain imagination—man picturing what he wants (see Rom. 1:21 KJV).

Evil imagination—man picturing demonic things (see Jer. 16:12 KJV).

Godly imagination—Man picturing things from God (see 1 Chron. 29:18 KJV).

Christian maturity is defined as—living as Jesus did, naturally and comfortably out of the Father's initiative, doing what you hear and see the Father doing (see John 5:19-20,30; 8:26,28,38). This is counter to the Western lifestyle that says we live out of reason (rationalism) and self-effort (humanism). So we step out of the Western worldview and step into God's anointing!

The Lord of All—Almighty God (trust Him, He even numbers the hairs on your head).

The defeated foe—satan (don't re-empower him by placing your faith in him).

New Age—People hungering for spiritual reality and not going through our Lord and Savior Jesus Christ to get it. Many of these people could not find spiritual reality in dead churches so they turned to the New Age. The Church should be offering them true spiritual encounters in the Holy Spirit.

Logos—the entire communication process; also, the Bible, the Word of God.

Rhema—when words leave one's lips.

Naba—the word for "prophecy;" it means "bubbling up," so when I want to prophesy, I posture my heart properly before God and speak forth the thoughts and words that are bubbling up within me.

Paga—God's voice leading me in prayer. It is sensed as spontaneous thoughts that light upon my mind while I am praying. So I fix my eyes upon Jesus, and tune to flow and pray, being guided by the flow.

The Law:

- Teaches us that we can never be holy without Jesus' shed blood (see Gal. 3:22).

- It **cannot** impart life/anointing to us (see Gal. 3:21).

- Keeps us from destroying ourselves before we learn to walk in the Holy Spirit (see Gal. 3:2-3).

- Is **not** the driving force of those who walk in the Spirit (see Gal. 3:25; 5:18).

Workers of the Law—an attempt to become spiritual through our own efforts (see Gal. 3:2-3).

Hearers with faith—believe you become spiritual by saying "yes" to what God has done (Gal. 3:2-8). You declare that everything was completed in Jesus, and now Jesus lives in you making you complete. Whenever you need anything, you ask for Christ to provide it through the indwelling Holy Spirit.

You tune to flowing thoughts, flowing pictures and flowing emotions, and because of the operation of the "Law of the Spirit of Life," you experience the Holy Spirit providing it. You thank Him for this wonderful provision. A miraculous transaction has taken place within you. You have stepped from your frame that is dust (see Ps. 103:14), to the power of God in your spirit (see 2 Pet. 1:4). You see yourself as dust fused to glory. You may take this step, from weak dust to divine anointing, hundreds of times a day.

Living and walking by the Spirit—(see Gal. 5:25) I live as Jesus, tuned to divine flow—flowing thoughts, flowing pictures, flowing emotions, and flowing power (anointing).

Ongoing warfare between workers of the Law and hearers with faith—Workers of the law are slaves. They persecute those who are free and who live by faith (see Gal. 4:21-31). They generally take satan's stance (the accuser's stance—see Rev. 12:10). So if you are living by faith, know that legalists will be persecuting you and calling you demonized just as they did Jesus (see Matt. 12:24). They will have websites against you. They carry the spirit of murder with them (see John 8:44), so they will be trying to kill you. I guess we just agree with Jesus, that they are sons of the devil, thinking they are doing God a service as they kill the prophets (see Acts 7:51-53).

God's exams—God tests us to see if there is faith in our hearts or if we are still grumblers (see Deut. 8:2).

God's plan for our lives—to prosper us (see Jer. 29:11-12).

Giving thanks always lets us pass God's tests—we are to give thanks *for* everything (see Eph. 5:20) and *in* everything (see 1 Thess. 5:18).

Journaling/Prophecy reveals potential—A promise from God in your journal reveals what is available to you. It is stating your potential. If you go after it, you can possess it. If you don't, you are likely to never realize it.

Checklist for Tuning in to God

I Am Living the Tabernacle Experience

- Altar—I have laid down my own initiative, self-effort, and strength.

- Laver—I cleanse myself regularly by meditating upon the Bible.

- Shewbread—My will is ground fine before God and I walk in fellowship with the Body of Christ.

- Lampstand—I have moved from my reasoning to Spirit-led reasoning.

- Incense—I am a continuous worshiper; in everything I give thanks.

- Ark—I wait before God in stillness to receive what He has for me.

I Am Applying the Tuning Dial of Habakkuk 2:1-3

- I am quieting myself down.

- I am fixing my spiritual eyes on Jesus.

- I am tuned to spontaneity.

- I am writing down the flow of thoughts and pictures that come to me.

I Am Applying the Fine-Tuning Dial of Hebrews 10:19-22

- My heart is true, honest, and sincere.

- I have absolute faith that God's river is flowing within me.

- My conscience is completely clear through Christ's cleansing blood.

- I have been obedient to God's previous *rhema*.

I Am Confirming My Journaling Through Other Ways God Speaks

- My journaling lines up with Scripture and the character of God.

- My spiritual advisors confirm my journaling is from God.

APPENDIX D

Personal Application Index

Ministry Information

You may feel led to host Mark Virkler in your community for a weekend seminar on "How to Hear God's Voice." Details can be found at:

www.cwgministries.org/seminars

Mark and Patti Virkler have written 60 books demonstrating how to take God's voice into area after area of life. These are available at:

www.cwgministries.org/catalog

They have also developed over 100 college courses for Christian Leadership University that put the voice of God in the center of your learning experience. These classes can all be taken from your home. View our complete catalog online at:

www.cluonline.com

Would you allow the Virklers to recommend a coach to guide you in applying God's voice in every area of your life? Information about their Personal Spiritual Trainer program is available at:

www.cwgministries.org/pst

We invite you to become a certified facilitator of this course and teach others to hear God's voice! Find out the details at:

www.cwgministries.org/certified

Share your journaling, dreams and visions with others who have experienced this training! Healing rooms, prayer counseling rooms and dream interpretation discussion threads are also available. Thousands are gathering to share their lives at:

www.KoinoniaNetwork.org

IN THE RIGHT HANDS, THIS BOOK WILL CHANGE LIVES!

Most of the people who need this message will not be looking for this book. To change their lives, you need to put a copy of this book in their hands.

> *But others (seeds) fell into good ground, and brought forth fruit, some a hundred-fold, some sixty-fold, some thirty-fold* (Matthew 13:8).

Our ministry is constantly seeking methods to find the good ground, the people who need this anointed message to change their lives. Will you help us reach these people?

> *Remember this—a farmer who plants only a few seeds will get a small crop. But the one who plants generously will get a generous crop* (2 Corinthians 9:6).

EXTEND THIS MINISTRY BY SOWING
3 BOOKS, 5 BOOKS, 10 BOOKS, **OR MORE TODAY,**
AND BECOME A LIFE CHANGER!

Thank you,

Don Nori Sr., Publisher
Destiny Image
Since 1982

DESTINY IMAGE PUBLISHERS, INC.

*"Speaking to the Purposes of God for This Generation
and for the Generations to Come."*

VISIT OUR NEW SITE HOME AT
WWW.DESTINYIMAGE.COM

FREE SUBSCRIPTION TO DI NEWSLETTER

Receive free unpublished articles by top DI authors, exclusive

discounts, and free downloads from our best and newest books.

Visit www.destinyimage.com to subscribe.

Write to: Destiny Image
             P.O. Box 310
             Shippensburg, PA 17257-0310

Call: 1-800-722-6774

Email: orders@destinyimage.com

For a complete list of our titles or to place an order
online, visit www.destinyimage.com.

FIND US ON FACEBOOK OR FOLLOW US ON TWITTER.

www.facebook.com/destinyimage   facebook
www.twitter.com/destinyimage   twitter